Trees of Inspiration

A danger from which there is no escape
is the penalty for felling
the noble sacred trees.

Legal poem, seventh century

TREES *of* INSPIRATION

Sacred Trees and Bushes of Ireland

CHRISTINE ZUCCHELLI

The Collins Press

FIRST PUBLISHED IN 2009 BY
The Collins Press
West Link Park
Doughcloyne
Wilton
Cork

British Library Cataloguing in Publication data
Zucchelli, Christine.
Trees of inspiration : sacred trees & bushes of Ireland.
1. Trees—Religious aspects. 2. Tree worship—Ireland—
History.
I. Title
299.1'61212'09415-dc22
ISBN-13: 9781848890138

This publication has received support from the Heritage Council
under the 2009 Publications Grant Scheme.

Design and typesetting by Anú Design, Tara
Typeset in Garamond
Printed in Spain by GraphyCems

Contents

Acknowledgements

I would like to record my thanks to all the people whom I approached during the preparation of this book, and whose efforts and contributions helped to ensure its completion.

A study of the role of sacred trees and gentle bushes in the folklore and traditions of Ireland would be unthinkable without the support and assistance of the Delargy Centre of Irish Folklore, at University College Dublin. I am particularly indebted to the head of the Centre, Dr Seamus Ó Catháin, for the permission to use the library and the archive with its unique collections of folklore accounts, and to the full- and part-time collectors who have brought together such a wealth of different aspects of Irish folklore. My heartfelt thanks go also to Dr Patricia Lysaght, Dr Dáithí Ó hÓgáin and Dr Crístóir Mac Cárthaigh for their encouragement and helpful advice, and to Dr Bo Almqvist, former Head of the Department of Irish Folklore, for long ago guiding my first attempts to understand and explore Ireland's sacred landscape.

For kindly helping me locate written sources, acknowledgements are due to the staff at the library at University College Dublin, and to public libraries all over Ireland; in particular, thanks are extended to the Local Studies Centre in Ennis and to Clare County Libraries in Kilrush and Kilkee for their constant assistance over the years.

While preparing this book, I have knocked on innumerable doors and asked for directions, information and permission to access trees that lie on private lands. I was overwhelmed by the kindness that I met throughout the country, by the willingness of people to give me their stories, and their helpfulness when it came to locating some little-known trees. So many individuals have thus become involved in the making of this book that I could not begin to name them all. Nevertheless, I would especially l like to thank Noel O'Neill of Castlebar, County Mayo, for his ongoing encouragement and for providing most valuable information on some lesser known trees; acknowledg-ments are also due to the late Gerry Cribben of Ballyhaunis, to Miheál Murphy, Ballina, and Michael O'Sullivan of Kiltimagh, all from County Mayo; to Denis Hogan of Rathkeale, County Limerick; to Fr Wilfrid Harrington at the Dominican Priory in

Tallaght, Dublin; to Barry Whelan at the 1798 Centre in Enniscorthy, County Wexford; to Philip Comer of Crann in Castlebellew, County Galway; and to Cormac Foley and Frank Lewis in Killarney, County Kerry. Thanks to all these people who went out of their way to help me prepare this book.

My thanks also to editor Adrienne Murphy for her great professionalism, patience and guidance; to all at The Collins Press; to Karen Carty of Anú Design for putting so much enthusiasm and dedication into the design of the book; and to Lisa Sheridan for the cover design.

Thanks also to my niece and friend, Daniela Deutsch, for joining me on several fieldwork trips, and for permission to reproduce some of her photographs.

Last, but not least, to my husband, Guenter, for his confidence, his support and for sharing my passion for the myths and folklore of Ireland. Without his support, this book could not have been produced.

Introduction

In early medieval times, when older religions had largely been replaced by Christianity and the monasteries of the Celtic Church had become centres of education, Irish history and ancient oral traditions were preserved in writing for the first time. Among the oldest surviving texts is a legal poem on the rights and duties of a king, composed in the seventh century by an anonymous scribe. He leaves us the earliest documentary evidence for the veneration of sacred trees in Ireland when he refers to the penalty for the felling of sacred trees and instructs, 'Ni bie fidnemed! You shall not cut a tree sanctuary!'[1]

The worship of trees is a phenomenon that occurs in cultures all over the world. It was an important component of ancient religion, remained a part of spiritual life in pre-industrial societies, and has survived down to our modern times.[2] Reverence for trees is based on the recognition of their practical and their spiritual value, although anciently no sharp distinctions were made between the sacred and the profane, and we can assume that practical and spiritual aspects were often entwined and overlapping.

From prehistoric times,[3] trees have met the basic needs of human beings. They provided shelter and firewood; timber and wattles to build houses, huts, bridges and fences; and fruits, nuts, leaves and bark for food and medicine. Later, when mining and metalworking developed, timber was used for smelting ore. For their practical value, certain species of trees were considered more important than others, and laws and regulations were established to protect them and to govern their use. When spiritual and magical ideas developed around these species, these particular trees began to play important roles in popular religion and folklore.[4] With the acknowledgement of the spiritual significance of trees, individual groves and trees were singled out for special veneration and reverence. Probably identified and consecrated by seers or priests, and protected from profanation by sacred prohibitions, these high status trees would have been left to themselves, visited by humans for spiritual reasons only.

Today, we can no longer fully understand the motives for choosing particular trees and groves over others, and thus making them part of the 'sacred landscape': a land-scape that is distinguished by the recognised presence of the *anima loci*, the spirit or

'Bleeding' trees at Raheen, County Clare (top) and Castlekeeran, County Meath (below)

Trees mirror in many ways the life cycle of human beings: they are born from seed, they breathe and drink, they grow to maturity, reproduce and eventually die from age or disease. Their branches, roots and the veins of their leaves resemble human blood vessels, and certain species even ooze a reddish, blood-like sap when damaged. The image shows 'tree blood' dripping from Brian Boru's Oak in 2008; the ash at Castlekeeran 'bled' in 1839.

essence of a place. The nature of the *anima loci* is always determined by the prevailing spiritual concept within a society and consequently changes with cultural, religious and historical developments. Folklore beautifully mirrors the changing perceptions behind the veneration of trees and groves, because it preserves earlier traditions by absorbing new ideas into existing beliefs, and by adapting older traits to new situations.

A belief probably held by the earliest inhabitants of Ireland and certainly pre-dating formal religions is the animistic tradition, which considers all natural features as spirited conscious beings, or as deities in their own right. Traits of the animistic understanding of nature survive in the folklore of bleeding and crying trees.

With an advance in religious thought, more formal and structured religions developed, and trees and other features of the sacred landscape were no longer essentially seen as living beings. Polytheistic concepts regarded trees as abodes of deities or spirits who could enter and leave at will, or as temporary dwellings of human souls between death and reincarnation. Elements of this tradition surface particularly in the folklore of other-world beings and spirits of the dead. Monotheistic religions attributed the sanctity of sacred natural features to blessings by members of the holy family, saints or prophets.

Massive stone tombs of the Neolithic period and impressive stone settings of the Bronze Age are material evidence for advanced religious ideas in pre-Celtic Ireland, but they do not reveal their exact ritual functions or the beliefs behind them, and they do not shed light on the role of sacred trees in the religious life of their builders. When the Celts gained power in Ireland and abroad, they took over the ritual structures of earlier cultures, reinterpreted them in the light of their own spirituality and used them for ceremonial purposes, but they also constructed circles of wood for ritual use, and worshipped their deities in sacred groves and forests.[5]

Early Celtic culture had not yet developed a script, and knowledge was passed down exclusively by word of mouth in verse form by specially trained women and men. For the earliest written records on the role of trees and groves in pagan Celtic spirituality we depend therefore on Greco-Roman and Roman descriptions of customs and religion in areas of Celtic settlement from Asia Minor to Gaul and Britain. Covering the period from the first century BC to the second century AD, these records refer repeatedly to the sanctity of natural features, often sacred groves or tree sanctuaries. The term most commonly used to denote a pagan Celtic sanctuary was *nemeton*.

The archaic Irish form of *nemeton* is *nemed*. It appears first in the composition *fidnemed* or 'tree sanctuary' in the seventh-century legal poem quoted at the start of this book. One century later, mention is made for the first time of a highly venerated individual tree. The most common medieval Irish word for such a tree was *bile*, plural *biledha*. The origin of the term is uncertain. It may have derived from the Celtic word *bilios* for champion, but it also seems to be related to the old Indo-European word *bala*, which denotes 'leaf' in Sanskrit literature. The modern Irish term for a leaf, *bileog*, is a derivative from *bile*.[6]

Bile, pronounced 'billa', survived in modern Irish only as an archaism. It features in nineteenth-century descriptions of highly venerated trees, such as the Bile of Ballinascreen in County Derry, and two trees in County Tipperary, the Bella-Tree – a venerable ash at Rath Rónán – and the Big Bell Tree of Borrisokane. *Bile* also features in place names all over the country. On its own, it appears for instance as Bellia, Billy, Billa or Bellew

Drowned Forest, Rinevella, County Clare
The interpretation of place names often contains a speculative element. Rinevella on the Loop Head Peninsula has been translated 'point of the mouth' (of the Shannon) from Rinn a Bhéal Átha, as well as 'point of the sacred tree' from Rinn a Bhile. There are no folk recollections or historical accounts of an individual sacred tree in the area, but the massive stumps and trunks of ancient trees in Rinevella lagoon testify to the former presence of an extensive pine forest.

in Counties Clare, Kerry, Sligo and Meath respectively. More frequent are compositions, often referring to the location of the tree: Knockavilla in County Westmeath is Cnoc an Bhile, hill of the sacred tree; Moville, in Counties Down and Donegal, is Magh Bhile, plain of the sacred tree; Altavilla in County Limerick is Alt a'Bhile, height of the sacred tree; and Gortavilly in County Tyrone is Gort an Bhile, tilled field of the sacred tree.

Occasionally, medieval scribes used the term *craeb* or *craebh* as an alternative name for a sacred tree. The modern form is *craobh*, plural *craobha*, and means literally 'a branch'. Anglicised versions are fairly widespread in place names, particularly in the northern half of the country, where they appear as Crew in Counties Antrim, Derry and Tyrone, as Creeve in Counties Antrim, Armagh, Donegal, Down, Longford, Mayo, Monaghan, Roscommon, Tyrone and Westmeath, or in compositions such as Crewbane from Craobh Bán, white sacred tree, in County Meath.

Medieval sources indicate that *biledha,* or individual sacred trees, were renowned and revered for a variety of reasons. Chronicles and annals refer to them as focal points for community assemblies and as sacred features at early Christian churches and monasteries. Biographies of Irish saints emphasise the spiritual role of sacred trees and groves. The composers of these biographies were often inspired by texts from the Old and New Testaments and by the lives of Continental saints, but their work also incorporated motifs of the native Celtic lore that were current in the transitional period between pagan and Christian times. Medieval prose and poetry reflect even earlier concepts of tree worship. These ancient myths, sagas, tales and poems survive largely in manuscripts from the twelfth century. Written almost entirely in the Irish language, many were copied from older manuscripts and contain story lines and other traits that may have been current in oral lore since the fourth century.

Today, the ancient sagas and tales are conveniently grouped into four cycles.[7] Three of them – the Ulster Cycle, the Fenian or Ossianic Cycle and the Historical Cycle or Cycle of the Kings – are typically heroic. They deal with the deeds of fictional and historical Celtic warriors and kings, and reflect the customs and traditions of the aristocratic society of the early centuries AD. Sacred trees appear repeatedly in the context of 'adventures' and 'voyages', two genres of narratives based on the otherworld experiences of their heroes.

The Mythological Cycle of tales offers a particularly good insight into the spiritual world of ancient Ireland. The *Leabhar Gabhála Éireann* or The Book of Invasions of Ireland – a compilation of pseudo-historical texts which reconstruct the conquest of the country by successive groups of peoples – is considered a central part of the Mythological Cycle.[8]

Medieval scribes, eager to establish a Biblical origin for the earliest race of Irish, related that the first ever people to arrive in Ireland were led by Cessair, a daughter or granddaughter of Noah. Cessair's people were drowned in the Flood, except for Fintan mac Bóchna, a seer who went through several transformations and survived into Christian times to relate the early history of Ireland. The *Leabhar Gabhála* begins with the arrival of Partholán of Greece and his sons in about 2678 BC. Centuries later, their descendants were wiped out by an outburst of plague.

Eamhain Mhacha or Navan Fort, County Armagh

Eamhain Mhacha was one of the most prestigious sites of ancient Ireland. Archaeologists have found evidence that human activity started in the area in the Neolithic period. In the Bronze Age, an enclosure was built, probably a royal seat. In Celtic times, Eamhain Mhacha was used primarily for ritual purpose, and around 100 BC, a new ceremonial enclosure was added to earlier structures. The circular construction, consisting of four concentric rings of oak posts with a gigantic upright timber pole sunk into a hole in the centre, may have been a sanctuary – a nemed – with the central timber post representing the sacred centre of the territory.[9]

Next to arrive were Nemed or Neimheadh from Scythia and his wife Macha. Macha was a land goddess and represented sovereignty. Nemed means sacred, and the word was used to describe a sanctuary in general or a sacred person. Nemed and Macha cultivated land in south Armagh, where tradition links them closely with the ancient royal seat and ceremonial centre of Eamhain Mhacha or Navan Fort.

Neimheadh's people were defeated by the demonic race of the Fomhóire or Fomorians, and his sons fled to different parts of the world. Generations later, two rival branches of their progeny returned: the Fir Bolg, reputed to have come from Greece, and the Tuatha Dé Danann, said to have arrived from Denmark or Greece. The Tuatha Dé Danann, the 'people of the goddess Danu', defeated the Fir Bolg and the Fomorians and took the sovereignty of Ireland, until forced to submit to the Sons of Míl, who came from Asia Minor and are considered to be the ancestors of the present-day Celtic people. The invasion was led by Míl's father, Bile or Bille, who drowned in a storm raised by the Tuatha Dé Danann; unfortunately, the myths have nothing else to say about him.[10]

Another important source for the medieval and indeed earlier understanding of sacred trees are the *Dindshenchas*, a twelfth-century collection of older prose and poetry explaining the place names of Ireland. Here five great individual trees or *biledha* – considered by medieval texts to be sacred above all others – are repeatedly mentioned and elaborately described.[11] In one poem of the *Dindshenchas* all five trees occur together:

> Tree of Rossa, Tree of Mugna
> How was the Branch of Daithi laid low?
> Its gentle shoots bore many blows.
> An ash tree of the skilful hosts,
> Its wind-lashed top bore lasting growth.
>
> An ash in Tortan, recount it well,
> An ash in Uisneach where the troops dwell,
> The branches fell, the truth is plain,
> In the time of the sons of Aed Slane.
>
> Oak of Mugna, bountiful treasure,
> Nine hundred bushels, its great measure.
> In Dairbre southwards it did fall,
> On Ailbe's plain of the cruel war.

Yew of Rossa, yew of the graves,
Plentiful its wooden staves,
Tree without any hollow or flaw,
O noble yew, how was it laid low?[12]

Since medieval literary sources are generally not accepted as historical fact, the celebrated trees became commonly regarded as the five 'mythical' trees of Ireland. It is nevertheless possible that most of them were real trees, functioning as tribal centres for assembly or religious ceremony. When medieval scribes exaggerated their wonderful properties to emphasise their magnitude and importance, they transferred these trees into the realm of myth and legend.

The Middle Irish text on 'The Settling of the Manor of Tara' links the origin of these five mythical trees with Fintan mac Bóchna. The story relates that on the day of Christ's crucifixion, a strange, otherworld character called Trefuilngid Tre-eochair appeared to Fintan and handed him berries from a magic branch which carried nuts, apples and acorns. Following the stranger's advice, Fintan planted the berries, and from them sprang five trees: Bile Tortan, Eó Rossa, Craeb Dháithí, Bile Uisnigh and Eó Mugna.[13]

Bile Tortan, a sacred ash on Ardbraccan in County Meath, was strongly associated with kingship and with communal assemblies and gatherings. Eó Rossa, the celebrated yew at Old Leighlin in County Carlow, is praised in a poem consisting of short ambiguous descriptions that evoke both pagan and Christian associations. Craeb Dháithí, or the Branch of Dáithí, was an ash, linked with the townland of Farbill in County Westmeath and apparently named after a poet Dáithí who was killed when the tree fell. Bile Uisnigh, also called Craeb Uisnigh, was an ash tree at Uisneach in County Westmeath, the mythical centre of ancient Ireland.[14]

Eó Mugna, the sacred tree of Mugna,[15] is the most controversial of the five mythical trees. References to its situation are vague. Based on the remark that it fell on the Plain of Ailbhe in central Leinster, proposed possible locations are Moone in County Kildare or Ballaghmoon in County Carlow. With regards to its destruction, some texts relate that Eó Mugna fell in a storm in the second half of the seventh century, during the reign of the sons of Aodh Sláine. Other texts suggest that the tree was destroyed by the satire of eighth-century poet Niníne.[16]

Medieval sources agree on the mysterious detail that Eó Mugna remained hidden from sight into the second century AD, when it was revealed at the birth of the great mythical king, Conn Céadchathach. The sources also agree on the marvellous fruits of Eó Mugna, thus creating another controversy. The term *eó* usually denotes a yew, and one

Three fruits upon Eó Mugna – apples, hazels, acorns.

A poem on the Plain of Mugna[17], preserved in the *Dindshenchas* collection of place lore, dwells in particular on the marvellous crops of Eó Mugna:

> O Mugna, host to a tree so fine,
> That God fashioned in ancient times.
> A tree so greatly blest with favour,
> With three fruits so choice in flavour.
>
> Acorn and slim nuts so brown
> And apple, wild and sweetly grown.
> The king would get without let up
> Three times a year a mighty crop.
>
> Tree of Mugna, great its worth,
> Thirty cubits full in girth.
> From far and wide glorious sight,
> Three hundred cubits full its height.
>
> So the pure branch was brought down,
> As a wind broke the Tree of Tortan.
> Thus life's quarrels pass away,
> Like the ancient tree of Mugna's plain.

would expect scarlet berries growing on the famous tree. But Eó Mugna is exclusively and explicitly described as an oak tree, which moreover inherited the abilities of Fintan's magic branch, producing three crops a year, one of acorns, one of apples and one crop of nuts.[18]

The fruits ascribed to Eó Mugna are remarkable for their symbolism. In medieval Irish literature, nuts represented sacred knowledge and mystic insight; acorns were symbols of kingship and assembly; and apples were associated with paradise-orchards and with the otherworld regions of the dead. With the deliberate choice of these fruits, medieval scribes have linked Eó Mugna closely with the ancient concept of a great mythical tree that represents the entire universe and links the different levels of existence and consciousness.

Collectively described today as 'cosmic' or 'world' trees, and regarded as fictional, anciently these mythical trees were known by individual names and understood to be real trees growing in the centre of the world, often within a protective enclosure or garden, guarded by a snake or a dragon representing the spirit of the earth. Reaching up into the heavenly spheres, a world tree's branches made it a channel of communication with the divine; a medium through which mystic inspiration and sacred occult knowledge could be transmitted and spiritual transformation gained. The tree's trunk formed the *axis mundi*, the centre of the world of humans and a focal point for ceremonial assembly; while finally, a world tree's roots, reaching deep into the ground, were a connection to the realm of death and spirits.

The idea of a world tree existed in numerous cultures around the globe, and is particularly well documented for Indo-European peoples. In ancient India, the sacred fig tree Asvattha was the symbol for the universe and the cycle of life, death and rebirth. Its leaves were called *veda* for wisdom. The *Rig Veda*, the earliest religious scripture of India, would often describe Asvattha as an inverted tree, growing downwards from its roots in celestial realms. The most prominent world tree of ancient Europe was Yggdrasil, the mythical ash of the ancient Norse. It was said to link Midgard, the world of the humans, to Niflheim and Asgard, the abodes of the dead and the gods respectively. Watered and cared for by the Nornes, the three goddesses of the past, the present and the future, Yggdrasil symbolised the continuous cycle of life. Deities assembled in the shade of the tree, and Odin ritually hanged himself from its branches to gain the sacred knowledge of runes.[19]

With the fruit of Eó Mugna symbolising the three levels of existence, the tree was possibly the medieval manifestation or interpretation of the archetypal Irish world tree and its spiritual functions. From medieval times, the ancient myths and sagas, legends and biographies of saints were read aloud, and consequently, various motifs and episodes from the literary tradition filtered back into folklore. Monastic orders from the Continent, as well as Normans, and English and Scottish settlers, introduced motifs from their own spiritual worlds. Their religious ideas were largely absorbed into the native Irish perceptions of sacred trees, although the role of trees in the context of assembly changed considerably with the historical development of Ireland.

From the mid-nineteenth century, influenced by Church reform and political changes, popular traditions and religious practices began to lose their significance in people's everyday lives. Old venerable trees of spiritual or historical importance decayed, and with them their stories. At about the same time, nationalist sentiments arose and scholars from various disciplines became keenly interested in the cultural heritage of the country. Antiquarian societies such as the Royal Irish Academy or the Royal Society of Antiquaries in Ireland were founded to research archaeological, historical and folkloristic aspects of the Irish culture. Their reports, together with the letters and memoirs of the Ordnance Survey, established in 1823, contributed significantly to the preservation and documentation of popular traditions.

An invaluable source of information on all aspects of folklore is the manuscript collection of the Delargy Centre for Irish Folklore at University College Dublin. Founded in 1927 as the Folklore of Ireland Society or *An Cumann le Béaloideas Éireann,* the Centre is committed to the systematic documentation of folk traditions and oral lore. In 1956, the Ulster Folk and Transport Museum in Bangor was established to illustrate and preserve the traditions of the people in the North. The most detailed data in these reports, surveys and folklore collections relate to the period from the early nineteenth to the first decades of the twentieth century; correlated with medieval historical and literary sources, and with recent investigations, they illustrate changes and continuity in the perception of sacred trees in Ireland from pagan and early Christian times to the urbanised and modern society of today.

PART I

Trees of Sacred Knowledge

ncient Irish tradition had a special name for the essence of sacred wisdom: *imbas forosna*, literally 'light that illuminates'. The concept of *imbas* included mystic insight, sacred inspiration and oracular visions, and was a quality that distinguished the high-ranking and privileged learned class of *aés dána* or scholars. In medieval Ireland, this class consisted of druids, poets and judges, though early medieval sources indicate that pre-Christian society did not necessarily differentiate clearly between the three professions. Seers are repeatedly shown to be composers of satire and poetry, with additional responsibilities for divination, judgement, religious ceremonies and the preservation of oral traditions. The mythological lore of Amergin, son of Míl, confirms that anciently a distinguished individual could fulfil the three main functions of a privileged scholar. Amergin, so the myths claim, together with his brothers Heber, Heremon and Ir, led the first group of Celts to settle in Ireland. Organising their government of the country, the brothers appointed Amergin as chief bard, druid and judge.[1]

Throughout the Celtic world, seers and sacred knowledge were associated with trees, and commentators on pagan Celtic customs and religion abroad have particularly linked druidry with oak trees. Pliny, the Roman historian and naturalist, describing this special connection, wrote: 'They choose groves formed of oaks for the sake of the tree alone, and they never perform any of their rites except in the presence of a branch of it; so that it is possible that the priests themselves may derive their name from the Greek word for that tree. In fact, they think that everything that grows on it has been sent from heaven and is a proof that the tree was chosen by the god himself'.[2]

Into the present time, Pliny's suggestion regarding the derivation of the term druid remains popular with some scholars, who argue that the initial element, *dru*, was the Gaulish word for oak tree. Combined with the Celtic root, *wid*, for knowledge or wisdom, 'druid' would translate as 'possessor of oak-wisdom'. However, more commonly accepted

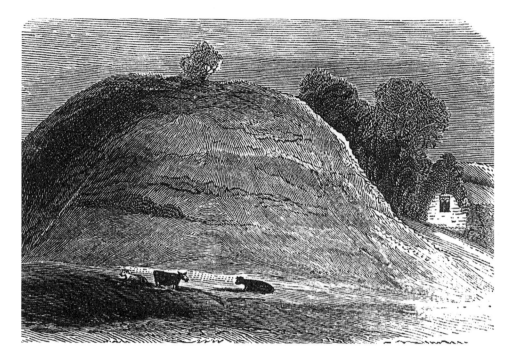

Motte of Killeshin, County Laois
The lone thorn tree on top of the motte evokes memories of 'glám dichenn', an old Irish practice of satire. The Book of Ballymote relates the story of a king who refused the proper award for a poem. To satirise him, the enraged poet first fasted on the land of the king. At sunrise, six other poets joined him on a visit to a hilltop on the boundary of seven lands; here all seven poets turned their backs to the hawthorn that was growing on top of the hill. Holding a perforated stone in one hand and a thorn in the other, each poet recited a satirical verse. Finally, they left their stones and thorns under the hawthorn, trusting that the ground would swallow up the king and his household if he was in the wrong, but that this fate would fall on themselves if he was not.[3]

today is the translation of druid as 'very knowledgeable', a compound of the Celtic roots *dru* for strong or great, and *wid* for knowledge.[4]

For ancient Ireland, where trees were firmly linked with the process of gaining mystic insight and sacred knowledge, we have no indications at all that the oak played a dominant role with regards to druidism and spirituality.

Medieval literature relates that the essence of *imbas forosna* was contained in the nuts of sacred hazel trees. Iubhdán's poem on the qualities of different trees explicitly refers to the rowan as *fid na ndruad*, the druid's tree. Geoffrey Keating's seventeenth-century *History of Ireland* notes that one method for seers to gain sacred wisdom was to lie on so-called 'wattles of knowledge', structures of branches from rowan trees; and a fourteenth-century text in the Book of Ballymote links the old Irish method of satire, *glám dichenn,* or 'satire from hilltops', with the hawthorn.

With the establishment of Christianity, the spiritual aspects of druidism were considered a serious threat to the new religion, and the disempowerment of druids is a recurrent motif in the biographies of early Irish saints. The saints inherited the religious role and functions of the seers, adapted several aspects of druidic wisdom and reinterpreted them in a Christian context. Druidic tree worship was thus channelled into the veneration of trees as powerful manifestations of the might of Christianity, and as media of communication between devotees and saints or the holy family. The functions of the seers as composers of satire and poetry, as guardians of ancient lore and as judges, were not regarded as threatening to Christianity, and survived in the guise of poetry and law-giving.

Trees of Religious Manifestations

The monastery of the monks of Iubhar-Chinntrechta was burned, with all its furniture and books, and also the yew tree which Patrick himself has planted.

Annals of The Four Masters for the year 1162[1]

Tree Worship and Christianity

The introduction of Christianity to Ireland is traditionally attributed to St Patrick, who began his missionary work in 432. According to his biographers, he had the entire island converted to the new faith by the time of his death in 463. But the Christianisation of Ireland was actually a gradual process that started shortly after 400 with pre-Patrician missionaries in the south, and took considerable time after Patrick's death to be completed.

Unlike his predecessors, Patrick precipitated a significant change when he separated political and religious powers, which were formerly in the hands of pagan kings. Following their conversion, the kings retained their full political supremacy, while their religious authority was transferred to the Church and executed by bishops. In the decades following Patrick's death, the early Church in Ireland deviated from Patrick's concept of a strictly organised Church based on Roman administrative principles and developed into a largely independent organisation, commonly known as the Celtic Church.

Structurally, the Celtic Church focussed on autonomous monasteries rather than bishoprics and dioceses. The monasteries resembled small towns with a guesthouse, a school and a refectory, cells for the monks or nuns, dwellings for the clergy, and small oratories and churches. Outside the monasteries, churches as such did not exist, and

St Patrick's Ash and Well, Tamlaght, County Fermanagh

we can assume that religious services for the converted laity were rather irregularly held in the open air at particular sacred places, that might often have been Christianised sanctuaries from pagan times.

Spiritually, the Celtic Church was distinguished by her ability to adapt pagan ideas into the complex of Christian principles and religious observances. The early Christian missionaries and founders of monastic settlements in Ireland were predominantly sons and daughters from influential pagan families; some of them belonged to the local aristocracy, others had possibly been druids or priestesses of the ancient religion before accepting baptism. After their deaths, they were venerated as saints.

Coming themselves from native pagan stock, the saints would have recognised and respected the sanctity of ancient ceremonial places and could easily transform them into Christian shrines by their blessings. From the earliest historical data found in manuscripts from the seventh and eighth centuries, to hagiographical texts from the later medieval period, indications abound for the religious veneration of trees and forest sanctuaries, and the tremendous significance of trees for the saints of early Christian Ireland.

On the Continent, the ascent of Christianity brought a major blow to the veneration of trees and to other forms of nature worship. Earlier, when the Jewish faith had emerged as the first monotheistic religion in the East, the worship of sacred natural features was acceptable; recurrent references to sacred trees in the Old Testament show that the Jewish religion had fully endorsed the concept of trees as transmitters of sacred knowledge. Adam and Eve tasted the forbidden fruit from the Tree of Knowledge in Paradise; the Lord first appeared to Moses in the vision of a burning thorn; Abraham settled near a sacred grove of turpentine trees, where the Lord appeared to him, and he had a vision while sleeping under an old and venerated oak tree; the prophetess Deborah dwelled under a sacred palm tree when the children of Israel came to her for justice, and was eventually buried beneath the sacred oak of Beth-El. Scriptures from the New Testament relate that Jesus taught his disciples in the sacred olive grove of Gethsemane, and retreated to the grove on the last night of his life.[2]

In Gaul and other places in Europe, the earliest Christian teachers preached under sacred trees and erected altars and churches beside them. For the first couple of centuries, the spread of Christianity was a slow process, repeatedly interrupted by periods of severe persecution. In the early fourth century, the Christian faith was formally acknowledged and protected for the first time; in 380, it was declared the official religion of the Roman Empire. With its official establishment, the Christian Church became increasingly intolerant towards other religious concepts and beliefs, and as early as 380, the Church started a campaign to wipe out and discredit pagan forms of nature worship.[3]

Trinity Tree, Fore, County Westmeath (above) **and Trinity Tree, Dingle, County Kerry** (opposite)

Fore Abbey, founded in the sixth century by St Féichín, has two sacred trees: a tree beside the holy well that reputedly does not burn, and an ancient ash tree with three main branches, said to represent the Holy Trinity. The Trinity Tree overhangs St Féichín's Vat, a box-like structure that was once filled with water. In this small pool the saint would spend his nights kneeling in prayer. Formerly, sick or weak children were bathed in the pool for a cure; this custom has long since ceased, but votive offerings of rags, ribbons and coins left at the tree are proof of the ongoing popularity of the ash.[4]

On 8 September 2000, on Lady of Dingle Day, Guatemalan artist Juan Carlos Lizana Carreno presented Dingle with his modern interpretation of a tree representing the Holy Trinity, with three branches growing from one stock. The stunning artwork combines Celtic elements with Inca traditions; a text alongside explains the symbolism of the individual carvings.

Ash at St Brigid's Well, Killare, County Westmeath (right)

The Hill of Uisneach was one of the most prestigious sites of pre-Christian Ireland, linked with the ancient division of Ireland into provinces, with a celebrated stone marking the spiritual centre of Ireland, and with the first ceremonial fire lit in the country. There are no early Christian antiquities on the hill, but medieval scribes were eager to interpret the sanctity of the place in a Christian context. They linked the area with St Patrick by claiming that he had brought the new faith to the region, and with the sixth-century St Aedh mac Bricc, who is attributed with the foundation of the first monastery at Killare at the foot of Uisneach. Aedh means fire, and evokes associations with the ceremonial fires on the hill. Fire also plays a role in the biographies of St Brigid of Kildare, who is said to have received the veil from Patrick at Uisneach. The holy well of Killare is dedicated to St Brigid. The old ash that grows over the well is hollow and has suffered severely from fire. Candles are burnt in the cavity, and visitors to the gentle place leave votive coins.[5]

One of most ferocious Christian missionaries to fight Celtic nature worship in Gaul was Martin of Tours. His biography relates that in 380 the saint began to Christianise pagan sanctuaries by smashing idols of pagan gods, polluting holy wells and cutting sacred trees. He was, in fact, the first historically recorded individual to destroy sacred trees for purely religious reasons. Others followed his lead, encouraged by synods and Episcopal instructions. Early in the fifth century, the bishop of Auxerre ordered the destruction of a sacred tree, to which local Celts would attach the heads of hunted deer as votive offerings to their gods. About 450, St Maurilius burnt down a pagan tree sanctuary at Angers; in 452, the Synod of Arles gave general orders to demolish ancient pagan sanctuaries with their holy wells, trees and stones; and the Synod of Tours in 567 carried the same demands.[6]

Into the eleventh century, the Continent experienced a systematic destruction of pagan Celtic and Germanic sacred trees and forests.[7] At the same time, Irish saints and missionaries were eagerly integrating trees into the new religion, and saw no contradiction between venerating trees and being devout Christians. It was only from the twelfth century, when ecclesiastic reforms from the Continent swept over to Ireland,[8] that the Church hierarchy began to change its attitude. Monastic orders from the Continent were encouraged to settle in Ireland and to bring the Celtic Church spiritually and structurally in line with the principles of the Papacy. All over the country, stone churches and monasteries were built, usually in the Irish Romanesque style with its arched doorways and figural carvings. Replacing earlier timber structures and open-air altars, the churches were intended to be venues for controlled and organised Christian observances. While the structural reform of the Church was successful, the spiritual concepts of the Celtic Church did not change significantly, and medieval biographers of Irish saints continued to celebrate sacred trees as manifestations of Christian power and supremacy.

Detail from Cong Abbey, County Mayo
(below) **and the Green Man, Jerpoint,**
County Kilkenny (left)

Whether desired by the reformers or not, medieval architecture apparently incorporated features of nature worship into the newly erected stone churches and monasteries of the twelfth century. Capitals and columns were often carved or painted with rich foliage, giving the impression of massive, petrified trees. Side by side with figural carvings of clearly Christian connotation were motifs of uncertain, probably earlier significance: mermaids, beasts, naked females, and male faces surrounded by greenery, commonly known today as Green Men. Carvings of Green Men are very scarce in Ireland, but popular in England, Scotland and Wales, where some thousand examples have been recorded. The origin and meaning of Green Men is uncertain, but there are suggestions that they may have been Christian interpretations of pagan tree spirits.[9]

Sacred Groves in Pagan and Early Christian Spirituality

When the seventh-century instructions for a king refer to the protection of a *fidnemed*, they employ the archaic Irish form of *fiodh-neimheadh*, a composition of the prefix *fiodh* for a wood, and *neimheadh* for sanctuary or consecrated place. The term denotes a grove or wood around a clearing, where ceremonial rites of a magical or religious nature were performed. Comparable concepts of sacred groves existed in pre-industrial cultures all over the world. In ancient Europe, they were particularly common among Indo-European people. Finnish-Ugrians, Lithuanians, Slavs, Greeks and Romans worshipped in forest sanctuaries. A sacred wood stood at Uppsala, once the religious centre of Sweden, and old German legal tracts list penalties for interfering with the trees in sacred groves.[10]

Latin commentaries on Celtic religion indicate that the Celts did not normally construct permanent temples, but worshipped their gods in the open, often in sacred forests.[11] Throughout the areas of Celtic settlement abroad, the term *nemeton* was used to denote a sacred ceremonial centre. *Nemeton* is the equivalent to the Irish *neimheadh* and appears as a component of place names from the eastern to the western fringes of the ancient Celtic world. Drunemeton was the prestigious assembly site for the Celts of Galatia in present-day Turkey. Vernementon, Nemetostatio and Aquae Arnemetiae were Celtic sanctuaries in present-day England, as were Medionemeton in Scotland, Tasinemeton in Austria and Nemetobriga in Spain, while Nemetodurum, Nemetocena and Nemetacum were Gaulish place names in what is now France. As a component of personal names, *nemeton* appears particularly in Gaul: in the northeast, Nemetona – a goddess of the woods – was worshipped in territories inhabited by the Celtic Nemetes; further south, dedications were made to the Matres Nemetiales, the divine 'Mothers of the Sanctuary'. The term *nemeton* is linguistically related to the Greek word *némos* for a wood and to the Latin term *nemus* for a forest sanctuary. There is, however, no direct evidence that the term *nemeton* was exclusively applied to ceremonial centres in sacred groves, and it is possible that it was sometimes rather loosely used as a synonym for any sanctuary.[12]

Our knowledge of Celtic sacred groves is based on explicit and often elaborate descriptions by Roman historians. Writing in about AD 60, Lucan relates how in 49 BC,

St Flannán's Shrine, Inagh, County Clare

In the seventh century St Flannán became the first bishop of Killaloe in east Clare. The saint used to travel a lot, and local legend has it that on a visit to the west of the county he took a rest in a grove near Inagh, where he left the imprints of his feet on a stone and his blessings on a well.

St Flannán's Shrine has become a popular place of pilgrimage, especially for the pattern on 18 December. It is a stunning sanctuary, a modern interpretation of an ancient ceremonial grove. The most striking features are the trees that shelter the holy well. Dominated by an old ash tree, locally referred to as the 'unusual tree', the majority of trees are adorned with devotional objects. Some have holy pictures or rosary beads attached to their bark or branches. More often, the trees carry small shrines made of plastic containers and decorated with religious statues, pictures and candles. Larger shrines, built from defunct washing machines, ovens and fridges, are set up between the trees, adding to the captivating atmosphere of the grove.

when Caesar's troops ventured into southern Gaul, they came across a Celtic sacred grove near Massilia, now modern Marseille:

> A grove there was, never profaned since time remote, enclosing with its intertwining branches the dingy air and chilly shadows, banishing sunlight far above. In this grove there are . . . altars furnished with hideous offerings, and every tree is sanctified with human blood . . . the birds fear to sit upon those branches, the beasts fear to lie in those thickets; on those woods no wind has borne down nor thunderbolts shot from black clouds; though the trees present their leaves to no breeze, they have a trembling of their own. Water pours from black springs and the grim and artless images of gods stand as shapeless fallen tree-trunks . . . Now it was rumoured that often the hollow caves below rumbled with earthquakes, that yew trees fell and rose again, that flames shot from trees which were not on fire, that snakes embraced and flowed around the trunks.

Altadaven Woods, Clogher, County Tyrone

Altadaven Woods is an ancient grove with both pagan and Christian associations. Local lore relates that the rocky outcrop in Altadaven Woods was an assembly site for pagan ceremonies, until one day St Patrick happened to pass soon after people had just gathered to worship their gods. The saint climbed a conspicuous chair-shaped rock to preach to the congregation. To prove the might of the new religion, he ordered a well to spring from a nearby bullaun stone, a large boulder with a small circular depression.

Altadaven has indeed been identified as an ancient assembly site for the harvest festival of Lughnasa. The Christianised version of the festival survived into the early decades of the twentieth century. The times of big communal gatherings at Altadaven are over, but people still visit the place individually to climb the rock-chair to make a wish, or to seek a cure at the healing well. The votive offerings of rags, ribbons and other objects attached to the old holly trees between the rock-chair and the well provide evidence of the ongoing special significance of Altadaven Woods.[13]

Caesar gave order to destroy the grove, but his terrified legionnaires refused to lay hands on the sanctuary, until Caesar himself took an axe and felled the first tree, an oak that seemed to reach the sky.[14]

Less elaborate is Tacitus' sinister account of the destruction of a Celtic sacred grove on the Isle of Mona, modern-day Anglesey off the coast of Wales. Writing in AD 115, the historian describes the Roman attack of AD 60: 'The groves devoted to Mona's barbarous superstitions he demolished. For it was their religion to drench their altars in the blood of prisoners and consult their gods by means of human entrails.' Referring to the same period, Cassius Dio noted that in the east of Britannia, the Celtic Iceni under Queen Boudicca had offered human sacrifice in the sacred grove of the goddess Andraste.[15]

Derryloran, County Derry

Early Christian missionaries often selected oak groves for the establishment of cells or monasteries. In County Derry, Doire Luráin or Derryloran, literally Luran's Oakwood, was the site of St Luran's sixth-century oratory; Kilcolman in County Offaly was originally called Derrymore or Doire Mór, after the big oak grove where St Colman built a cell at the turn of the sixth century; and around 550, St Colmcille of Derry, attracted by an oak grove, founded the monastery of Durrow or Dairmhaigh, the 'Plain of the Oaks', in County Offaly.[16]

TREES OF INSPIRATION

EDYTHE M MEMMOTT
28 LOCUST AVE

WEST LONG BRANCH, NJ 07764
USA

| er Number | 38563764 – 198071 | | | Date: | 9/01/2012 |
| tomer Reference: | | | | Despatch Note: | 20120104165401 |

N	Title	Qty	Status	Returns Reason
1848890138	Trees Of Inspiration	1		

Distribution Center

Returns Department
5520 Brick Rd.
South Bend, IN 46628
United States

Distribution Center

Returns Department
5520 Brick Rd.
South Bend, IN 46628
United States

83704 – 198071

CUSTOMS/DOUANE
DESCRIPTION   BOOKS
VALUE   17.99
NET WEIGHT   1.01 kilos
TOTAL VALUE   17.99
SIGNATURE

*** PALLET TL ***

ffica use only | EDYTHE M MEMMOTT
28 LOCUST AVE

WEST LONG BRANCH, NJ 07764
USA

0000

20120104165401

For pre-Christian Ireland, the only reference to the significance of sacred woods is a vague remark in an Old Irish glossary from the fourteenth century, which claims that the seers used to perform rituals in forest sanctuaries. Elsewhere, sacred groves appear exclusively in a Christian context, linked with monastic settlements of the early Celtic Church. From the tenth century, entries in annals and chronicles[17] report repeatedly that forest sanctuaries were accidentally destroyed by fire or wind. For the year 995, the Annals of Ulster and the Annals of the Four Masters state that lightning struck the monastic settlement of Armagh, a foundation of St Patrick. The ensuing fire destroyed the monastery along with its tree sanctuary. In the year 1077, the Annals of the Four Masters note that the monastic site of Gleann Uiseann – today Killeshin in County Wicklow – was burned with its yews. The chronicler of this incident does not explicitly speak of a tree sanctuary, but the fact that he considered the destruction of the yews memorable might indicate that they were considered to be a sacred grove.

Entries for 1146 and 1178 in both the Annals of the Four Masters and the Annals of Ulster record violent windstorms that felled numerous trees in Doire Choluim Chille, St Colmcille's beloved oak wood of Derry. In Adamnán's *Life of Colmcille*, the grove is called Roboretum Calgali or Doire Chalgaidh, and it is possible that it was a place of Christian worship before Colmcille arrived in the sixth century. Derry, however, has become firmly and exclusively linked with Colmcille. A quatrain, ascribed to the saint in Manus O'Donnell's biography, renders his respect and affection for the wood:

> *Though I am affrighted, truly,*
> *By death and by Hell,*
> *I am more affrighted, frankly,*
> *By the sound of an axe in Derry in the West.*[18]

The Lismore biography of St Colmcille relates that the saint received the oak wood, together with a fort in its centre, as a present from a local king. Before building his monastery, St Colmcille burnt the fort, but when the fire threatened to destroy the oaks, he composed a hymn to protect them. St Kevin left a protective spell on the Holy Wood, today Hollywood, in County Wicklow, where he had his first hermitage. When he decided to move eastwards into Glendalough, he found the dense forest impenetrable. So he started to pray, and the trees bent down in front of him to give way, only to rise again after the saint had passed. Similarly, St Brigid gained control over a forest by means of her blessings. It hence became Ross na Ferta, the Wood of the Miracle, north of Kildare.[19]

Eager to assign a purely Christian origin to the sanctuaries of early Christian Ireland,

St Colman mac Duach's Hermitage, Slieve Carran, County Clare

St Colman mac Duach was renowned for his reclusive character. When he first retreated from public life around AD 600, he built an oratory in a dense and remote hazel wood at the foot of Slieve Carran in the Burren area of County Clare. Today his hermitage lies in ruins, and only a few pilgrims visit the holy well in the peaceful grove. Barely able to infiltrate the thick foliage, the sun casts a diffuse light on the rounded boulders, which are overgrown with mosses and lichens.[20]

hagiographical texts would naturally maintain that it was only the link with particular saints that turned ordinary forests into sacred groves. Several Irish saints are portrayed by their biographers as characters with an extreme desire for solitude. St Kevin of Glendalough, for instance, and St Colman mac Duach were among them, and it is very likely that they both selected specific groves for their retreats for the mere sake of remoteness and inaccessibility. Most Irish saints were less reclusive, and their biographies present them eagerly travelling to spread the new faith. St Patrick, St Brigid, St Colmcille and other great missionaries who throughout Ireland are linked with sacred groves and individual trees, would hardly have selected a remote forest in which to establish a Christian place of worship. In these cases, it is reasonable to assume that the main motivation for the selection of a site was the presence of a pagan sanctuary.[21]

Sacred Trees and the Celtic Church

As well as groves and forest sanctuaries, individual sacred trees must have played an important role in pagan Celtic religion. Lucan, describing the sacred forest of Massilia, noted that 'grim and artless images of gods stand as shapeless fallen tree-trunks'. Writing in the second century AD, the Greco-Roman scholar Maximos of Tyros reported that the Celts of Galatia venerated Zeus as their uppermost god, and that his idol was a tall oak tree. Inscriptions from Gaul show that the Celts of Aquitaine made dedications to Sexarbor Deus, 'god of the six trees', to Deus Robur, 'oak god', and to Deus Fagus, 'beech god'.[22] The most compelling evidence for the tremendous importance of sacred trees in pagan spirituality, however, are the edicts and instructions of the official Christian Church that these trees be destroyed.

In Ireland, a few literary sources from medieval times refer to sacred trees of pre-Christian significance. An oracular tree occurs in the biography of St Berach; a druidic priest of Crann Greine, or 'sacred branch of the sun', is mentioned in another text; and Eó Rossa, referred to as 'fuel of sages', is associated with druidism through the seer Eohy, who reportedly crafted a shield made of wood from the tree.[23]

Because early Irish missionaries saw no contradiction between the veneration of trees and the doctrine of the new religion, medieval scribes could easily utilise the cult of mythical otherworld trees, interpreting them within the framework of Christian ideas without detaching them from the world of imagination and wonder. A description of a tree with nine branches, growing downwards from heaven like an inverted world tree, and emitting sweet melodies listened to by white birds, is for example used as an allegory for Christ, the nine grades of heaven, and the pure white souls of the just.[24]

The 'Voyage of Snedgus and Mac Riagla', preserved in a fourteenth-century manuscript, makes mention of another wondrous tree. The text tells how two of Colmcille's clerics went off course when travelling from Ireland to Iona, and 'Thereafter the wind wafts them to an island wherein was a great tree with beautiful birds. Atop of it was a great bird with a head of gold and with wings of silver … And the bird bestows on the clerics a leaf of the leaves of that tree, and the size of the hide of a large ox was that leaf. And the bird told the clerics to take that leaf and place it on Colmcille's altar. So that is Colmcille's flabellum. In Kells it is.' A version of the story appears in the fourteenth-century tale, 'The Adventure of St Columba's Clerics', in the Yellow Book of Lecan. It describes the tree as 'having a frame of silver and golden leaves upon it, and its summit spread over the whole isle.'[25]

TREES OF INSPIRATION

St Maelruan's Tree, Dominican Convent, Tallaght, Dublin (opposite)

Into the nineteenth century, St Maelruan's walnut tree was popularly thought to have been planted by the eighth-century saint and founder of Tallaght monastery. Walnut trees, however, are not indigenous to Ireland; since they were only introduced around 1760, it is generally understood today that the present tree was planted when the original tree or its descendant had decayed. In 1795, the walnut tree was struck by lightning, and split into several parts. But it survived, and the parts took root and grew into a magnificently wide-spreading tree that still produces plentiful crops.[26]

Entries in annals and chronicles provide documentary evidence for historical *biledha* or individual sacred trees at early ecclesiastic sites. For the year 1013, the Chronicum Scotorum mentions the destruction by storm of the great oak of Regles-Finghin, a church attached to the monastic settlement of Clonmacnoise. For 1149, the same source records that lightning struck and fell the yew tree of St Ciarán at Clonmacnoise. The Annals of the Four Masters note for the year 1056, that 'Lightning came and killed three persons at Disert-Tola and a student at Sord and broke down the bilé'. For the year 1162, the Annals report the burning of the yews of Iubhar-Chinntrechta or the 'yew at the head of the strand', which is modern-day Newry in County Down. Some monastic foundations that perpetuate the names of highly revered individual trees are long lost; Craibh Laisre or Laisre's Bush near Clonmacnoise, for example, is only remembered in archival sources. Other foundations such as Cill Dara or Kildare, the 'church of the oak', are still prominent, even though the name-giving trees decayed in medieval times.[27]

The shrine of Kildare is believed to have originally been a pagan sanctuary, guarded by vestal virgins and presided over by a female druid or priestess that bore the name of the Celtic goddess, Brigid. The last Brigid in the line of pagan priestesses would have accepted Christianity and consequently have re-dedicated the site, with its perpetual fire and sacred tree, into a Christian place of worship. It seems likely that similar transformations took place elsewhere, particularly where saints took on the names of pagan deities: St Nechtan of Dungiven in County Derry carries the name of the aquatic god Nechtan or Nuadhu; Bronach was the name of a goddess and of the sixth-century foundress of Kilbroney Church in County Down; and several saints were called Molua, an affectionate version of Lugh or Lughaidh, who was a fictional hero and ancient Celtic deity.

As with sacred forests, we can assume that saints and missionaries frequently adopted revered trees of pagan significance. The earliest references for the transformation of a sacred tree of apparently pre-Christian significance into a Christian shrine are contained in the eighth-century Book of Armagh and the ninth-century *Tripartite Life of St Patrick*. They relate that Patrick built the church of Ard Breacáin – today anglicised as Ardbraccan, in County Meath – near Bile Tortan, one of the most prestigious assembly trees of ancient Ireland.

According to his biographers, St Patrick through his blessings Christianised several ancient Lughnasa assembly sites with their wells, stones and trees. Among these trees is the predecessor of the young thorn that grows today over St Patrick's Well in Oran in County Roscommon; an ancient ash tree that still thrives beside the healing well in Miskaun Glebe in County Leitrim; and the old and gnarled Críocan Thorn high up on the Offaly side of the Slieve Bloom Mountains.[28]

St Patrick's Tree, Miskaun Glebe, County Leitrim (above)

St Patrick's Well in Miskaun Glebe is considered particularly effective as a cure for warts and other skin ailments. The old custom to bathe the afflicted part of the body with a rag dipped into the water, and then to tie the rag to the tree beside the well, is still occasionally practised. The well-tree, a beautiful old ash, is believed locally to pre-date Christianity. Tradition has it that St Patrick said Mass under its branches.[29]

St Patrick's Bush, Oran, County Roscommon (opposite)

Oran has been identified as an old Lughnasa assembly site, and to this day the shrine is most frequently visited at the beginning of autumn. Like many other Lughnasa sites, Oran is firmly linked with St Patrick, who, according to local tradition, rested at a whitethorn beside the spring and left his blessings on the place before resuming his journey. Today, pilgrims begin and end their rounds at St Patrick's Bush, a successor of the original thorn, but the custom of tying votive ribbons to its branches has died away.[30]

TREES OF INSPIRATION

A popular motif in the biographies of St Patrick is his encounter with 'holy men', presumably pre-Patrician Christians, dwelling in or under trees. Bishop Tíreachán's account of St Patrick's mission relates that the saint built a church in a place called Nairniu on the Roscommon-Mayo border, where he had come upon a holy man named Iarnascus, sitting under an elm tree. Patrick continued his journey to a well called Mucno – present-day Tobar Makee in Drumtemple in County Roscommon – where again he met a holy man, Secundinus, sitting under an elm tree, and founded a church before heading on.[31]

The life of St Patrick in the Book of Lismore relates that the saint was approaching Clonmacnoise, when he met a leper sitting in a hollow elm at a place now known as St Ciarán's Well. In another story, Patrick's servant Muinis arrived at this tree at night-fall and put some relics into its hollow. Next morning, when Muinis found that the tree had closed over the relics, Patrick foretold that a man would come soon who would need the relics. The man in question was St Ciarán, the founder of Clonmacnoise. A tree used for a retreat occurs also in the biography of St Kevin, who spent a number of years as a hermit in a hollow tree near the Upper Lake before moving to found the monastery of Glendalough.[32]

References in medieval biographies and modern folklore accounts say that early Irish saints, when travelling to spread the faith, preferred to spend the night in or under trees, and would hang relics and other valuables from their branches, thus creating tree sanctuaries all over the country. St Colmcille is popularly associated with several trees and thorns in the northern half of Ireland. One of them is a thorn into which the saint hung his books, known as Drum a Leabhair or the Bush of Books, in Croaghross near Kilmacrenan in County Donegal. An episode in St Colmcille's biography in the Book of Lismore, compiled in the fifteenth century from older sources, indicates that the saint preferred to sit and contemplate under a particular oak tree in Kells in County Meath, close to his monastic foundation. St Ciarán of Seir was associated with numerous sacred ash trees and thorn bushes in Counties Laois and Offaly, many of them long decayed and forgotten.[33]

Hagiographical texts abound with accounts of sacred trees that owe their existence to the blessings or miracles of saints, but known to date, there is not one single reference in the biographies of saints actually planting trees. Curiously, in oral tradition the motif of sacred trees planted by the hands of saints is extremely popular and was current from the twelfth century. The tale was attached to trees of local significance, such as St Cuimin's Yews in Rutland in County Offaly and St Latiaran's Whitethorn in Cullen in County Cork,[34] as well as to widely known and celebrated trees. Famous for its protective

St Ciarán's Thorn and Well, Clonmacnoise, County Offaly

The Long Station pilgrimage at Clonmacnoise was traditionally done in bare feet. It was a considerable circuit, taking in two wells, several praying stations inside the monastic enclosure, and a small church on the old pilgrimage route. The circuit started at St Ciarán's Well with prayers, rounds of the well, and reverence paid to the carved stones beside it. One of the carvings is said to represent St Ciarán. Before moving on, pilgrims may hang offerings of rags or religious objects to the old tree that stands beside the well – a whitethorn that has no thorns. Clonmacnoise has remained a notable place of pilgrimage, especially around the saint's feast on 9 September. The Long Station is no longer undertaken by most devotees, but a visit to St Ciarán's Well and Thorn is still part of the pilgrimage.[35]

virtues was St Kevin's Yew in Glendalough in County Wicklow. The tree stood near the portals of the cathedral. It was severely damaged around 1835 by a landowner who cut off its major branches and used the timber to make furniture. People from the area gathered the fragments of the yew to keep them as precious talismans.[36]

In 1758, the English cleric Richard Pococke was the first to describe in writing the

Churchyard Yew, Muckross Abbey, Killarney, County Kerry

In the 1840s, local folklore had a lot to say about the celebrated Muckross Yew. The Anglo-Irish journalists Mr and Mrs Samuel Hall wrote that the yew was believed locally to have been planted by the monks who built the abbey. They also recorded the commonly held belief that anyone who dared to injure the tree would not be alive on that day twelvemonth. In 1842, the English illustrator William Henry Bartlett published his account of *The Scenery and Antiquities of Ireland*. He, too, refers to the folklore of the Muckross Yew, and notes that the tree was supposedly 'planted by the blessed hands of Colmkille [sic] himself, who left a strict order and command to all thrue [sic] believers not to touch so much as a leaf from it.' Bartlett also renders the tale of a young man who ignored the sacred prohibition. The next morning he was found dying in the cloisters of Muckross, lying on the ground steeped with blood that was dripping from the yew, and clutching the twig that he had broken.[37]

extraordinary yew tree in the centre of the cloisters of Muckross Abbey in County Kerry. In 1776, the English historian and writer Arthur Young praised 'the most prodigious yew tree I ever beheld, on a great stem, two feet diameter, and fourteen feet high, from whence a vast head of branches spreads on every side, so as to form a perfect canopy for the whole space.' To the German traveller Johann G. Kohl, who paid a visit to Muckross in the 1840s, the tree was 'the finest and most handsome Irish yew tree' he had ever seen. The earliest accounts of the tradition that the yew was planted by St Colmcille date from about this time. Botanists strongly question these accounts and reckon that the tree may have been planted between the foundation of the friary in the fifteenth century and its dissolution in the course of the Reformation during the sixteenth century, or after Muckross was burned by Cromwellian troops in 1652.

Tree Miracles and Miraculous Trees

When the saints of the early Celtic Church took over the religious functions of druids, they also inherited their knowledge of sorcery and magic. Interpreted in a Christian context, incantations were regarded as prayers to either bless or curse, while acts of magic and sorcery became miracles. Medieval biographies of saints are basically compilations of tales describing miracles and wonders, written with the intention of demonstrating the might and power of the new religion.

Moving Trees and the Power of Prayer

Among the special powers attributed particularly to saints from the late sixth and early seventh century was the ability to move or uproot trees by prayer. A lovely episode in the lives of St Maedhóg and St Molaise relates how, when the childhood friends were trying to decide whether they should stay together or go their separate ways to spread the faith, they prayed for a sign from heaven sitting down under a tree each. When the trees fell in different directions, the friends bid each other farewell and travelled in the directions indicated by the trees. St Maedhóg went south to Leinster where he founded the monastery of Ferns; St Molaise turned north and established a monastery on Devenish Island on Lough Erne.[38]

As a means of emphasising the superiority of the Christian religion, miracles involving trees of pre-Christian significance were sometimes performed in contests with druids.

At the turn of the sixth century, St Berach or Barry was reportedly challenged by a druid, whereupon the saint, through his prayer, moved a pagan oracular tree from a place called Rathin to another assembly place, and had it firmly rooted in its new location.[39]

Early in the seventh century, St Laserian, the first bishop of Leighlin, wanted the timber of Eó Rossa to build a church. The sacred yew – which apparently stood near Old Leighlin in County Carlow, close to Dind Ríg, the ancient seat of the kings of Leinster[40] – is regarded as one of the most notable mythical trees of ancient Ireland, and was very likely a real tree of pagan importance.

A biography of St Laserian tells of how a number of saints had assembled under the tree and prayed for it to fall. At each prayer, the roots of Eó Rossa seemed to move a little, but only the prayers of St Laserian managed to uproot the tree. He kept some timber for himself and distributed the surplus to other saints who wanted it for building purposes. Among them was seventh-century St Moling. A biography of the saint relates that he sought and obtained some timber of Eó Rossa for the roofing of his oratory, which became known as Tech Moling in St Mullin's in County Carlow. Another biographer tells of a mighty oak tree with which St Moling wanted to build the church of St Mullin's. When cut, the tree fell into the ditches and dense woods beside the River Barrow, and the workmen were unable to recover it. Upon a prayer of the saint, however, the tree was miraculously transported into its proper place.[41]

Trees of Miraculous Origin

The biographies of early Irish saints abound with stories that attribute the origin of sacred trees to miracles performed by patron saints and founders of places of worship. The motifs from hagiographical texts were readily adopted into the oral tradition of local saints. Antiquarian reports and folklore surveys indicate that legends of trees created through acts of magic and miracles were widespread and popular throughout the nineteenth century, but from around 1900, when the majority of the legendary trees had begun to decay from old age, their stories often died with them.

Particularly popular among medieval scribes was the motif of a saint's staff or walking stick, taking roots and growing into a venerable tree. This story is reminiscent of the legendary origin of the famous Glastonbury Thorn in England, a hawthorn which supposedly grew from the walking stick of Joseph of Arimathea, who came to England as a metal merchant accompanied by the child Jesus. When Joseph drove his staff into the ground on Christmas Eve to pray with his followers, God responded by causing the staff to bud and eventually grow into a tree. Plants grown from cuttings from the original

Young yew tree at Old Leighlin, County Carlow

A litany of thirty-one epithets, attributed to Druim Suithe, the poet, is preserved in the Dindshenchas and praises the famous tree. The poem stands in the Christian tradition, but some of the epithets seem to echo earlier concepts. They link the Yew of Rossa with the idea of a 'world tree' and its association with kingship and victory, heaven and doom, sacred knowledge and mystic insight. There is also a reference to Banba, the ancient land goddess and personification of Ireland.[42]

Yew of Rossa,
Royal wheel,
Regent's rule,
Wave's sound,
Best of beings,
Straight, strong tree,
Stout, strong god,
Door of heaven,
Building's strength,
Crew's captain,
Man of pure words,
Plenteous bounty,
Trinity's might,
Measure of matter,
Mother's good,
Mary's son,
Fruitful sea,
Beauty's honour,
Mind's master,
Diadem of angels,
Cry of Life,
Banba's renowned,
Vigour of victory,
Decision's basis,
Doom's decision,
Fuel of sages,
Noblest tree,
Fame of Leinster,
Gentlest bush,
Champion's cover,
Vitality's vigour,
Spell of knowledge,
Yew of Rossa.

Glastonbury Thorn survive to our day, and the legend and history of the tree are still well remembered.[43]

Around 810, St Colman mac Duach – born under a sacred ash in Kiltartan, County Galway – retreated to a hermitage in a hazel grove, then founded the monastery of Kilmacduagh in County Galway. His biography relates that the saint had an extraordinary tree there, Cuaille Mhic Duach or Mac Duach's Stake, which had the reputation for saving people from an untimely death.[44] The term *cuaille* or stake for a tree was usually reserved for trees that had miraculously grown from staffs or walking sticks. Cuaille Cianacht, the Stake of Keenaght, is another example. It is mentioned in an entry in the Annals of the Four Masters for the year 1157, and identified with Coolkeenaght near Faughanvale in County Derry.

Very little is known today about St Mochoemóg's Stake in Eile, County Offaly, a tree that grew from a staff planted in the ground by the saint to mark the burial place of a victim of murder. St Brandon's sacred ash in Thornback, County Kilkenny, overshadowed a holy well known as Tubber-a-crinn, or the Well of the Tree, until it decayed from old age in the nineteenth century. The tree reportedly grew from the staff of the local patron saint, Brandon, a contemporary of St Patrick. St Patrick himself left a walking stick stuck in the ground beside a well in the townland of Tully near Kilcorkey in County Roscommon, which also grew into a venerable ash tree that shadowed the local holy well.[45]

'The Petrified Woman', Garranes, County Kerry (above)

The legend of sixth-century St Fiachna tells of a woman who cheated on the saint by secretly selling the butter from his cows on the market. Fiachna soon discovered her disloyalty, and through a curse petrified the woman, turning her into a pillar stone. The rope that she was carrying grew into a thorn beside the pillar.[46]

St Moling's Walking Stick, Mullennakill, County Kilkenny (right)

The biographers of St Moling link the seventh-century saint with several tree miracles. One of them relates to Moling's Tree beside his well in Mullennakill. The original tree, described as a thorn, a hazel or an oak, reputedly grew from the saint's staff which he planted in the ground. In reverence for the tree, the well was originally known as Tobar Crann Mo-Long, or the Well of Moling's Tree. The tree has renewed itself many times in the shape of different tree species. Today it is an alder tree, and pieces of its bark and twigs are taken as talismans against fire.[47]

Crann Cholmáin or St Colman's Tree in old Kilcolman graveyard near Ardmore, County Waterford, disappeared around 1840. The once highly revered tree was locally believed to stem from a dry stick which the saint had stuck into the ground. The tree was thought to be immortal and indestructible, and it was considered extremely unlucky to remove so much as twigs and branches that fell from the tree for firewood. One story has it that a man who broke some twigs off the tree to use as kindling found his house burnt to the ground when he returned home.[48]

A legend that is still current – even though the tree had rotted away by 1838 – concerns St Patrick's Walking Stick in Rathnaleugh, County Louth. According to local legend, Patrick once visited the area and being thirsty took a rest at the well. Before resuming his journey, he blessed the well and planted his staff of yew in the bank beside it. When the stick began to grow into a tree, the well became popularly known as the Yew Tree Well, and the adjoining graveyard of ruined Kilklienagh Church as the Yew Tree Graveyard.[49]

During the birth of St Senan in the second half of the fifth century, his mother clutched a stake of rowan. At his birth it took roots, burst into flower, and soon grew into a venerable tree, which was a visitors' attraction until the end of the nineteenth century. Later in his life, St Senan founded a monastery on Inis Cathaigh or Scattery Island on the Shannon Estuary in County Clare. Local lore, based on the biography of the saint, recounts how when the island was suffering a severe drought, Senan dug a well with a stick of hazel or holly and set the stick beside the well. The dry wood took roots immediately, so that the following morning the brethren found a fully-grown tree on the edge of the well.[50]

An interesting variant of the motif in Manus O'Donnell's *Life of St Colmcille* explains the origin of a holly tree that once stood in Meenaneary in County Donegal. The biography was compiled in 1532, but is based on earlier texts and oral traditions of the saint. It tells of Colmcille's encounter with demons, who occupied this part of County Donegal after St Patrick expelled them from Croagh Patrick in County Mayo. When Colmcille approached, the demons covered the area with fog, and out of the fog they hurled a holly spear which killed Colmcille's servant, Cerc. Colmcille took the spit and hurled it back into the fog, and the mist lifted. The spit took root where it struck the ground and grew into a fine holly which would not wither until Doomsday. In 1835, when John O'Donovan visited Meenaneary for the Ordnance Survey, the holly tree was thriving on the bank of the River Glinne. In the 1940s, folklore records indicate that the holly and its story were still alive; sadly, the tree has since vanished and its history is hardly remembered in the area.[51]

Sacred Ash Tree, Tubberberrin, Woodtown, County Meath

In the eighteenth or nineteenth century, the miracle of a tree growing from dry timber is said to have occurred in Woodtown and is still remembered locally. The story has it that after a vision, a mother brought her unfortunate son, Bernard or Biorrán – who was barely able to walk – to a particular spring. Bathing in the well healed his limbs to such an extent that he was able to walk away, leaving his crutches behind. The spring was forthwith called Bernard's Well or Tubberberrin, and from the crutches grew two wondrous trees, which produced oak leaves in the first year, ash leaves in the second, and elm leaves in the third, all in a continuous cycle, so that it was impossible to establish the species of the trees. The eventual decay of the trees is attributed to the custom of sticking pins into their bark, and breaking off twigs and branches as talismans for house protection. Around 1950, only the half-rotten remains of the trees were left. Strikingly, the decaying stump of one of the trees took on the shape of a cross, and visitors to the well continued to take portions of the stump home, until it, too, literally disappeared. The well is still visited, particularly for the annual pilgrimage on 1 August. An ash tree nearby has one major branch growing over the well, while its smaller branches grow in rectangular shapes and resemble crutches.[52]

The growth of a sacred tree from a saint's staff was a particularly popular theme with medieval biographers, but they also used other colourful motifs to explain how a venerated tree came into being. Several of these tales have become current in local folklore.

Crannahulla, from Crann a'Shúile or the Tree of the Eye, was the old name for one of the sacred ash trees in the parish of Clenor in County Cork. Its origin is linked with the legend of beautiful St Craebhnat, who – in spite of her vow of virginity – was promised to the prince of Munster. When the groom came to carry her off, she tore out one of her eyes to disfigure herself and threw it to the ground. From the eye sprung the sacred ash, which was said to be distinguished by its immortality and its incombustible timber.[53]

St Naile's Apple Tree in Kinawley in County Fermanagh thrived into the early years of the twentieth century. The tree's origin was traditionally associated with the arrival of sixth-century saints Naile and Ninion, and with their argument over who had the right to become the patron of the area. To decide the matter, each saint marked an apple and threw it into a pool on top of a hill. An underground stream connected the pool with a nearby spring, and St Naile's apple came up first in this well. He thus won the honour to be the patron saint, and founded a church, Cill Náile, which was later anglicised to Kinawley. By the saint's blessing, the spring turned into a holy well with healing properties. A crab-apple tree sprang up beside the well from the seeds of Naile's apple. Pilgrims, seeking a cure at the well, believed that hearing a robin singing in the tree was a sign that their prayers would be answered.[54]

The name of Tobar an Deilg or the Well of the Thorn, on the east side of Lough Foyle in County Derry, refers to an episode from the life of St Colmcille. The saint, so the story goes, had a thorn in his foot and bathed it in the well to soothe the pain. The thorn came out and grew into a venerable whitethorn tree beside the well. In another legend, sixth-century St Ita pulled a thorn from under her donkey's hoof and thrust it to the ground, ordering the thorn to never harm her animal again. Obediently, the thorn grew into a large whitethorn tree whose thorns all pointed downwards. The tree – known as St Ita's Thorn – stood close to the saint's church in Killeedy in County Limerick; it decayed shortly before 1895.[55]

Trees of Wondrous Virtues

In 1185, the historian Giraldus Cambrensis or Gerald of Wales accompanied Prince John, later King John of England, on a visit to Ireland. In *Topographia Hibernica*, his account of their journey, Giraldus gives a description of Glendalough in County Wicklow, writing in detail of an extraordinary tree that owed its virtues to a miracle performed by St Kevin at the turn of the seventh century:

> At the time when St Kevin was distinguished for his life and sanctity in Glendalough a noble boy, who was a student of his, happened to be sick and to ask for fruit. The saint had pity on him and prayed for him to the Lord. Whereupon a willow tree not far from the church brought forth fruit that was health-giving to the boy and to others that were sick. And to this day both the willow tree and others planted from it around the cemetery like a wall of willows bring forth fruit each year, although in all other respects, in their leaves and branches, they retain their own natural qualities. The fruit is white and oblong in shape, health-giving rather than pleasant to the taste. The local people have a great regard for it. Many bring it to the farthest parts of Ireland to cure various diseases, and it is called the first fruit of St Kevin.[56]

In the twelfth century, the fruit were also known as St Kevin's Apples. Current popular renditions of the tale claim that the young man had begged the saint for an apple to cure his illness. Kevin, with a prayer to God, plucked three fruits from a willow tree which immediately turned into apples and cured the patient. The tale is reminiscent of an episode from a biography of St Patrick, who made apple blossoms appear on an ash tree – which became known as Crann Comhaita or the Tree of Power – in order to demonstrate the might of Christianity to the pagan prince of Munster. St Brigid is attributed with blessing an alder which consequently produced apples and sloes, and cursing a fruitful apple tree, making it barren.[57]

St Carthage of Lismore was a contemporary of St Kevin. A description of his life recounts that he was preaching in the Rathan area of present-day County Offaly when a druid approached him. The magi challenged Carthage to make an apple tree produce leaves, even though it was winter. The saint blessed the tree and it did produce leaves. The druid then asked the saint to make the tree bloom, then to make it produce fruit, then to order the fruit to ripen. The saint answered each request with a blessing, and every time the tree immediately responded. Finally, when the druid tasted an apple and found it bitter, the saint blessed the fruit and suddenly it tasted as sweet as honey.[58] Another legend holds that St Colmcille had an apple tree that bore only bitter fruit at his monastery in Durrow in County Offaly. When Colmcille blessed the tree and ordered it to let all bitterness depart, the apples became delightful and sweet.[59]

The abbey of Lorrha in present-day County Tipperary, established in the sixth century

'A tree by the name of Tilia', Tuamgraney, County Clare (left)

The medieval biographers of St Colm of Terryglass, or Colm mac Crimthainn, wrote that in the sixth century, the saint came to Inis Cealtra in Lough Derg on the Shannon. On the island he met an old man called Maccriche, who had a wondrous tree by the name of Tilia, 'whose juice distilling filled a vessel and that liquor had the flavour of honey and the headiness of wine.' Tilia is the Latin name for the lime or linden tree, and the delicate flavour of honey produced from lime tree blossom is well renowned. A beautiful example grows through a crack in the lime-stone base in the memorial park of Tuamgraney, close to Lough Derg and Inis Cealtra.[60]

Linden blossom (right)

Lime or linden trees feature very seldom in the medieval lore of Irish saints and their miraculous trees. The tree is not indigenous to Ireland, and must have been extremely rare at the time. The first specimints were possibly introduced from the Continent, where linden trees have been treasured for their blossom since the Middle Ages. Lime-blossom honey — valued for its superior quality — is used almost exclusively as medicine or in the manufacture of liqueurs; lime-blossom tea is appreciated for curing colds.

by St Ruadhán, was in medieval times one of Munster's most renowned religious centres and a popular place for pilgrimages. Lorrha was particularly famous for St Ruadhán's lime tree, from which reputedly dripped a sweet-tasting sap. The liquid was said to provide enough food for monks and visitors alike, and everyone found the flavour he or she desired in it. Unfortunately, not all the monks of Lorrha were pleased with the miraculous tree, and several saints from other places were jealous of the popularity of Ruadhán on account of it. Eventually, Ruadhán was ordered to put a stop to the miracle. He made the sign of the cross over the tree which stopped the dripping immediately.[61]

In the 1870s, John O'Hanlon paid a visit to Seir Kieran in County Offaly and noted: 'There is a bush on top of this hill, which is believed to have vegetated since the time of St Kieran.' Immortality was a miraculous quality often attributed to the sacred trees of early Irish saints. It was believed up until the nineteenth century that the trees had survived from the times of the earliest Irish saints and missionaries.[62]

A coppiced tree

To some degree, the belief in the immortality of sacred trees arose from the impressive age that certain species can reach, their resistance to severe weather conditions, and their ability to coppice, or grow anew from the stump, as long as their roots are not damaged.

The notion of immortal trees was regularly supported by reports of sacred trees that renewed themselves after they had seemingly died. Some of these are trees of rather local significance, such as the immortal hawthorn at Tubber Patrick near Muff in County Donegal,[63] which continued to grow even after being cut and uprooted. Other reports concern widely known and revered trees. St Maelruan's Tree in Tallaght was struck by lightning and split into several parts, which took root and grew into an impressive and still fruitful tree. St Fintan's Money Tree – by the roadside near Clonenagh in County

Laois – was a sycamore which lodged a well in one of its forks. The sycamore apparently died from metal poisoning caused by money stuck into its bark. Soon after the tree fell, a shoot began to sprout from the stump and has since grown into a fine young tree. The same phenomenon can be witnessed in Fore in County Westmeath with St Féichín's sacred ash tree, and at Seir Kieran in County Offaly, where a strong thorn grew from the roots of its decayed ancestor.

The Tree that would not Burn, Fore Abbey, County Westmeath (right)

Fore Abbey, established in the sixth century by St Féichín, was once renowned for its seven wonders. These were the construction of the monastery in the bog; an image of an anchorite in stone; a mill without a stream; a stream that flowed uphill; well water that would not boil; a massive stone lintel raised by an angel; and a tree that would not burn. The tradition of a fire-resisting tree had particular meaning in Fore, since the monastery was burnt no less then twelve times between the eighth and the twelfth centuries. Pilgrims used to tie rags and other votive offering to the branches of the tree that would not burn, but they also hammered coins into its bark (above). Eventually, the old tree died from metal poisoning, but a new, fresh one has since grown from the stump.[64]

Trees of
Spiritual Transformation

One solitary tree, the only one that meets the eye on this secluded spot, overshadows the well, and it is covered with pieces of cloth in all colours. These pieces of cloth have been tied to the branches of the tree by grateful pilgrims, who have experienced the beneficial influence of the water beneath.

John O'Hanlon, *Lives of the Irish Saints* (1875)[1]

Pilgrimage and Church Reforms

Sacred places accredited with the power of spiritual and physical transformation are especially sought out in times of crisis. Some shrines have gained a special reputation for healing specific ailments, while others are considered helpful for a range of complaints and problems, for granting any type of wish, or for offering protection from perils and catastrophes.

Sacred trees of transformation stand almost exclusively at old places of Christian worship, particularly near holy wells, or in graveyards that have survived from early monastic settlements. Most likely many of these places were successors of ancient pagan shrines, ceremonially visited by people who would have sought the divine by appealing to the spirits or deities connected to the place.[2] With the coming of Christianity, magical rites were transformed into Christian devotion, and ceremonial pagan worship became pilgrimage. The ritual release of the indwelling power of sacred trees and places

St Brigid's Ash, Mullennakill, County Kilkenny

With the spread of Christianity, shrines and sacred places became firmly and exclusively linked to saints and missionaries. Trees, stones and wells were seen as channels of communication between pilgrims and local patron saints, enabling devotees to communicate with God and the Holy Family through the intercession of the respective saint.

has considerable regional variants, depending on localised customs, the religious persuasion of the applicants, and the problems they wanted to solve. In their present form, the observations at sacred places are a legacy of the early Celtic Church, but they preserve ancient traits and practices that certainly pre-date the arrival of Christianity in Ireland.[3]

On the Continent, the Christian Church radically changed its attitude towards nature worship in early medieval times, initiating a campaign to eliminate what it considered a symbol of heathendom and a threat to Christianity. The destruction of openly pagan sanctuaries was followed by Church reforms. From the twelfth to the late eighteenth century, the Church was eager to erase all remnants of any semi-pagan practices that may have survived within Christian devotion. Offerings at sacred trees were discredited in favour of financial contributions to the Church; venerated trees were built into the masonry of churches and chapels to prevent people from interacting with them; and trees were adorned with sacred pictures and linked to legends of the Holy Family in an effort to suppress older, more archaic cults of local saints.

In Ireland, the survival of ancient traits and customs in Christian observances was aided by the political and social development of the country from the late medieval period. In the twelfth century, ecclesiastic reforms from the Continent reached Ireland and influenced the attitude of the official Church towards archaic religious practices. In 1155, English-born Pope Adrian IV granted the sovereignty of Ireland to the Anglo-Norman King of England, Henry II, as a tactical move to aid Church reforms and to copperfasten the influence of the Papacy on spiritual matters. His grant was in fact a licence to invade Ireland, but while the ensuing Norman and English conquests eradicated the Gaelic political system, religious and spiritual matters were hardly affected. The authority of the Papacy in Irish affairs decreased considerably from the 1530s, when King Henry VIII set up an independent reformed Church – in Ireland established as the Church of Ireland – under the supremacy of the English monarch. The Church of Ireland lacked the cultural insight and the language for large-scale conversions and soon became the Church for those loyal to the English Crown, while wide sections of the native Irish population held on to the Catholic faith which still contained many elements and views of the early Celtic Church. With Cromwell's offensive in 1649, Papal influence came to an end. The prosecution of the Catholic faith under Cromwell's regime, followed by oppressive laws in the aftermath of the Battle of the Boyne at the end of the century, deprived the Irish Catholic Church of the structure and means to modernise herself in line with the principles of Rome. It was only after Catholic Emancipation in 1829 and especially after the Famine years in the 1840s that the Church hierarchy in Ireland had the power to eliminate unconventional practices from Catholic devotion.

One reason for the Church's growing hostility towards traditional religious observances was certainly the misconduct and disorderly behaviour that reportedly developed around pilgrimages. However, contemporary reports also indicate a conscious and deliberate elimination of archaic pagan traits, which were vilified as superstitious practices. Paul Cullen, Archbishop of Armagh from 1840 to 1870, was the most ferocious reformer of Irish Catholicism. He banned pilgrimages to holy wells, suppressed the outdoor celebration of Mass and ordered or encouraged the removal or destruction of several sacred stones and trees, the veneration of which was considered particularly incompatible with Catholic principles.

In the 1840s, when John O'Donovan travelled Ireland for the Ordnance Survey, he regretted in a letter from County Roscommon that the priests, 'inclining very much to Protestant notions, are putting an end to all those venerable old customs.'[4] Thomas O'Conor, who worked with O'Donovan, described the traditional pilgrimage to Lough Ciarán in County Mayo on the last Sunday in July, relating how pilgrims would swim horses in the lake for protection, and throw offerings of butter into the water to safeguard the well-being and productivity of their cows. Also for protective purposes, ropes and chains used for tying animals were fastened to a nearby sacred tree. Shortly before 1838, following orders by the Catholic bishop of the diocese who wished to end the old ceremonies at the lake, the revered tree was cut down.[5] At about the same time, the sacred ash at St Olan's Well in Aghabullogue, County Cork, was felled by order of the parish priest. Local tradition held that the wood of the tree did not burn, and the men who cut the tree never had 'a day's luck' afterwards. In Belcoo, County Fermanagh, the dangers involved in interfering with a sacred tree were taken more seriously, and when the local priest attempted to end the 'pure paganism' of hanging rags and religious objects to a bush beside St Patrick's Well, he could find no one willing to cut the bush.[6]

In the period of nineteenth-century Church reform new churches were built, with the intention of transforming religious worship from an outdoor affair into well-organised public services in consecrated buildings. Often of impressive size, the new churches demonstrated the rise and increasing power of the Catholic Church in Ireland.[7] Characteristically, there was a tendency to dedicate these new churches to the Virgin Mary rather than to a local patron saint. A passionate veneration of Mary had spread throughout western Christendom from the times of the Crusades and on the Continent, countless sacred places were rededicated to Mary. In Ireland, rededications are scarce, but devotion for the Virgin is evident in Lourdes grottoes throughout the country, and in her intense veneration in the context of apparitions.

St Ciarán's Tree, Seir Kieran, County Offaly

Legend has it that St Patrick gave a bell to St Ciarán and advised him to build a monastery at the place where the bell started to ring. The monastic site selected with the help of the bell was Seir Kieran. The spot where the bell gave its sound is marked by a whitethorn that was formerly called Bell Bush, but has long become commonly known as St Ciarán's Tree. Despite Church reforms and modernisations, St Ciarán's Tree is still held in enormous veneration, and its branches are covered with votive offerings, especially rags and religious objects, left by visitors who pray at St Ciarán's for a cure or for help in other difficult situations.[8]

Tobermurry, Mary's Well, Rosserk, County Mayo

This beautifully-kept shrine near the mouth of the River Moy, not far from Rosserk Abbey, owes its existence to an apparition of the Virgin Mary around 1680. According to a Latin inscription, the small chapel lodging the holy well was built in 1684; however, a second inscription in English claims that it was built in 1798. Curiously, there are no legends regarding the origin of the hawthorn that grew in the early twentieth century from the vaulted stone roof of the chapel, but the fact that it survived in this exposed position is considered a miracle in itself. Seemingly without roots, yet firmly clinging to the roof, local tradition maintains that the hawthorn has withstood numerous severe storms without suffering any damage to its branches or prematurely losing its haws.[9]

Sacred Trees and Holy Wells

Most of the sacred trees of early Christian Ireland stood close to wells. Since wells played an important role in pagan Celtic spirituality, attested by archaeological finds of water shrines, offerings and inscriptions, it is reasonable to suggest that the presence of sacred wells often influenced saints and missionaries in their selection of locations for the establishment of Christian shrines. Ireland has about three thousand holy wells, and devotional practice at many of these would involve the sacred trees growing beside them; however, the trees, important as they may be, are usually of secondary significance to the water of the well.

An indication of the close link between wells and their adjoining sacred trees are place names deriving from the Irish term *tobar a bhile* or 'well of the sacred tree'. It occurs in the names of townlands such as Toberbilly in County Antrim, and in the names of holy wells, such as Tobaravilla for a well near Kilkee East in County Clare, or Tobar a Bhile at Kilcrohane in County Kerry. Both of these wells have long lost their adjoining sacred trees. The traditions of the Clare well and its *bile* are entirely forgotten, though the tree in Kilcrohane – a huge ash which was once considered to be the largest ash tree in Ireland – remained an object of veneration into the twentieth century. While the tree was still standing its branches were covered in rags, left by pilgrims who visited the well, especially for the annual pattern day on 30 July. By 1945, when the tree had fallen from old age, the rotting trunk was left beside the well, and pilgrims stuck coins into it as votive offerings. Nothing remains of the tree today, and the well became popularly known by the name of the local patron saint, Crohán.[10]

Folklore accounts describe how the waters of holy wells were also thought to interact with particular sacred trees. When wells dried up for no apparent reason, explanations were sought for the disappearance of the water. Some legends claimed that a well had left its position in response to the adjoining tree being cut. St Patrick's Well in Carnagh in County Cavan, for instance, disappeared after its highly revered tree – to which pilgrims would attach rag offerings – was cut. St Gobnait's Well in Ballyvourney, County Cork, migrated for no apparent motive from its former position to the present location, and a whitethorn sprang up to mark the site of the well.[11]

More common in popular tradition and current into the middle of the twentieth century, were local legends of holy wells that left their original positions, to emerge again in the forks or trunks of trees, or from under their roots. Consequently, the tree would function in place of the well and maintain its healing properties.

Toberara, Kilbarry, County Kildare (above)

In 1875, John O'Hanlon in his *Lives of the Irish Saints* gave a short description of the celebrated well that emerged from under a tree near old Kilbarry cemetery, and associated it with St John and St Crunnmael. There are no memories of the well today.[12]

St Cuan's Well, Toberchuain, County Waterford (right)

St Cuan's Shrine is dedicated to the sixth-century saint, who was the founder or the second abbot of nearby Mothel Abbey. St Cuan's Well, also known as the Well of Mothel, seems to rise from the roots of a mature ash tree. In the nineteenth century, an annual pattern was held at the shrine from 9 to 11 July. It used to attract up to two thousand attendants, but was eventually suppressed by a parish priest who objected to the disorderly behaviour and misconduct of pilgrims during the social part of the pattern. Today, individuals still visit to avail of the curative power of the water.[13]

Tree-Well, Ballydeloughy, County Cork

The holy well of Ballydeloughy was originally situated closer to the old church and graveyard. But when it was filled in some time before 1905, the well migrated into the trunk of a sycamore tree on the nearby fence bordering the public road. And there it has remained since, always carrying some water, even in the driest of summers when other wells have dried up. The tree-well is renowned for its curative power for sore eyes, but there are neither votive offerings nor any other signs of ritual visits to it.[14]

St Patrick's Well, Dromard, County Sligo (left)

St Patrick's Well at Dromard is the oldest holy well in Connacht, said to have been consecrated by St Patrick himself. Mass is traditionally celebrated here on 29 June, the feast of St Peter and St Paul. Local belief has it that on this occasion an additional holy well would miraculously appear in the fork of one of the mature ash trees that shelter the sacred enclosure. Pieces of bark from these trees were formerly carried as talismans to relieve backache.[15]

St Fintan's Tree, Clonenagh, County Laois (below)

St Fintan's Well was originally close to the ancient monastery of Clonenagh. When the landowner filled in the well to get rid of the devotees, the water reportedly moved to an old church some miles away. A drop from the migrating water fell on a mature sycamore by the roadside and produced a new well in the fork of the tree. The tree-well gained a reputation for healing, and pilgrims who found a cure at Clonenagh left votive rags and crutches at the tree. For wishes and good luck, people started hammering coins into the trunk of the tree, and the sycamore consequently became known as the Money Tree.

Old age, metallic poisoning and damage to the bark eventually weakened the venerable tree, and it was blown down in 1994. For a while the broken bole remained by the road, and pilgrims took pieces from it as relics. The bole has been removed, but from the stump of the old tree a strong shoot has grown in recent years, supporting the belief in the immortality of sacred trees. The stump is still attributed with the power of granting wishes, and people often stop to press a coin into it for luck.[16]

In the Irish language, a tree-well of this type was called *tobar igcrann*, 'well in the tree'.[17]

An explanation for a well's migration could often be found in the local folklore. A frequently cited reason was that the well was initially on private land, and when the owner – typically a Protestant landlord – started refusing access to pilgrims or had the well filled in and closed up, it was forced to move. Another explanation for the phenomenon of moving wells was that the water had been polluted, insulted or profaned by people using it for domestic purposes. This is said to have happened to Mary's Well in Rockspring, County Cork, to St Margaret's Well in Cooraclare, County

Clare, to Our Lady's Well in Skirk, County Laois, and to tree-wells in the Ballycastle area of County Antrim and Tartaraghan, County Armagh.[18]

While most migrating wells were thought to remain in their newly selected positions, a few tree-wells were renowned for moving several times. An account from Derrynalester near Killinagh in County Cavan describes a terrible storm in June 1861 and the remarkable effects it apparently had on the local holy well, Tobar Mhuire. First the water left the well and emerged in a house nearby, where it remained for some time. Then it moved to the foot of a mighty ash tree said to date from the time of St Patrick. When the water caused the roots of the ash to wither, the tree fell over the well in the form of rainbow, and the water migrated back to its original position. In the twentieth century, the ash tree was cut and left on the ground to rot because people still held it sacred and would not use its timber for any purpose.[19]

The water of St Patrick's Well on Knockroe in County Galway was said to interact with a hollow tree near Mountbellew village. Into the early twentieth century, the well was thought to leave Knockroe every year shortly before Garland Sunday, the local name for Lughnasa, and to emerge for a few days in the tree near Mountbellew. It was a custom for people to take water home from the tree-well and to sprinkle it in their houses for protection, before the well returned for another year to Knockroe. The site of the tree-well is overgrown today, and the migrating well is no longer remembered.[20] The tree species most closely linked with migrating holy wells are the ash, with its ability to withstand water around its roots, and the sycamore, with its tendency to hold water in its forks. But while ash trees can live to a great age in extremely wet ground, sycamores are not as resistant to water, and most of the sycamores described as tree-wells in the early decades of the twentieth century have since decayed.[21]

Releasing the Power of Sacred Trees

Trees primarily associated with healing usually, though not exclusively grow by holy wells and places of early Christian worship. The shrines are characteristically named after the local patron saint and a ceremonial visit involves prayers to the saint, asking him or her to intervene on behalf of the pilgrim.

In the northern part of Ireland, several trees credited with the combined power of healing and granting wishes have lost their original links to saints and Christian devotion, even when they appear in the environment of graveyards, monastic sites or healing

Wishing Tree, Dungiven, County Derry (left)

In the twelfth century, the Augustinian order established a friary at the site of an early monastery in Dungiven, founded in the seventh century by St Nechtan, but more popularly linked with St Colmcille and St Patrick. The Wishing Tree on the grounds of the friary is commonly believed to grant wishes if rags or ribbons are offered to its branches. The tree overhangs a small bullaun stone, the cavity of which always contains some water, reputed to have the cure for warts.[22]

wells. Often known as 'wishing trees', to access their power it is considered sufficient for visitors to solemnly formulate their wishes and leave a token of good faith behind. In the southern counties, the term 'wishing tree' is less common and of rather recent origin; most sacred trees renowned for answering any type of request in the south are still popularly known under the name of the local patron saint, and visitors traditionally formulate their wishes in the form of a prayer. As with sacred trees renowned for their healing qualities, wishing trees are often found at holy wells. Others stand seemingly unattached by the roadside, though one can usually find the overgrown remains of monastic settlements or dried-up wells nearby.

Solemn visits to sacred places may be taken whenever the need arises, and people resort to shrines individually at any time of the year, but pilgrimages are considered particularly effective when made at set dates for communal devotion, usually the feast

Rag Bush, Kilmogg, County Kilkenny

Earlier, the veneration of this roadside tree – known as the Rag Bush or the Raggedy Bush – was linked with St Patrick and the water of the bullaun stone beside it. The bullaun is dry and widely neglected today, but the tree has not lost its miraculous virtues. It is covered in all kinds of votive offerings, and the objects left behind by devotees are often clues as to their wishes or their problems and challenges.[23]

day of the local patron saint. The common term 'pattern' for a pilgrimage is a deriva-tion from the Irish word *pátrún* for patron saint.[24] Other popular dates for communal pilgrimage are Good Friday, the feast of St Peter and St Paul on 29 June, and the times that correspond with three of the four main seasonal assembly days of pagan Ireland. Anciently, these seasonal festivals were held at the days that divided the year into quarters. The Celtic year began around 1 November with Samhain, literally the 'end of

St Bernard's Well, Rathkeale, County Limerick

Set in peaceful quiet surroundings a few miles outside Rathkeale, St Bernard's Well seems to emerge from the roots of a magnificent ash tree that has one major branch growing over the well like a bow. The traditional dates for a visit to the healing well are the feast of St Bernard on 20 August, and Good Friday. Into the early decades of the twentieth century, pilgrims tied rags to the branches of the ash, or drove pins into its trunk. Today, they tend to leave religious objects in or beside the tree or stick coins into its bark.[25]

summer'. Samhain had strong associations with death and the otherworld, and plays no role in the context of sacred trees. Imbolc or Oimelg marked the beginning of spring-time and was celebrated around 1 February. Imbolc was the feast of the Celtic goddess Brigid, a deity linked with fire and water, fertility and healing. Her namesake saint inherited the feast day and many characteristics of the goddess, and trees and wells dedicated to St Brigid are still highly revered as places of pilgrimage. Around 1 May, Bealtaine celebrated the beginning of summer with sacred ceremonial fires. The belief in the special qualities of water from holy wells on May Day, and the custom of putting up May Bushes, are probably remnants of ancient traditions.

A popular time for communal pilgrimage to shrines associated with St Patrick is Lughnasa, the ancient Celtic harvest festival and start of autumn, held at the beginning of August. Myths illustrate the antiquity of the Lughnasa gatherings. They tell that the pre-Celtic land goddess, Tailtiu, died from exhaustion after clearing plains for cultiva-tion, and that her foster-son, the Celtic god Lugh, established the festival of Lughnasa in her honour. With the Christian conquest, St Patrick took the patronage from Lugh, when he reportedly destroyed the main pagan idol of Ireland – a pillar stone entirely decorated with gold and called Crom Dubh – at Lughnasa, transforming the ancient harvest festival into a celebration of Christian victory over paganism. Among Gaelic speakers, this date is widely known as *Domhnach Chrom Dubh* or the Sunday of Crom Dubh.[26]

A pilgrimage to a sacred place is a ritual walk or sacred journey, commonly known as a *turas*. It takes in several stations such as trees, wells, stones or church ruins, where pilgrims stop to pray and to perform certain prescribed rituals. Since the *turas* is always a circular walk, from station to station, and around the individual station markers, making a pilgrimage is also known as 'doing the rounds'. Of crucial importance and of ancient origin is the direction in which the ceremonial circuits and rounds are carried out. The clockwise or sunwise direction, also known as right-handwise or *deiseal*, is in Ireland, as in many parts of the world, generally considered lucky and appropriate for constructive magic and blessings; consequently, it is reserved for the releasing of the benevolent powers of a sacred place. The reverse, anticlockwise direction, popularly referred to as left-handwise, widdershins or *tuafal*, is regarded as unlucky, but suitable for sorcery and destructive magic.[27] The custom of circumventing trees right-handwise has survived to our days in many places of Christian devotion.

Physical contact is also believed to release the indwelling powers and virtues of sacred places. Devotees would establish this contact by drinking from a well, for example, or washing sore parts of the body in it, kissing a stone, or touching a tree.

Tobernalt or Tobar an Ailt, County Sligo

Tobernalt, outside Sligo town, is an ancient Lughnasa assembly site and is closely linked with St Patrick. Some small circular indentations on the top slab of a simple stone altar are considered to be imprints of the saint's fingers. Prayers said while holding one's fingers into the impressions are trusted to be answered through the intercession of the saint. During the Penal times, Mass was read from the stone altar.

Tobernalt or Garland Sunday, over the last few decades celebrated once again with a communal pilgrimage on the last Sunday in July, attracts a considerable number of devotees. The place is also frequently visited throughout the year by individual pilgrims seeking cures and leaving votive offerings in an old holly tree.[28]

Rag Trees, Well of Doon, County Donegal

The origin of the pilgrimage to the Well of Doon is traditionally attributed to Father Lector O'Friel, an eighteenth-century healer who discovered the curative powers of the well, and to Father Gallagher, who blessed the well for the use of the local people in times of sickness and need. Since then, the Well of Doon has become one of the most popular healing shrines in County Donegal. A well-trodden path testifies to the customary circumvention of two small birches, a ritual carried out in bare feet while reciting the prescribed prayers. In addition, before leaving the place, rags or personal items are tied to the branches of the trees.[29]

St Ciarán's Well, Castlekeeran, County Meath

In 1839, news spread that the large ash over St Ciarán's Well near Kells in County Meath was bleeding. People flocked to the well to witness the miracle and to collect the precious sap to obtain a cure. About ten years later, W. Wilde paid a visit to the well and praised the size and beauty of the sacred ash tree. In the early decades of the twentieth century, the tree decayed and fell. Today a young ash tree has been adopted as the sacred well-tree, and visitors tie rags and ribbons to its branches.[30]

Jaundy Well, Stonebridge, County Monaghan

Once renowned for having a cure for jaundice, the healing well at Stonebridge is still popularly known as Jaundy Well. It is no longer the custom to take a bath in its water, or dip a piece of undergarment in the well, wring it out and wear it, but the well has not lost its healing reputation and is still popular with visitors seeking a cure for various ailments. Before leaving, people often follow the old tradition of fastening a piece of cloth to one of the bushes overhanging the well.[31]

TREES OF SPIRITUAL TRANSFORMATION 65

Occasionally, the contact was established by taking relics from a sacred tree to bring about a cure. The leaves of St Patrick's Bush in Meenamalragh in County Donegal, for example, were applied to heal sore feet, while the bark of the trees at St Patrick's Well in Dromard, County Sligo, was used to relieve backache. General healing virtues were ascribed to the sap of St Ciarán's Tree at Castlekeeran, County Meath, when it appeared to bleed in 1839.[32]

Curative clay or soil was also taken from the base of sacred trees. Highly popular is the Clay of Gartan at St Colmcille's birthplace in County Donegal, which is supposed to be dug exclusively by natives of the area. A passage in Manus O'Donnell's *Life of Colmcille* relates that the clay once fled into the trunk of the tree when a stranger attempted to dig it. Only when the tree was sprinkled with holy water was the clay released. In Aghagower, County Mayo, curative soil was taken from the base of the holy tree that grew over St Patrick's Bed.[33]

The act of literally connecting with the indwelling spirit of a sacred object is an ancient component of associative magic. It is based on the belief that the essence of the spirits or people to which an object owes its virtues, is still alive within that object. This archaic principle survives also in the belief in the protective powers of tree relics, and in the practice of making offerings at sacred shrines as symbols of the ailments and problems that an applicant wishes to leave behind. The belief that anyone removing such an offering will automatically be stricken with the ailment it represents is still strong today.

Tree Relics, Amulets and Protection

To remove so much as a twig or a chip of dead wood from a sacred tree for practical purposes was a commonly acknowledged taboo. It was, however, completely acceptable to take pieces of sacred trees as relics or amulets in order to meet spiritual needs, and several trees were once widely renowned and sought out for the protective powers of their relics during times of great challenge.[34]

The earliest reference to relics taken from sacred trees occurs in a tenth-century biography of St Brigid. The author, Bishop Animosus, refers to Brigid's beloved oak tree in Kildare and notes that 'no one dares to cut it with a weapon but he who can break off any part of it with his hands deems it a great advantage, hoping for the aid of God by means of it, because through the blessing of St Brigid, many miracles have been performed by that wood.'[35]

Animosus did not reveal the nature of these miracles, but more recent references to protective trees indicate that pieces of bark and twigs were predominantly carried as charms or talismans during journeys or other activities that were considered risky or perilous, or as charms to ward off natural disasters.

Pieces of Cuaille Mhic Dhuaich or Mac Duach's Stake, at Kilmacduagh in County Galway, were attributed with the power of saving people from an untimely death. A seventeenth-century biography of St Colman mac Duach relates the remarkable story of a man who survived three successive hangings thanks to a small piece of the tree that he carried concealed in his mouth; unfortunately, he died on the fourth attempt, after the executor had detected and removed the talisman. In the eighteenth century, Bishop Pococke visited Kilmacduagh and noted that people took bits of the tree as relics. The tree was gone by the early decades of the twentieth century, but it was still remembered that the attendants of funerals in Kilmacduagh graveyard had once made sure to bring home pieces of the sacred tree as talismans.[36]

Crann San Lionairt or St Leonard's Bush in the County Kilkenny townland of Dunnamaggan was an old whitethorn beside a holy well. In the nineteenth century, natives of the area who were emigrating would not have left without a piece of bark or a twig from the thorn, trusting in the local custom that it would protect them from shipwrecking and drowning. The well is still surrounded by impressive mature trees, but the old thorn bush has long since decayed.

St Craebhnat's sacred ash tree in the townland of Killuragh in Clenor parish in County Cork was also highly revered for protecting people from drowning. So popular was the tree with emigrants, that they had literally chipped it away by the 1860s. In west Clare, emigrants and sea-going people trusted in the unfailing protection attributed to St Senan's blessed alder tree on Inis Cathaigh or Scattery Island on the Shannon Estuary, and carried a sprig or a few leaves from the tree on their journeys. The custom of cutting initials into the bark of the alder eventually killed the tree, and the dead trunk stood for several years, until some people uprooted the stump looking for treasure.[37]

While the habit to carry tree talismans on journeys has almost entirely disappeared, pieces of individual sacred trees are still used as charms to protect homes from fire. At St Moling's Well in Mullennakill in County Kilkenny, a tree with such protective virtues allegedly grew from the saint's walking stick. It was, however, considered extremely dangerous to profane this tree, and local lore knows of a man who chopped some branches for firewood, only to find his house turned to ash when he returned home.[38]

St Colman's Well and Ash, Kiltartan, County Galway

Bile Mhic Dhuaich, the sacred ash of sixth-century St Colman mac Duach, is believed to mark the place of the saint's birth. The dead tree stands beside an oratory which lodges St Colman's Well, and portions of its timber are still highly valued as charms to protect homes from lightning and fire.[39]

St Moling's Walking Stick, Mullennakill, County Kilkenny

Tobar Crann Mo-Long, the Well of St Moling's Tree, was the old name for the holy well in the parish of Mullennakill. There is still an annual pattern held on 20 August, and it is customary for visitors to take home some leaves, twigs or a piece of the bark from the alder tree that overshadows the small altar at the shrine, in order to protect their property from fire. The association with fire is probably based on an episode in a biography of the seventh-century saint, which relates that Moling once went into a burning house and extinguished the flames with his prayers.

Cures, Wishes and Votive Offerings

The most notable element in the spiritual worship of trees is the practice of leaving offerings in or around them. This phenomenon occurs in cultures all over the world, irrespective of the prevailing religious concepts, and has apparently developed from the universal need and desire to honour and appease the *anima loci*, the spirit of the place.

For pagan Celtic religion abroad, the practice of offerings and sacrifice to the gods is well documented by finds and historical accounts, although the offerings were primarily deposited in water.[40] References to offerings associated with trees and groves are scarce. They relate to the time between 49 BC and AD 60, and stem from Roman historians, who put sacred Celtic trees into the context of human sacrifice. Lucan gave a lively description of the sacred grove of Massilia as it stood in 49 BC with 'altars heaped with hideous offering, and trees sprinkled with human blood'. A later commentator on Lucan's text claimed that the Celts of Gaul appeased their main deities originally with human and then later with animal sacrifice. The victims were either drowned to appease the god Teutates, burnt in hollow tree trunks to honour Taranis, or hanged from sacred trees if offered to Esus. A relief of Esus on a stone altar from the first century AD shows him in the process of tree-cutting; a relief from Paris and one from Trier show human and animal heads hanging from trees. Tacitus, referring to the time around AD 60, makes mention of human sacrifice in a Celtic sacred grove on Anglesey off the coast of Wales; at around the same time, according to Cassius Dio, the Celtic Queen Boudicca sacrificed prisoners to a goddess of war in a forest sanctuary in the east of Britannia.[41]

Well-Trees at St Cooey's Wells, Portaferry, County Down

In the eighth century, St Cooey built a monastery close to the southern tip of the Ards Peninsula. Nothing remains of his foundation, and today only a few walls of a small church dating from the later medieval period are left standing. However, the beautifully-kept shrine is still very popular for the healing properties of its wells. They are clearly marked and assigned to the cure of various ailments. Each well has its own tree for votive offerings. The well for bathing the eyes flows from under a thorn covered in rags and pieces of cloth; the well for drinking in order to cure internal problems is located under a money tree; and the well for washing sore parts of the body has a thorn on which pilgrims leave metal offerings such as nails and chains.[42]

For pagan and early Christian Ireland, we have no written evidence at all of offerings associated with trees and sacred groves. From the Middle Ages, there is archaeological evidence that pilgrims were expected to leave offerings at famous shrines. Among the earliest finds are devotional bronze objects and pins, dating from between the tenth and the twelfth century, unearthed at St Ciarán's foundation of Clonmacnoise.[43] Documentary evidence for the custom comes later. The earliest references to the tradition of tying offerings to the branches of sacred trees and bushes stem from eighteenth- and nine-teenth-century descriptions of Catholic religious devotion at holy wells. They indicate that these offerings were left as symbolic presents by grateful pilgrims, as tokens or reminders of their requests, or in fulfilment of semi-magical practices. The commentators – church representatives, state officials and visitors to Ireland – came predominantly from Protestant backgrounds or from the Catholic hierarchy, and their accounts were essentially hostile.

When William Shaw-Mason, a statistician who conducted a parochial survey of Ireland, visited Tubber Patrick in Dungiven, County Derry, in 1813, he wrote: 'The absurd and superstitious ceremonies which are here practised, to this day, would scarcely be credited without ocular testimony . . . [The visitors to the well] walk around it a certain

Rag Tree at Tubber Grieve, Portlaw, County Tipperary

In the 1840s, writers Mr and Mrs Hall visited Portlaw and noted that 'adjoining the Suir towards Clonmel, is the picturesque well of Tubber Grieve, a holy well in high repute with the peasantry.[44]

Clootie Tree, St Olcan's Well, Cranfield, Antrim

St Olcan's Well – close to the ruins of thirteenth-century Cranfield Church on the northern shore of Lough Neagh – is dedicated to St Olcan of Armoy, a contemporary of St Patrick. The well was once famous for its healing qualities, and for the miraculous power of the amber-coloured pebbles from its depths, which were believed to protect women during childbirth, to protect men from drowning and to safeguard homes from fire and burglars. Until 1828, a pattern was held on three consecutive days between May Eve and 29 June, when the water and pebbles were said to be most effective.

Revived in the twentieth century in its original three-day form, since 1979 the pattern was reduced to a one-day celebration of Mass on the Sunday next to 29 June. Throughout the year, pilgrims visit Cranfield individually to avail of the curative properties of the well; following the old custom, they wash the affected part of the body with a rag dipped in the well, say a prayer, and finally tie the rag to one of the overhanging thorn trees. As the rag decays, the affliction is said to disappear.[45]

number of times, repeating during their progress, a stated measure of prayers, and then they wash their hands and feet with the water, and tear off a small rag from their clothes, which they tie on a bush, overhanging the well.'[46]

Rag offerings were – and indeed still are – the most common way to honour a sacred tree in order to affect a cure or to have a wish granted. The custom is well documented in all parts of Ireland, and was so popular that special names evolved for trees and bushes honoured in this way. In the north, they are popularly known as 'clootie trees', in the rest of the country as 'rag trees'.

Some pilgrims say that rag offerings are a way of leaving a bit of oneself behind, as a reminder of a request to the local patron saint. This is the Christianised version of the archaic idea of leaving a personal article in the possession of a benevolent power, to encourage the spirit of the place to keep the person in mind and look out for them. In the context of healing, rags were occasionally said to be symbolic presents, taken from the cured parts of the body and left by grateful pilgrims. Canon O'Hanlon, for instance, noted this purpose behind rag offerings around 1840 in Aghade in County Cork; the Irish Folklore Commission recorded the same principle around 1940 in Ballygonigan in County Donegal.[47]

Generally, clooties and rags play a direct and crucial role in obtaining a cure. From the earliest reference to the most recent accounts, all over Ireland people seeking a cure would wash the afflicted part of the body in a healing well using a piece of cloth. In earlier centuries, pilgrims would have torn a small rag from the garment they were wearing when they visited the well. In 1902, the scholar W. G. Wood-Martin described this custom around a pattern at the holy well near Tinahely in County Wicklow, noting that the devotees tore shreds from their garments and hung them on St Patrick's Bush, a sacred thorn beside the well. Today, pilgrims usually bring along handkerchiefs, rags, ribbons or pieces of underwear especially for that purpose. Before leaving the healing shrine, the rag is tied to a tree or a bush at the well, in the hope that as the cloth withers away, the disease will leave the body.[48]

Getting rid of a disease by transferring it from the body to another object echoes traits of pagan associative magic, which is based on the notion that what was once connected remains spiritually or energetically linked. The cloth is hence used to link the sick part of the body with the healing power bestowed to the well by a saint, and the maladies are hence symbolically rubbed off with the cloth. When the rag is left at the tree, it evokes the ancient notion that trees are capable of taking on diseases from people. The common belief that pain and disease will fade as the rag withers is also a remnant of magic, based on the principle of simultaneity and correspondence.[49]

Offerings at St Gobnait's Well, Ballyvourney, County Cork and at the Well of Doon, County Donegal

Crutches and walking sticks – left by grateful pilgrims who no longer needed them having found a cure at a shrine – or by sufferers hoping to get rid of their ailments by discarding their walking aids, were once a common sight at holy wells. Still highly venerated as places of pilgrimage, St Gobnait's Shrine and the Well of Doon both have a reputation for healing rheumatism and various other diseases.[50]

Regionally, considerable thought formerly went into the most effective colour for rag offerings. While rags in different colours were traditionally left in some places, in others they had to be exclusively of one colour, particularly white or red. Unfortunately, it is impossible to establish with certainty the original purpose behind the choice of particular colours, since from the earliest surveys of the custom until today, the reason given for choosing certain colours is always simply 'tradition'. Today, pilgrims are generally less concerned about the colour of their rag offerings, but in many places the majority of the cloths are still either white or red.

Tobernafiaghanta, Termon, County Clare

In some places the old custom has survived of using pieces of red wool or ribbon to tie white rags to the branches of sacred trees. White, the colour of purity, and red, believed to protect against the power of evil spirits, were anciently regarded as colours of the otherworld.

These days, an increasing number of rag or clootie trees are festooned with such an eclectic array of offerings that their branches are barely visible. As with the rags torn from an individual's garment, the offerings are usually very personal yet materially valueless items, put there in the belief that leaving a bit of oneself behind will have a beneficial effect. Among these offerings, we find ordinary personal possessions such as buttons, brooches, pipes and hair pins. Some of the offerings reflect the applicants' individual desires: bottles and cigarette packs stand for the desire to give up bad habits, while spiritual support for the favoured sports team is sought by leaving jerseys or ribbons in team colours. Photos and memorial cards, or small toys, soothers and baby clothes are signs of prayers and good wishes for relatives and friends.

Particularly in the southern half of Ireland, rag trees are often adorned with religious objects, such as holy pictures, rosary beads, small crosses, holy figurines and small holy water containers, left as presents by grateful visitors, but more often as reminders of prayers and requests. Sometimes votive rags occur alongside offerings of metals such as pins, nails and coins.

Pine trees, more common in the northern parts of Ireland, have often lost their original links with saints. They are generally considered to have the combined power of granting wishes and precipitating cures for toothache or warts. The Toothache Tree that once stood at Beragh Hill in County Tyrone was linked with neither saint nor well, and no day in particular was designated as a special time to visit. Local people used to hammer small denomination coins, pins or nails into the trunk to affect a cure for toothache.[51]

The custom of hammering pins or nails into the bark of sacred trees is possibly more archaic than offering rags. The origin and meaning of pin and nail votives are no longer known, and speculations vary widely. The suggestion that the practice derives from pinning as opposed to tying rags and other votive offerings to sacred trees denies any spiritual significance to the pins and nails as such. Suggestions of a possible connection between nails and the crucifixion of Christ can be dismissed, since pin and nail offerings certainly pre-date Christianity, and were also practised in non-Christian areas of the world. More plausible is the idea that the nails and pins were substitutes for more costly offerings.[52]

The ritual offering of nails existed from very early times in Rome, where it was customary to drive a nail into a particular wall of the temple of Jupiter on the Capitol. On the Continent the ritual survived in the tradition of 'nail trees', into which every passing craftsman would drive a nail for luck. These trees occur exclusively in regions that once stood under Roman control, but there is no documentary evidence of a direct derivation from Roman custom.[53] In Ireland and abroad, bronze pins were found in pagan sacrificial hoards, indicating a long tradition of metal offerings. Bronze pins were also among the earliest Christian votive offerings deposited at important shrines in medieval Ireland.

**Wishing Tree, Mullandoy,
County Monaghan**

The Wishing Tree in the graveyard
of ruined Mullandoy Abbey by the
shore of Muckno Lake in County
Monaghan was popular into the
early decades of the twentieth
century. To have a wish granted,
applicants were supposed to
focus on their wish while walking
around the tree, then stick a pin
into its bark as an act of good
faith. The same procedure was
thought to bring about a cure
for toothache.[54]

Nail and pin offerings, St Coda's Mass Tree, Killarney, County Kerry

Anciently, votive pins and nails may have been offerings to the indwelling power of a tree. A strong pagan aura is retained at Christian shrines, where pins and nails are hammered into trees as tokens of an applicant's trust in the positive effect of a personal item left in the possession of a benevolent power, or as channels for the transference of maladies and problems. When pin offerings were used to affect a cure for skin ailments and humpbacks, the afflicted part was pricked with the pin, which was then inserted into the tree. Often pins and nails were stuck into trees lodging healing wells in their trunks or forks. According to local lore, these wells had usually migrated into the trees from their original positions. In the north, these particular trees were commonly known as 'pin wells'. A famous example – on Coney Island in County Armagh – was the Pin Well, a beech lodging healing water in its fork. The tree is still standing, though the tradition of sticking a pin in its trunk while making a wish has largely died out. Equally popular into the twentieth century, but now decayed and gone, were the Pin Well in Tartaraghan in County Armagh, the Pin Tree of Ardboe in County Tyrone, and the Pin Well of Magherinagaw in County Antrim.

The practice of sticking pins and nails into sacred trees has gradually been replaced by the custom of hammering coins into their bark. Money offerings as part of patterns and pilgrimages to holy wells were common practice during the seventeenth and eighteenth centuries in the form of donations for the priest, who would not have had any other opportunity to collect the tithes of his parish. Like the money left by pilgrims in collection boxes at Christian shrines, these offerings should be understood as financial contributions to the Church rather than as votive offerings in a spiritual sense. Only when people began to deposit coins in the waters of holy wells, under adjoining stones, or hammered into sacred trees, could their money offerings be regarded as spiritually-motivated votives to a sacred place.[55]

Pin Tree, Ardboe, County Tyrone

The Pin Tree of Ardboe – once the most popular wishing tree in the northeast of Ireland – stood on the grounds of ruined Ardboe Abbey overlooking Lough Neagh. The beech was a typical pin tree, with a hollow that always contained some water. Records trace ritual visits to the tree back to the eighteenth century, and relate that it was the custom to put a pin or nail into the bark of the tree to make a wish come true, and to prick a wart or a hump-back with a pin before sticking it into the tree to make the problem disappear. In the 1940s, the bark of the tree was studded with pins and nail heads, but by the mid-1960s, the tree had fallen, and people took to hammering coins into an adjacent beech tree. When the photo was taken in 1995, this tree too had decayed, but remained an object of reverence. Unfortunately, the Pin Tree was blown over in a storm in 1998, and only the memory of the beautiful tree remains.[56]

After several decades of decline, money offerings are presently experiencing a revival. In several places, coins are left in addition to rags and other objects. Particularly in the north, money offerings to trees have replaced the earlier pin and nail offerings. These days money trees are throughout Ireland associated with making wishes, and tend to be visited for good luck rather than cures. Their coins are generally of small denomination, tokens as opposed to valuable offerings; there is nevertheless the firm belief that anyone collecting the coins for his or her own use will acquire the diseases or problems left behind by the pilgrims who made the offerings.

St Lassair's Ash Tree, Kilronan, County Roscommon

Situated by the shore of Lough Mealy or Meelagh, the beautifully-kept shrine of St Lassair, the daughter of local saints Rónán and Ailbhe, is renowned for its healing powers. The well was once overshadowed by an ash tree studded with votive coins, rosaries and pins, left by grateful pilgrims. The ash has died, and although a collection box is in place at the shrine, people have recently begun to stick coins into the remnants of the well-tree.[57]

In the long run, pins, nails and money cause trees to decay from metal poisoning, and the custom of honouring trees by offering money and other metal objects has resulted in death for many a venerated wishing tree. When only the stump remains, people often continue to revere it in the same way. The stump of St Fintan's Money tree in Clonenagh in County Laois is still a highly revered wishing tree. Another example is the Pin Well in Magherinagaw graveyard in County Antrim. A hollow in the sycamore's trunk had always contained some water, attributed with healing powers for various ailments, and said to have migrated into the tree from a closed-up well nearby. The trunk of the tree was festooned with pins, nails, coins, rags and other objects. When the tree died shortly before 2000, a last fragment was left at the side of the graveyard, and people continued to push coins into the rotting wood.[58]

The Danger from which there is no Escape

A ceremonial visit to a shrine is considered to be a sacred ritual, an acknowledgement of the spirit and the sanctity of the place. The belief is that, if the visit is carried out with respect, the shrine's benevolent powers are released. But if the sanctity of the place is insulted or violated by people using its water or wood for profane purposes, then the powers released are malevolent.

Since medieval times, hagiographical texts and local legends have imaginatively described the dangers that would inevitably follow the violation of sacred trees. In the twelfth century, Giraldus Cambrensis recorded the fate of archers who dared to cut several sacred trees at Finglas, now in County Dublin, which were 'planted by the hands of holy men with their own hand around the graveyards for the ornament for the church… They were forthwith smitten by God whose divine indignation reserves vengeance to himself and condescends to vindicate the injuries offered to his saints on earth by a sudden and singular pestilence: so that most of them miserably perished within a very few days.'[59]

According to his biographers, St Kevin promised 'hell or short life to anyone who should burn either green or dry wood' from the trees in Hollywood Forest in Wicklow, and St Forannan ordered that 'not so much as a cloak-pin should be cut from his wood'. A sixteenth-century biography of St Colmcille relates that when the saint's oak at Kells had fallen, some bark was taken to tan leather, which was then worked into a pair of boots. The unfortunate man who wore the shoes was smitten with leprosy. Colmcille also cast a protective spell on his beloved oaks of Derry. Twelfth-century chronicles relate that in 1188, a certain Donnell O'Cannanan hurt himself while cutting a tree in the sanctuary of Derry. When he died from his wounds shortly afterwards, the chronicles blamed Colmcille's spell or a curse by the clergy of Derry.[60]

Luggela, Lough Tay, County Wicklow

In the nineteenth century, there was a local tradition that St Kevin, when retreating from public life, selected the remoteness of Luggela Valley to build his first hermitage by the shore of Lough Tay. Ruins of a small monastic settlement, long overgrown with thicket, are held to be the sacred place, and it was considered unwise to destroy or profane the trees here. As evidence of the seriousness of the taboo, the story was told of a man who began clearing away brambles from the site in the summer of 1855, until his eye was nearly taken out by a rebounding thorn.[61]

Folklore accounts show that into the twentieth century, the ancient sacred prohibition against using hallowed trees for profane as opposed to spiritual purposes was taken very seriously. This taboo extended to fallen twigs and wood from trees that died from natural causes. Consequently, decaying sacred trees were usually left alone and allowed to rot where they lay.

Originating as a means by which to protect sacred trees from being cut for firewood in times of scarcity, the medieval motif of a miraculous tree that would not burn — known from the biography of St Féichín of Fore — became popularly attached to sacred trees throughout Ireland. Trees or thorns that would not burn stood at St Laghteen's Well and St Olan's Shrine, both in Donaghmore parish, and beside the Holy Well, Kilclogh, all in County Cork. There were variations on the motif: for example, logs from tabooed trees were said to explode in the fire, as apparently happened in Kiltegan parish in County Wicklow. In County Wexford, the sacred oak tree that grew over St Munn's Well in Cooraun was cut down and sold for firewood. Local lore does not recall what happened to the culprit, but holds that the person who bought the timber was unable to lift it from the ground, eventually leaving it to rot where it lay by the well.[62]

Echoing the ancient magic principle of correspondence, it was believed in many parts of Ireland that the inevitable result of burning wood from a sacred tree inside a house would be the destruction of that house by fire. Local legends tell the fate of men who foolishly ignored the taboo, collecting twigs or branches from sacred trees for firewood. A story relating to St Colman's Tree near Ardmore in County Waterford is typical. A man broke some twigs from the saint's tree and carried them home to burn. As he approached his house, it appeared to be in flames, so he dropped the bundle of twigs and ran home to put out the fire. But when he reached his cabin, there was no sign or smell of fire. So the man went back, lifted his bundle, and just as before, saw a vision of his house on fire. Again he dropped the bundle and ran home to extinguish the flames, only to find no sign of fire at all. When the same thing happened a third time, the man was determined not to be fooled again, and walked home carrying his bundle of firewood.

Big Bell Tree, Borrisokane, County Tipperary

This time, however, the flames were for real, and when he reached home, he found his cabin burnt to the ground.[63]

Almost identical versions of this popular tale were associated with the sacred ash tree at St Patrick's Well in Kellistown in County Carlow; the sacred tree at St Fintan's Well in Sutton, County Dublin; the yew tree at Tobar an Iubhair or the Well of the Yew at Roughgrove, County Cork; the sacred trees at Tobar Álainn in Graigavine and at St Moling's Well in Mullennakill, both in County Kilkenny; the whitethorn at St James' Well at Corbally Hill in County Kildare; and the Big Bell Tree at Borrisokane in County Tipperary.[64]

A related local legend told of a man who took no chances when he needed firewood during a severe winter. There was a huge ash tree in the townland of Coolnamooneen in County Sligo. It was known as Crannavilla or the Honey Tree, after a hollow in the trunk which was said to have contained honey in ancient times, and in later times water. The tree was considered sacred, but one winter in the late 1930s, fuel was scarce,

St Ciarán's Tree, Seir Kieran, County Offaly (right)

St Ciarán's Tree is protected by a sacred taboo that even today no one would think to interfere with it. But in the eighteenth or nineteenth century, legend has it that a landlord became angry when the whitethorn scraped his carriage as he drove past, and asked his workman to remove the offending branches. The workman refused, so the landlord took an axe in his hands to chop the branches off himself. As he struck his first blow, he got a stroke of facial paralysis which disfigured him for the rest of his life.

St Ciarán's Tree originally stood by the roadside. When the road was widened, local authorities respected the sanctity of the thorn and diverted one lane slightly, leaving the tree in a green spot in the middle of the road. Traditionally, the tree is always passed right-handwise, that is on the left side. The tree is understood to be immortal, and local memory recalls that whenever the old tree dies, a young one grows up beside it.[65]

Biddy's Tree, Mountbrigid, County Cork (left)

The sacred ash tree at St Brigid's Well near Buttevant is affectionately called Biddy's Tree. Folklore claims that long ago, a Protestant policeman from County Galway had ridiculed the local community's high regard for the sacred place. To show his scorn, he went to swing in the branches of the sacred tree. Back in the police station at nearby Churchtown, he felt violent pains in his limbs; six month later, he was dead.[66]

TREES OF INSPIRATION

and a man decided to cut it. The night before he intended to fell the ash, he left his hatchet at the tree; when he found the hatchet still there in the morning, he took it as permission from the spirit of the place to cut the tree, which he did without any consequences.[67]

The violation of sacred trees out of an urgent need for firewood is rarely linked with severe injuries or death. Exceptions are the tales of a man who took branches from the trees at Tobar Rí an Domhnaigh outside Abbeylara in County Longford, who fell sick and died shortly afterwards; or of a Limerick man who, ignoring his wife's warnings, cut part of the tree at St Patrick's Well in Knockainey, and was struck blind by a branch. It is said that when people began cutting a sacred tree for firewood, or to remove branches that were in the way, they would usually have understood any sudden pains, strange voices or the sudden death of horses or cattle as warning signs, and left the tree alone.[68]

Swift and severe retribution was traditionally reserved for those who violated the sanctity of trees out of ignorance or spite. Legends of drastic consequences almost invariably involved Protestant landlords or officials, who either ignored warnings because they had no time for what they considered to be superstitions, or else profaned sacred places to mock Catholic devotion. The officer who interfered with the sacred bush at St Colmcille's Well at Sandyford in County Carlow, and the landlords who chopped branches from St Ciarán's Tree at Seir Kieran in County Offaly and from St Colman mac Duach's sacred ash in Corker, Kiltartan, in County Galway, were all punished with permanent disfigurement.[69] Often death was the price for the violation of the sacred taboo.

A grim story current around 1900 in Kanturk, County Cork, told of a man who mocked local people when they paid their rounds at the local holy well and sacred tree. Out of spite, he cut the venerated tree and saved the timber for firewood. Soon afterwards, the man died – and the wood of the sacred tree was burned at his wake.[70] St Hugh's Shrine in Rahugh in County Offaly – which is linked with St Brigid and her contemporary, Bishop Hugh or Aedh mac Bricc – is the source of another taboo-breaking tale. The shrine has a sacred stone which is still reputed to cure headaches, and a healing well overshadowed by a hawthorn. In the nineteenth century, the landlord wanted to end pilgrimages to the shrine, and set fire to the tree. Folklore recalls the man sitting in his armchair to watch the tree burn – and dying the moment it went alight.[71]

Trees of Bardic Inspiration

A hedge of trees surrounds me…
May the Lord protect me from Doom!
I write well under the greenwood.

Anonymous scribe (ninth century)[1]

Tradition had it that *imbas forosna* – translated as 'encompassing knowledge' and 'light that illuminates' – was contained in the nuts of hazel trees which grow at otherworld wells of wisdom. Medieval texts describe these wells as the sources of Ireland's main rivers. They link the wells and hazel trees firmly with the divine race of the Tuatha Dé Danann, and with bardic inspiration.[2]

A prose tale in the *Dindshenchas* describes how the Tuatha Dé Danann lady Sinnan, in search of magic wisdom, visited the Well of Connla in Tír fá Thonn, the Land beneath the Wave. The well, said to be the source of the River Shannon, was overhung by the hazel trees of 'musical poetry', which belonged to the seer Crimall. Every year, the trees would drop their ripe fruit into the well, raising *bolg imbais*, bubbles of inspiration. The nuts were eaten by salmon that lived in the well, and any person who tasted from those salmon or drank the bubbles of wisdom would gain mystic knowledge and artistic skills. In a poem in the *Dindshenchas,* the source of the Shannon is alternatively called the Well of Segais, and attributed with the same qualities:[3]

> *Here the inspiration of Segais is found*
> *At the true spring's excellent ground.*
> *Over the well of the graceful flow*
> *Where the hazel of musical poetry grows.*

The source of the River Boyne, known as Nechtan's Well, was traditionally believed to lie hidden in Sidh Neachtain, the mound or otherworld dwelling of Nechtan, outside the village of Carbury in County Kildare. Nine hazel trees grew around it, and they too bestowed their magic property to the water when they dropped their nuts into the well, so that anyone who drank water from the river in June would become a poet.[4]

The medieval text called *Macgnímartha Find* links Fionn mac Cumhaill with the hazel trees at Nechtan's Well, when it tells how the hero went to the Boyne to learn the art of poetry. When he sucked his thumb, which he burnt while cooking a salmon from the river, Fionn obtained mystic insight by chance, because the fish had eaten the hazel nuts of wisdom that had dropped into the water.[5]

The close link between poetry and mystic insight in early Irish literature is echoed in the Irish word for a poet, *file*, plural *filid,* a derivation from the Celtic root for 'to see'. Poets or *filid* were also official historians, genealogists to ruling families, and preservers of ancient traditions. They belonged to the learned class of the *aés dána* or scholars – a class traditionally affiliated with trees of inspiration – who were undoubtedly responsible for the introduction of writing to Ireland.

The young River Boyne, Carbury, County Kildare

The River Boyne is named after the goddess Bóinn of the Tuatha Dé Danann, a patroness of poetry and wife of mythical King Nechtan or Nuadhu. Medieval texts relate that Nechtan took great care to allow only a few chosen men to visit his magical well of inspiration, because the sight of its water would blind everyone else. Ignoring the taboo – which was based on the archaic notion that the light of inspiration could cause blindness – Bóinn went secretly to drink from the well. Insulted, the water rose up in a gush, blinded Bóinn in one eye and fled from the well, forming the River Boyne.

Celtic culture was initially an oral one, and writing was only introduced in areas of Celtic settlement through contacts with the Roman world. In Ireland, this happened first through a script called Ogham. Ogham is based on the Latin alphabet, and it is very likely that pre-Patrician Christians and an acquaintance with Roman culture influenced its development. Nevertheless, Ogham is an alphabet in its own right, and was in use from about the fourth until the seventh or eighth century. The script consisted of sets of up to five strokes or notches, which were marked along a central line, usually the sharp edge of a stone pillar or a piece of wood. The notches went from the bottom upwards, and if necessary, down the opposite side.

Traditionally, the invention of the Ogham script is attributed to the mythical Oghma of the Tuatha Dé Danann, who was noted for his speech and poetry. Oghma was the Irish adaptation of the Gaulish deity of eloquence, Ogmios. A derivation of the word Ogham from the name of the deity, however, has been rejected by scholars on linguistic grounds.[6]

No longer unequivocally accepted is the well established and widely held belief that the letters of the script were named after native Irish trees. The notion of tree-derivation for Ogham is based on several medieval texts. A passage in *Auraicept na nÉces*, or the *Scholar's Primer*, a collection of medieval manuscripts on Ogham, associates the script with trees when it explains that Ogham is 'read as a tree is climbed, treading on the root of the tree first.'[7]

Other texts deal explicitly with the meaning of the individual letters' names. Since some names are rather obscure, there is room for widely differing interpretations. Consequently, several medieval forms of Ogham interpretation have come down to us, linking the letters for example with the names of animals, colours or plants. The association of tree names with the letters is maintained in three medieval lists that explain the letter names in the form of *bríatharogaim* or 'word-oghams', cryptic and almost impenetrable two-word descriptions. The *Bríatharogaim Morainn mic Máin*, for instance, defines the oak as *arddam dossa* or 'highest of bushes'; the *Bríatharogaim Mic in Oícc* uses for the oak the description *greas sáir* or 'work of a carpenter'; and in the *Bríatharogaim Con Culainn*, the oak is *slechtam sáire* or 'most carved of craftsmanship'.[8]

Ogham inscriptions are typically short and commemorative, giving the name of a person and details of his ancestry. Their exact purpose is unknown, and may have had pagan or early Christian connotations. In any case, we can safely assume that the script was developed by members of the learned class, and that it must have been a tremendous experience for them to see the sound of words expressed in symbols for the very first time. Given the high esteem in which trees were held in early Ireland for their spiritual value,

Ogham stones, Dunloe, County Kerry

Modern studies and scholars question the existence of an Ogham alphabet named exclusively after trees, maintaining that only eight or ten out of the twenty Ogham letters were originally named after trees. The medieval perception of Ogham being a tree-based alphabet is nevertheless still popular today, with the interpretation of the letter names corresponding largely with those given in the Bríatharogaim. The list below gives the common traditional interpretations of the Ogham letters, with the undisputed and widely agreed ones marked in bold letters.

B beith	**birch**
L luis	rowan
F fern	**alder**
S sail	**willow**
N nin	ash
H huath	**hawthorn**
D dair	**oak**
T tinne	**holly**
C coll	**hazel**
Q quert	apple
M muin	buckthorn
G gort	ivy or furze
Ng ngegtal	broom
ST straif	blackthorn
R ruis	elder
A ailm	**fir**
O onn	**ash**
U ur	heather
E edad	aspen
I ídad	**yew**

it is easy to imagine that those responsible for the development of Ogham chose tree names as at least one way to name their first ever alphabet.

Ogham by its nature was unsuitable for long inscriptions or texts. When poetry and prose was first written down in medieval times, it was in an early form of Irish through the Latin alphabet. The eleventh-century romance, 'Scél Baile mac Buain', suggests that early writings were inscribed on tablets of timber. The story concerns doomed lovers, a Leinster princess named Aillinn and Ulster youth, Baile mac Buain. When they were buried, an apple tree and a yew tree grew from their respective graves. Seven years later, the trees were cut down and worked into writing tablets, on which the poets of Ulster and Leinster wrote down the stories and tales of their provinces.[9] Similarly, tradition has it that Germanic tribes made their first writing tablets from beech, and later wrapped their first real books in beech covers. The modern English word, book, is in fact a derivation from the German term *Buch* for book, which in turn is a derivation from *Buche* for beech; in Scandinavian languages, the term *bok* denotes both a book and a beech tree.[10]

Like the pagan seers and druids before them, the poets and bards of Christian Ireland were often inspired by the splendour of trees and groves. They left us some enchanting celebrations of trees and their wondrous attributes. In the tenth century, the following tale – which is still current in folklore – was associated with the legends of Labhraidh Loingseach, a mythical king and ancestor of the people of Leinster. This unfortunate king had the ears of a horse, and hence wore his hair very long to conceal his embarrassing deformity. Once a year, the king called for a barber, and had him executed as soon as his job was finished, to ensure that his secret remained safe. One day, the job fell to a widow's only son. The woman persuaded the king to spare the boy's life on the condition that he would never ever disclose to anyone what he had seen. The burden of the secret, however, weighed so heavily on the boy that he fell seriously ill. To recover his health, the boy followed the advice of a druid. He went to a cross-roads, turned to the right, and told his secret to the first tree he met. Thus relieved, the boy soon recovered. The tree happened to be a willow, and it was not very long afterwards

Silken Thomas' Yew, Maynooth, County Kildare (left)

Thomas Fitzgerald, known as Silken Thomas, was a member of the Kildare branch of the powerful Geraldine family. One of his ancestors, Maurice Fitzgerald, built Maynooth Castle in 1176. A row of five fine yew trees stands on the lawn close to the castle ruins, and some nineteenth-century commentators have suggested that the largest of the trees might be as old as the castle. In 1534, Silken Thomas led an unsuccessful rebellion against England. Tradition has it that on the last evening that he ever spent in Maynooth Castle, he sat beneath the spreading branches of the marvellous yew, and played the harp that he loved so much.[11]

that Craiftine, the king's harpist, chose that very tree for the making of a new harp. When Craiftine went with his new harp to play before the king and his court, the only sound that would come from the instrument were the words, 'Dhá chluais chapaill ar Labhraidh Loingseach! Two ears of a horse has Labhraidh Loingseach!'[12]

A beautiful piece of nature poetry is preserved in the twelfth-century text *Buile Shuibhne* or *The Frenzy of Suibhne Geilt*. The oldest version of this story is dated to the ninth century, though the poem itself is attributed to Suibhne Geilt or Mad Sweeney, a fictional seventh-century king of Dál nAraidhe in the northeast of Ireland. Cursed by St Rónán for having attacked the saint and his clerics, Suibhne went mad during the Battle of Magh Rátha in AD 637, and fled to the wilderness, where he lived in trees. The ballad in which he praises the trees of the forest begins:

> A dhair dhosach dhuilledhach,
> At ard os cionn crainn.
> A chólláin, a chraobhacháin,
> A chomhra cnó cuill.

> Thou oak, bushy, leafy,
> Thou art high beyond trees.
> O hazlet, little branching one,
> O fragrance of hazel nuts.[13]

Sir Walter Raleigh's Yews, Youghal, County Cork (opposite)

In the 1840s, the writers Mr and Mrs Hall visited Myrtle Grove and noted: 'In the gardens there is a group of four aged yew trees, which tradition states to have been planted by Raleigh, and where it requires no stretch of fancy, at least, to believe that he has many a time, sat, read, and talked, or lolled in the summer time.' Sir Walter Raleigh (1554–1618) is best known as the English adventurer in the service of Queen Elizabeth I, but he was also an acknowledged writer of prose and poetry. For his help in ending a rebellion in Munster in 1580, Raleigh was awarded knighthood and land in Ireland, and during his stays in the country, he resided in Myrtle Grove. Raleigh is popularly remembered for having grown the first potatoes and for having smoked the first tobacco in Ireland, and for being dowsed with water by a panicking servant at Myrtle Grove, who thought he was on fire.[14]

Thomas Moore's Tree, Meeting of the Waters, County Wicklow (left)

One of the most famous works of Dublin-born poet Thomas Moore (1779–1852) is *Irish Melodies*, a collection of 130 songs. It contains the celebrated lyric 'The Meeting of the Waters', a lovely tribute to the scenic confluence of Avonbeg and Avonmore in the Vale of Avoca, composed by Moore in 1807 in the shade of a large tree at the meeting of the two rivers. Today, only the skeleton of the tree survives. It still carries the poet's name, and is cherished and well protected. It is possible that tree was a whitethorn, though the species can no longer be identified with certainty.[15]

A text from around the thirteenth century, dealing with the death of the fictional Ulster king, Fergus, contains a poem on the qualities of various types of wood. The poem is recited by Iubhdán, king of the land of leprechauns, who visits Fergus at his court in Eamhain Mhacha. Terrified to see a servant burning a piece of woodbine, he instructs in verse form which trees to burn and which to spare. The following extract of the poem refers to the species of trees that occur in several other manuscripts in the context of druidic or bardic inspiration.[16]

> Ná loisc sailig sáir, fid deinim na nduan,
> Beich na bláth deol, mian cáich an cró caem.
> Caerthann fid na ndruad, loisce caemchrann na gcaer,
> Seachain an fid fann, ná loisc an coll caem. . . .

> Do not burn the noble willow, enduring in verse,
> Bees the blossom suck, all love its graceful curves.
> Rowan the druids' tree, burn the fair tree of berries,
> But avoid the weak wood, the fair hazel, for fire. . . .

Poetry and music were from ancient times understood to be inspired arts, which could be refined to perfection by the artist, but never acquired if the capacity was not there in the first place. Irish folklore tells of poets with inborn capacity and of clans where artistic skills were inherited over generations; but there are also numerous tales of poets and musicians said to have been endowed with their skills during adulthood, in the form of gifts from otherworld sources.[17]

One such was the blind Mayo poet, Antoine Ó Reachtabhra, who is today more popularly known by the anglicised version of his name, Anthony Raftery. Ó Reachtabhra was born around 1780 near Kiltimagh in County Mayo, in the townland of Killeaden, which is dominated by the conspicuous hill of Lissard. An old oak tree at the foot of Lissard was believed to be a popular assembly place for local fairies, and it is under this tree that the fairies are said to have offered Raftery the gift of music or poetry, and he chose the latter. Raftery's affinity with trees and their bardic inspirations surfaces in his work. In one poem, for example, an ancient thorn tree tells the poet the history of Ireland in verse.[18]

Writing in the shade of trees, and drawing inspiration and stimulation from their beauty and magnificence, was a habit cherished by many artists and scholars. An aged yew tree in the garden of Glebe House in Newcastle, County Dublin, is locally known as the Dean's Tree after Jonathan Swift, the Anglo-Irish writer and Dean of St Patrick's in Dublin, who often sat under the tree to study or to converse with his friends. Dean Swift had a keen interest in politics, and was renowned for his satirical prose with its sharp criticism of the English role in Irish poverty and deprivation.[19] In the second half of the nineteenth century, Professor Thomas Andrews, the first vice-principal of Queen's University in Belfast, liked to work under a laburnum tree in the university's grounds, and reportedly wrote much of his momentous work on the liquefaction of gas in that very place.[20] Several Irish and Anglo-Irish bards and poets, from Thomas Fitzgerald to Thomas Moore to the literary circle around Lady Gregory, are firmly linked with their particular trees of inspiration. Lady Gregory is today primarily associated with the Autograph Tree in Coole Park, though she preferred to sit and contemplate under a catalpa tree nearby. This tree is dead, but in 1995, a new catalpa tree was planted by Lady Gregory's descendants in her memory.

Autograph Tree, Coole Park, Gort, County Galway

Coole Park was the home of Lady Augusta Gregory (1852–1932), the famous Anglo-Irish playwright, folklorist and co-founder of the Gaelic League and the Abbey Theatre in Dublin. Within the walled garden of the estate grows a magnificent mature copper beech known as the Autograph Tree, which is celebrated for the initials carved in the bark by Lady Gregory's famous guests and literary friends. Among them are the initials of William Butler Yeats, Douglas Hyde, George Bernard Shaw, Sean O'Casey and John Millington Synge.[21]

PART II

Trees of Assembly

*I*N ANCIENT IRELAND, communities held regular seasonal meetings and festivals that fulfilled a variety of religious, ceremonial, political and commercial functions, but doubtlessly served social and communicative purposes as well. Into medieval times, these assemblies were held in the open air, at designated assembly sites, usually on easily accessible hills, and often linked with Neolithic or Bronze Age monuments or outstanding natural features. These assembly sites were considered sacred, and there is literary and historical evidence that sacred trees were often of central focus in these special places.

The most beautiful literary account of an assembly tree in ancient Ireland is a twenty-one-stanza poem in the *Dindshenchas* that mourns the loss of Bile Tortan, the sacred ash tree that once grew on Ardbraccan near present-day Navan in County Meath. Bile Tortan is usually listed as one of the 'mythical' trees of Ireland, but it seems very likely that it was once a real tree, attributed with wondrous qualities by medieval scribes, to emphasise and enhance its importance. Whether real or imaginary, Bile Tortan was considered one of the most important assembly trees in early medieval Ireland, a territorial marker and focal point, with associations with kingship, fairs and battle.

Bile Tortan

The Tree of Tortan is no more
Its edges battered by raging storms.
Rival crowns gather in common plain
Grieving long after they part again.

Tree of Tortan, proud its display
Mid roaring winds forever a-sway.
Firm it stood here from its green youth
Until its death, so barren of growth.

The men of Tortan are forlorn
For that unique tree they mourn.
The sight before them valued most
Over all things that have been lost.

Tribe of Tortan, in a great mass
Under the outstanding tree so vast.
From the rainstorms they were spared
Until the day it was old and bare.

Though it is now sapless wood
A great age on earth it stood.
The king who once raised up its frame
Has brought it back down again.

Fifty cubits its girth so strong
Rearing over the forest throng
And three hundred, a perfect number
The full height of its great timber.

Three ramparts of Ireland, you see
Are shorn of their security
Tree of Rossa, Tree of Mugna wide,
Tortan's Tree strong on every side.

Tree of Tortan, deep is your roar
Through the peril of fierce storms.
From it torn great swarms of litter
By the winds of nights in winter.

Residing over great Tortan's Plain
When the fine sons of Mil did reign
Until it fell when its strengths waned
In the reign of the sons of Aed Slaine.

The wind did cause the tree to fail
Only the hard heart could bear the tale.
Three times fifty Conaille were killed
When at their fair the tree was felled.

Though you, O bent over old crone
Take firewood from it for your home
Once many a fair youth was blest
Under its bright branches to rest.

When winter loosed her snowy locks
She loosed fair sticks in circling flocks
Deathly horrid her gleeful scorn
At the felling of the Tree of Tortan.

As all the eye can see must fall
So they joined in unending war.
The wind never once did stay her hand
'Til the tree's pride was at an end.

All things fade and lose their worth
Death comes to every thing on earth.
They are red earth, but withered clay
All who gathered about the tree.

The plain of Tortan is a kingless land
Since the fair tree no longer stands.
Two thirds of its wealth now gone
Since the great tree was brought down.

Vain pride of Adam, the first man
Destroyed the sons of the noble clans.
The same fate is for us in store
Now their mighty tree is no more.

Fair Ochann and Tlachtga are wastelands
Without Ailell of the warrior bands
Son of Nathu, just ruler of Meath
Law giver and great champion tree.

I Mochua, with Cróin do plead
Please do not grieve excessively.
From the bare stump so grey in hue
Many a tree might spring anew.

On a particular summer's day
I was in the wood of bushy leaves.
In a burst of rain I was kept dry
Under the Tree of Tortan's eaves.

I have no comfort, though winds shake
The fertile woods in cheerful play.
Alone a ghostly woman takes
Wood from the Tree of Tortan today.

Though the wind may sport against it
While it was young, it could not break it.
But it brings all old things to earth:
So the Tree of Tortan met its death.[1]

The earliest references to Bile Tortan are given in the eighth-century Book of Armagh and the ninth-century *Tripartite Life of St Patrick*. They relate that St Patrick built a church beside the venerable tree.

Saints and missionaries would frequently appear at communal gatherings to preach the new religion to the pagan attendants. During the course of conversion to Christianity, the sacred, religious components of the assemblies were separated from the secular parts. The spiritual aspects were transformed into pattern and pilgrimage, while the mundane elements – such as installing chieftains, trading or holding law-courts – were permitted to continue much as before. The sacred furniture of assembly places, such as wells, stones and trees, usually cleansed from pagan associations by the blessings of the missionaries, were allowed to remain in place as a central focus for the new religious and the old secular activities.

Medieval Irish law tracts contain valuable information about the different types of assembly in Gaelic Ireland, and define their purposes and rights.[2] With the Anglo-Norman conquest, Gaelic political assemblies began to lose their purpose. From the sixteenth century the Tudor administration interfered with the traditional Gaelic judicial and commercial assemblies. Out of fear that the Irish might use outdoor conventions as occasions to organise plots against England, assemblies were often vilified or banned. From the seventeenth century, following severe religious, social and political repressions, Irish Catholics often chose trees as meeting points for secret religious conventions or military assemblies. At about the same time, English tradition began to link landmark trees in Ireland with important English people such as King William III.

Today, assembly trees have almost entirely lost their original sacred or spiritual significance. Now revered primarily for their historical value, they are more often referred to as 'monument' trees or 'heritage' trees.

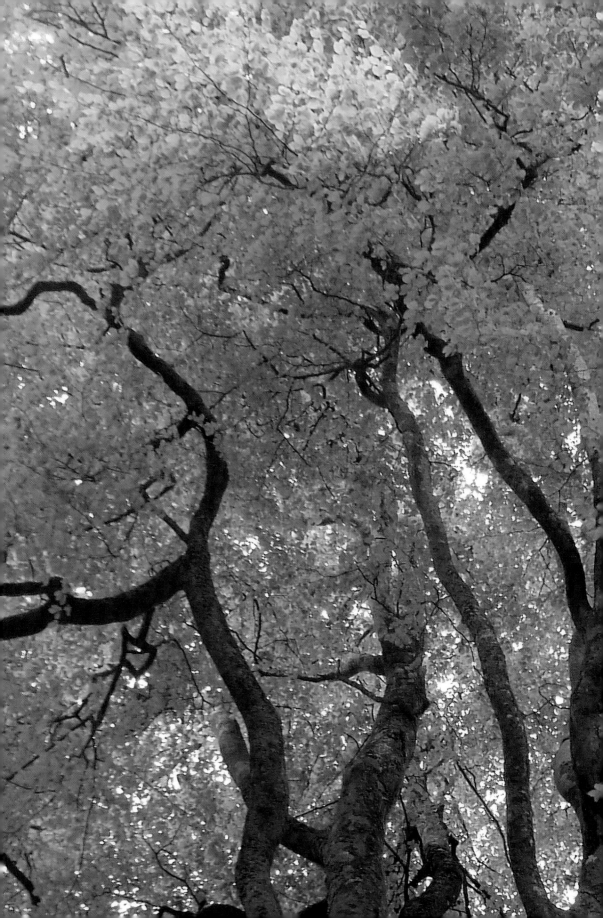

Chieftain Trees
and Royal Oaks

Tree of Mugna, great and fair,
Highest its top beyond compare,
Thirty cubits, no small count,
The measure of its girth's amount.

Three hundred high, tree without stain,
A thousand could gather in its shade.
In the Northeast hidden from sight,
Until Conn of the Hundred Fights.

A hundred score warriors, no idle boast,
A thousand and forty more at most
Could gather there with raucous noise,
'til the satire of poets it destroyed.

Poem in the *Metrical Dindshenchas* (twelfth century)[1]

Every year, on the night of Samhain – so a ninth-century text informs us – the seer Fínghein was visited by a woman, Rothniamh, who arose from an earthen mound. On one such occasion she foretold the birth of Conn Céadchathach or Conn of the Hundred Fights, one of the great mythical kings of Ireland. She prophesised that on his birth, several wonderful phenomena would occur, among them the discovery of an ancient tree called Eó Mugna, the archetypal world tree of ancient Ireland. A poem claims that all five 'mythical' trees of Ireland remained hidden from view until the night of Conn's birth, when 'Dathin's branch, and Mughna's sacred bough, and Uisneach's tree of copious rich produce, the trunk of Tortan, and the Yew of Ross, were on this night first known to rise in air.'[2]

In medieval Irish literature, kingship is often linked with the cult of great individual trees, and sacred trees are also used by medieval scribes as metaphors for kings and chieftains as champions and protectors. The derivation of the Irish word for such a tree, *bile*, cannot be established with certainty, but it seems to be closely related to the Indo-European root *bilios* for a champion.[3]

The poem mourning the loss of Bile Tortan equates the sacred ash with a king when it laments that the plain of Tortan was a kingless land since the tree has fallen. Another poem in the *Dindshenchas* refers to the Leinster king, Cathaoir Mór, and his dream of a marvellous tree, laden with fruit and emitting music.[4]

A tree of gold on the hill free from battle,
Its crown reached the cloudy welkin;
Thence the music of the men of the world
Was heard from the tree's crown.

Whenever the violent wind would beat
On the soft fresh foliage of the tree
There would be vast plenty, O men!
Of its fruit on the soil of the earth.

Every fruit the hosts would choose,
From east, from south, and from north,
Like the food-tide of the lazy sea,
Would come from the top of that one tree.

A druid, explaining the dream to Cathaoir, said that the tree represented the king himself, with the music symbolising his eloquence in assemblies and gatherings, and the abundance of fruit standing for his magnanimity. Eloquence and generosity were attributes thought to distinguish a proper king; and links between generous kings, trees and bountiful crops occur repeatedly in medieval literature and historical sources.

An entry in the Annals of Connacht for the year 1442 praises the children of King Ardgar Mór mac Mathgamna and likens them to 'fragrant trees and mighty oaks of bounty, for they distributed horses and treasure and money to every suppliant.' The sons of Tuireann describe Tuis, King of Greece, as 'the oak above the kings' and explain that 'as the oak is beyond the kingly trees of the wood, so are you beyond the kings of the world for open-handedness and for grandeur.' Tree metaphors were also used to describe the unworthiness of a king. The Annals of the Four Masters relate that the reign of undeserving leader Cairbre Caitcheann was marked by several disasters, among them rivers without fish, cattle without milk, and oak trees bringing forth but one single acorn.[5]

The metaphorical understanding of a king as a great tree, often an oak, standing at the centre of his realm and his people, was in all likelihood a reflection of the spiritual function that was anciently linked with his office. The king was meant to act as an intermediary between heaven and earth, between the divine and the mundane, in this way safeguarding his people's welfare and prosperity through his rightful, wise and generous reign. In this context, it is no surprise to find clear indications for the presence of highly revered sacred trees at palace sites and at assembly places of the chieftains and kings of medieval Ireland.

Recurrent references to a *bile rátha* in medieval texts imply that a 'sacred tree of the fort' was once a common feature at these enclosed dwelling places, particularly at high status forts. A commentary to the ancient laws of Ireland refers to a sacred wood at the fort; a tenth-century text on the colloquy between King Guaire and his hermit brother Marbhán mentions a sacred tree at the fort; and in the *Táin Bo Cuailnge*, Cúchulainn's charioteer Lóeg compares the height of an approaching warrior to the 'noble trees on a main fort's green'.[6] Place names from all over Ireland back up the literary references for affiliations between forts and sacred trees. *Ráth bhile*, 'ring fort of the sacred tree', appears in names such as Rathvilly in County Carlow and Rathvilla in County Offaly; while *dún bile* or 'fort of the sacred tree' was the Irish name for Dunbell in County Kilkenny. Lisnabilla in County Antrim, Lisnabill in Counties Longford and Tipperary, and Lisavilla in County Roscommon are anglicised versions of *lios na bile* and *lios bhile*, or 'enclosure of the sacred tree'.[7]

From the tenth century, annals and chronicles refer explicitly to sacred trees at important assembly sites. Historians and archaeologists have established that in medieval

Rathmore, Clogher, County Tyrone

When Ptolemy drew his map of Ireland in the second century AD, he marked Rathmore under the name of Regia, indicating a capital or a residence of kings. The oldest part of the Rathmore complex is a hill fort dating to the pre-Christian Iron Age. Traditionally, Rathmore was associated with the Three Collas, mythical brothers accredited with the establishment of the kingdom of Airghealla or Oriel. In the fourth and fifth century, nearby Clogher was the capital of the kingdom, and local tradition has it that the kings of Oriel were inaugurated at Rathmore. There is no written evidence to support this view, but a curious stone known as the Golden Stone or Cloch Óir, which is preserved in Clogher Cathedral, was reputedly one of the highly renowned oracle stones of ancient Ireland, and may have played a role in the inauguration ceremonies of local kings.[8]

times, several of these sites were also used for the ceremonial inauguration of territorial rulers. In ancient Ireland, communities were based on clans or *túatha*, ruled by local chieftains and provincial kings. In medieval times, the national or high kingship of Ireland was introduced. Chieftains and kings were selected from the leading families and installed at specific inauguration places, which were usually the main assembly or palace sites of the respective territories. It appears that for their prestigious inauguration sites, the Celts favoured places of earlier spiritual significance, distinguished by cairns, burial mounds and other Bronze Age monuments. They linked these sites to their own mythical ancestor, however, and would have added specific insignia of tribal power such as sacred stones and highly venerated trees.

The earliest references to a sacred tree at a royal assembly site relate to the Bile of Magh Adhair near Quin in County Clare. The plain is named after the legendary Fir Bolg hero Adhar, and was from early medieval times a noted place of assembly and inauguration for the Dál gCais sept and their O'Brien descendants. Entries in annals report that around 980, Mael Sechnaill, King of Meath and High-King of Ireland, plundered the territory of the Dál gCais, which was then ruled by Brian Boru. In the course of the raid the 'tree of Aenach-Maighe-Adhair' was cut, after 'being dug from the earth with its roots'. It must have survived the attack or been replaced by another tree, because around 1050 the Bile was cut down again, this time by Aodh O Conchobhair of Connacht.[9]

For the year 1099, entries in the Annals of the Four Masters, the Annals of Ulster and the Annals of Loch Clé report the destruction of the Craeb Tulcha, the Sacred

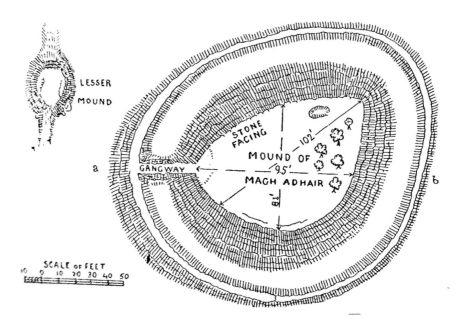

　🌿　TREES OF INSPIRATION

Magh Adhair, Toonagh (left), **and Brian Boru's Oak, Raheen** (above), **both in County Clare**

Locally, the magnificent oak at the fringes of Raheen Woods in east Clare is thought to be around a thousand years old. Not surprisingly, folklore has linked the tree with the most important son of the area, Brian Boru. Born in 926, the son of a Dál gCais chieftain, Brian was either born or raised in the ring fort Beal Boru, about 10 km from Raheen by the shores of Lough Derg. He was installed chieftain of the Dál gCais sept at Magh Adhair, presumably in the vicinity of the sacred tree, and resided at the royal palace of Kincora, present-day Killaloe, a short distance south of Beal Boru. In 1002, Brian became High-King of Ireland and his previously local campaign against the Vikings of Limerick grew into a nationwide struggle. Brian Boru was murdered in 1014 in the aftermath of the Battle of Clontarf.

Branch of the Mound, which stood at the inauguration and assembly place of the Ulaidh tribe of Antrim. Archaeologists have identified the mound as Crew Hill in the parish of Glenavy in County Antrim. The attack on the Craeb Tulcha was led by Domnall uí Lochlainn of the O'Neill sept from Tyrone. In IIII, the Ulaidh of Antrim took revenge for the destruction of the Craeb Tulcha. They ventured into O'Neill territory, still ruled by King Domnall uí Lochlainn, and cut down the sacred trees of Tullahogue, the inauguration site of the O'Neills, near present-day Dungannon.[10]

Ruadh-bheitheach or the Red Birch was sacred to the chieftains or kings of Uí Fhiachrach Aidhne in south County Galway. The tree was destroyed in 1129 by invaders from Munster. A substitute must have been planted or allowed to grow, because in 1143 chronicles report again that the tree was uprooted, this time by a joint army of men from Munster and Connacht.[11] The entry on the destruction of the Ruadh-bheitheach in the year 1143 is the last historical reference to a sacred tree at a royal inauguration site. Local tradition claiming that Lisnaskea, the Fort of the Thorn Tree in County Fermanagh, was named after the sacred thorn at the inauguration place of the influential Maguire clan, seems to be folklore rather than historical fact.[12]

Beech trees, Tullahogue, County Tyrone

The hilltop fort of Tullahogue was the prestigious inauguration site of the O'Neills of Tyrone. A map of Tullahogue, drawn on the eve of its destruction in 1602, shows a couple of mature trees inside the enclosure, and several others growing on its outer banks. It is possible that these trees were the successors of the sacred trees cut down in 1111 by invading enemies from Antrim. The tall beech trees that grow on the banks of Tullahogue today were only planted some hundred years ago.[13]

The early Irish terms for an inaugural assembly were *oirdneadh* or *ríoghadh*. The installation ceremony of the chieftain or king was known as *banais ríge*, the king's wedding, and was considered his symbolic marriage to the sovereignty of the land. Historical and literary sources indicate that there were considerable regional variants of the ritual, which may have involved bathing or drinking rituals, trials, ceremonial circuits, standing or sitting on sacred stones, and the bestowal of royal insignia to the king or chieftain.

While the precise function of sacred trees in the inaugural ceremonies of early medieval Ireland is not fully understood, there is reason to believe that the *slat na ríghe*, or 'rod of kingship' – the archetypal symbol of legitimate royal authority – may have been cut as a matter of course from a sacred tree growing at an inauguration site. *Slat na ríghe* is well documented in a description of a royal inauguration ceremony in the twelfth-century biography of St Maedoc of Ferns. The text specifies that the rod handed to the King of Bréifne in the course of his inauguration had to be cut from the sacred hazel tree of St Maedoc on Mount Seskin in Leinster.[14]

The effort apparently made by rival tribes to destroy the sacred trees at each others' inauguration sites indicates the significance of these trees as symbols of tribal identity and royal authority. This destruction or uprooting was clearly the greatest symbolic insult that an invading enemy could inflict upon a king and his people.[15]

From the thirteenth century, the Anglo-Norman concept of lordship began to gradually replace the Gaelic system of kingship. The old inauguration sites and rites became obsolete. But trees surfaced again as symbols of influential clans and families when the Anglo-Normans introduced a previously unknown tradition to Ireland: hereditary coats of arms and crests. Originally of military purpose, born of the need to identify friend and foe in battle, the coat of arms had by the thirteenth century developed into an emblem of family identity and distinction, used on seals, documents, possessions and tombs. The social meanings of hereditary coats of arms fitted in very well with the important role of genealogy in early Irish society, where septs and clans based their identity on myths of a common origin from legendary heroic ancestors. Gaelic families readily adopted the concept of arms and crests to emphasise their affiliation with an extended family group or sept, and by the fifteenth century, a heraldic tradition was firmly established in Ireland.

For their coats of arms, the more high-ranking Gaelic families tended to choose symbols with strong mythological allusions, such as stags, boars, serpents, salmon and trees. Given the close link between Gaelic kingship and oak trees in medieval Irish literature, it is not surprising to find that the oak is the most prominent tree in Irish heraldry. Oaks appear on their own, in groups or in combination with other symbols;

they are depicted growing out of mounds or torn up by their roots; sometimes, oak leaves or wreaths of oak are used.[16]

An intimate link between chieftains, kings, leading families and the oak tree is not peculiar to Ireland. Treasured for its impressive growth, strength and longevity, the oak is considered a superior tree throughout Europe.[17] Ancient religions associated the oak with their major deities. In Christian times, oaks became the fitting symbol for legendary and historical kings, and 'royal oak' trees occur even in countries where monarchy has long been abolished. In Ireland, the tradition of designated Royal Oaks is exclusively associated with two English monarchs, King Charles II and Queen Victoria.

King Charles II was the older brother and predecessor of King James II. Following his defeat in the Battle of Worcester in 1651, Charles II fled from Cromwell's Parliamentary troops to escape capture. For several days and nights, he hid in a large oak tree near Boscobel House in Shropshire, before continuing his flight to France. On 29 May 1660, Charles made a triumphant return from his exile to restore monarchy in Britain. Soon the story of the oak that had saved the king began to spread. Charles himself acknowledged the tree by adopting the oak as his emblem, and by ordering that the date of his return be celebrated annually as Royal Oak Day. The oak at Boscobel was hence known as the Royal Oak, and in honour of the tree and the king, 'The Royal Oak' became a popular name for public houses and inns throughout his realm.[18]

Charles II, however, did not generalise his respect for oak trees, and it was during his reign that the finest trees of the famous oak wood of Shillelagh in County Wicklow were felled. There were nevertheless a few public houses in Ireland named after the Royal Oak, but today their original link with King Charles II is almost entirely lost. In the County Kildare village of Enfield it is hardly recalled that the old name, Innfield, was a reference to the local Royal Oak Inn. Likewise the derivation of the name for the Royal Oak Inn in Mooncoin in County Waterford is no longer remembered, and in the small village of Royal Oak near Bagenalstown in County Offaly, local lore associates the name with the nearby stronghold of the ancient kings of Leinster at Dind Ríg, or else with the faded memory of an unnamed king that passed through the village long ago. Only the small Oak Grove Millennium Park in the village links the name with Charles II and Royal Oak Day on 29 May.[19]

In 1861, Queen Victoria paid a short visit to Killarney in County Kerry, and the royal visit is reflected in several local names, such as the Royal Oak near O'Sullivan's Cascade and the Queen's Oaks in the gardens of Muckross House. Other names are Queen's Drive, a panoramic route with great views over the Lakes of Killarney; the Queen's Cottage, where Victoria allegedly took a rest; and Ladies' View, where her ladies-in-waiting stood to enjoy the scenery of the lakes.[20]

The Queen's Oaks, Muckross (above)**, and the Royal Oak, Killarney, County Kerry** (right)

During her long reign from 1837 to 1901, Queen Victoria had numerous commemorative oak trees planted at places she visited. While she stayed in Killarney, the queen lodged in Muckross House, and on the occasion of her visit, a group of five or six oaks were ceremonially planted between the House and the Lower Lake; three of them, known as the Queen's Oaks, survive today.

The Royal Oak on the western shore of the Lower Lake is one of the biggest oaks in the Killarney area. It must already have been an impressive specimen in 1861, when Queen Victoria was reportedly brought to see the spectacular cascades of the nearby triple waterfall. It is said that she held a picnic in the shade of the stately oak tree by the lake shore.

Judgement Trees

The druid insisted to have the lawsuit heard in a place called
Rathin, under a particular large tree which was renowned
for giving oracular responses to its pagan worshippers.

John O'Hanlon, *Lives of the Irish Saints* (1875)[1]

Brithem, literally 'maker of judgment', was the old Irish name for a judge. Brehon is the anglicised version. In early Irish society, brehons belonged with poets and druids to the privileged group of scholars, a learned class whose members owed their high-ranking status to their sacred insight and wisdom as well as to their knowledge acquired by learning. Brehons were responsible for the preservation and transmission of Brehon Law, the old instructions and guidelines for the delivery of justice, which, like the genealogical narratives and historical traditions, were originally passed on by word of mouth. Brehons acted as judges in public lawsuits, and they advised kings on legal decisions.

The *Críth Gablach*, a legal tract written around AD 700, states that 'A king must have a judge with him, or be a judge himself.' Only a few kings were credited with special judging abilities and with the composition of legal tracts; among them was the legendary Cormac mac Airt, whose reign is dated in the third century AD. According to a fourteenth-century text, the king was lured by the divine Manannán mac Lir to Tír Tairngire, the Land of Promise, where he found true and sacred wisdom in the hazel nuts growing over the Well of Segais.[2]

The sacred nature of justice in early Irish society was expressed in the ancient belief that a brehon who passed judgement without listening to both sides, or without having a profound knowledge of the law, would cause crops to fail in his territory and disease to befall his people. Geoffrey Keating, in his *History of Ireland*, wrote that all the oak trees lost their acorns prematurely if King Fachtna mac Seancha Macuill gave a bad judgement, but they retained their fruit if his judgement was good.[3]

Our information on early Irish law and judges comes from law tracts, which were written down during the seventh and eighth centuries. The archaic language of the texts, however, indicates that the contents are in fact much older. Legal tracts were essentially based on the social structure of society, and on the status of its members. Typically, compensation in the form of payment could atone for almost any crime in secular law; when the payment could or would not be delivered, enslavement or the death penalty were possible alternatives. Canon Law was stricter, and crimes such as the murder of high-ranking clergy or scribes, or the violation of monastic sanctuaries, were principally punished with execution, especially with hanging.[4]

In the context of venerable trees, there is a medieval law tract which regulated the use of trees and shrubs, and listed the penalties for damaging or cutting trees without the landowner's permission. This text is preserved in the eighth-century legal tract *Bretha Comaithchesa* or Laws of Neighbourhood, but probably derived from the earlier but lost law tract *Fidbretha* or Tree Judgements, which is mentioned in a text from the seventh century.

Based on the social structure of medieval Ireland and on the laws relating to the status of people, the *Bretha Comaithchesa* classified trees into four categories, each comprising seven species, and determined special fines for the interference with each class of trees. Commentaries on the laws indicate that the classification was mainly determined by the practical importance and economic value of the trees' timber and fruit, and only secondarily by their symbolic significance. It is nevertheless striking that the species regarded most valuable by law were also the most prominent species in terms of individual sacred trees.[5]

The most precious species of trees – oak, hazel, holly, yew, ash, pine and apple tree – formed the *Airig Fedo*, the 'Nobles of the Wood' or 'Chieftain Trees'. Compensation

Oak tree and holly blossom

for interfering with a tree from this class was a one-year-old heifer for branch-cutting, a two-year-old heifer for fork-cutting and a cow for base-cutting.

The oak was protected by additional regulations. For the cutting of a young tree, a compensation of a two-year-old heifer was fixed. For stripping off enough bark to tan a pair of woman's or man's sandals, compensation was one cow-hide or one ox-hide respectively; in addition, the culprit had to dress the wound of the tree with a mixture of clay, cow-dung and new milk until it healed.

The laws explain that the oak, valued for its acorns which formed the staple diet of pigs in autumn, was also held in high esteem for the excellence of its timber and for its dignity and impressive size. Spiritually, we find individual oak trees closely linked with kingship and the monastic foundations of early Irish saints.

The hazel's denomination as a Chieftain Tree was attributed to its rods, which were worked into wattles for fences and houses. Hazel nuts are mentioned for their nutritious quality, but not for their association with *imbas forosna*, the essence of sacred knowledge. Commentaries on the classification of the holly refer rather cryptically to 'grass for another and chariot shafts'. The first part of this description might mean that the upper branches were cut for winter-fodder for cattle, a practice that was still carried out in parts of County Kerry in the 1940s.[6] Venerable holly trees are a common feature at ancient assembly places for the harvest festival of Lughnasa.

Yew trees – in religious contexts, the archetypal trees of life and death – owe their position in the class of Noble Trees to the figurines, domestic vessels, spears and arrows that were crafted from their timber. The ash was listed among the Nobles of the Wood because it was 'support of a royal thigh and half-material of a weapon', meaning that the timber of ash was used to make handles of weapons, and possibly seats or chairs for kings. Sacred ash trees often grew beside holy wells, and two of the most venerated 'mythical' trees of ancient Ireland were ash trees.

Apart from a few scattered groups of pine that might have survived until the twelfth or thirteenth centuries, the pine is believed to have become more or less distinct in Ireland by the time the laws were written down. The inclusion of the pine in the law texts was

Ancient pine tree, Céide Fields, County Mayo

Neolithic or New Stone Age people settled in Ireland from about 4000 BC. They were the earliest farmers and the first to interfere with the land and its resources when they cleared woodlands to make plots for grazing livestock and growing crops. In a once densely wooded area now known as Céide Fields, Neolithic farmers cleared plots of the extensive pine forest with stone axes and by burning. The trunk of one massive pine from this forest is preserved in the Céide Field Visitor Centre. The tree probably grew from around 4200 to 4400 BC, and was blown over when it was 150 to 200 years old. Hidden for millennia under a cover of bog, it was only discovered in 1940.

Whitethorn fruit

In earlier tree lists, the hawthorn or whitethorn appeared occasionally among the trees of 'Lower Divisions of the Wood'; later, its status was elevated. Since the timber of whitethorn is of little value, and its fruit was probably only eaten in times of scarcity,[7] the rise of its status was possibly due to the tree's considerable spiritual value.

TREES OF INSPIRATION

possibly made with reference to Scotland, where the pine never became extinct, and where Irish Brehon law was introduced in the fifth century by invaders from Ulster. Regarding the significance of the apple, the law mentions its fruit and bark; unfortunately, it does not state what the bark of apple trees was used for. In medieval literature, apple trees and their fruit appear recurrently in the context of mythical otherworld experiences.

The second category of trees, titled *Aithig Fedo*, the 'Commoners of the Wood' or 'Peasant Trees', included alder, willow, hawthorn, rowan or mountain ash, birch, elm and wild cherry. Compensation for branch-cutting was a sheep, for fork-cutting a one-year-old heifer, and for base-cutting a cow. Highly venerated individual hawthorn trees are linked with saints and holy wells, with death and burial, and with the world of the fairies. Rowan trees were associated with druidism, and elms and alder occur occasionally in the hagiographical texts concerning early Irish saints. Willow, birch and cherry trees rarely feature in the lore of individual sacred trees.

The two remaining tree categories comprise shrub trees and bramble trees. *Fodla Fedo*, the 'Lower Divisions of the Wood', are blackthorn, elder, spindle, whitebeam, arbutus, aspen and juniper. *Losa Fedo*, the 'Bushes of the Wood', are bracken, bog myrtle, gorse, bramble, heather, broom and wild rose or gooseberry. They play no role at all in the veneration of individual trees and bushes.[8]

The *Bretha Comaithchesa* indicates an enormous esteem for trees in medieval Ireland, a regard and respect that encouraged lawmakers to categorise trees and to protect them by decrees and regulations. But the tract does not reveal whether the brehons of medieval Ireland chose individual sacred trees as venues for holding law courts. Historical and literary sources from Ireland and abroad, on the other hand, suggest that the ancient Celts frequently conducted the business of lawsuits in the shade of designated trees.

The Greek scholar Strabo described an assembly of three hundred Celts in the sacred oak grove called Drunemeton in Galatia in Asia Minor. He wrote that a council passed judgement upon murder cases, while the territorial chieftains and judges were responsible for all other judicial decisions.[9] Around AD 400, an anonymous Latin author of a comedy referred to an oracular oak tree in Gaul where the Celts carried out capital punishment.[10]

In Ireland, an oracular tree of judgement is mentioned in the biography of St Berach or Barry. In the course of his missionary work during the late sixth and early seventh centuries, the saint was challenged by a local druid. When the case was brought before a judge, the druid insisted that the lawsuit be heard under a renowned oracular tree in a place called Rathin. The judge, obviously unwilling to travel to Rathin, ordered the druid to bring the tree to the place of the assembly. The druid declined this request but Berach said a prayer, whereupon the tree miraculously moved to the assembly place and became firmly rooted there.[11]

In County Derry we find a comparatively recent historical reference to a venerable tree being linked with the delivery of justice. The old Irish name for the Black Hill in Ballinascreen parish was Cnoc na Daróige Duibh, or 'Hill of the Black Oak'. In 1835, when the Ordnance Survey visited the area, the oak had long since decayed, but it was still remembered locally under the name of 'Oak of the Assembly', or Daróg an Aireachtais. In medieval times, *aireacht* or *oireachtas* were the common terms used to describe assemblies that were held to hear lawsuits and to settle disputes between lords and rebellious subjects.[12]

Brehon Law, the old Gaelic legal system, was commonly executed in Ireland into the fourteenth century. The Anglo-Normans, who in many ways fully adapted to Irish culture and lifestyle, adopted the Irish judicial and legal system, and Anglo-Norman earls employed Irish brehons to speak law in their constituencies. In 1351, England issued an official order for her English and Anglo-Norman subjects in Ireland, urging them to abolish Irish Brehon Law in favour of English Common Law. The Statutes of Kilkenny, decreed in 1364–1366, reiterated this instruction.

As late as 1598, the English poet Edmund Spenser referred to the 'custom of the Irish to assemble in a rath or on a hill to settle disputes', suggesting that Brehon Law continued to be the legal system of the Irish. It was only with the English conquest in the early years of the seventeenth century that native Gaelic structures and law systems were eradicated.[13]

Hanging Trees

English Common Law, unlike Brehon Law, carried the death penalty for a number of crimes and misdeeds, among them treason. Historical documents provide detailed information on trials and executions from the time of the Plantations in the sixteenth century to the Irish War of Independence in the twentieth century. In Irish folk memory, the delivery and execution of English Common Law was long preserved in the lore of 'hanging trees'. These were usually considered haunted or cursed, and it was often said that gallows trees never produced leaves, blossom or

The Tory Bush, Kingscourt, County Cavan

The Tory Bush is a well-known place name for a crossroads between Kingscourt and Bailieborough in County Cavan. The bush, a hawthorn, stands carefully protected from grazing cattle in a field. The name of the tree derives from the Irish word *tórai* for a fugitive or outlaw, and was used from Cromwellian times onwards for the dispossessed and expelled Irish; later, it became a derogatory term for the followers of Catholic King James II and supporters of the monarchy.

The traditions that surround the Tory Bush are kept alive in stories, poems and ballads. Some claim that the tree was an assembly point for the dispossessed, before they attacked those who had driven them from their land; but there are also gloomy tales of several Tories hanged from the tree by the English in the seventeenth and eighteenth centuries.[14]

fruit, that birds never sang in their branches, and that meddling with them brought bad luck.

The majority of Ireland's hanging trees have decayed, and often their stories have disappeared with the trees. The Hangman's Bush near Rathcoole Bridge in County Wicklow is no longer remembered; forgotten also are the Hangman's Tree in Derry City, or the Hanging Tree in Currin in County Cavan. Others were well known into the early decades of the twentieth century. As folklore accounts from all over the country show, these hanging trees were particularly associated with the time from Cromwell's conquest of Ireland in 1649 to the Irish Rebellion in 1798.[15]

Given the records of Cromwell's persecution of the Catholic clergy, hanging trees were often associated with the murder of priests or clerics. A well-known example was the Bile of Carraigadroichíd, a pear tree near Macroom in County Cork. In 1650, the Bishop of Ross was hanged on the tree; consequently the tree never bore fruit again, and when some of its branches were cut off by the owner, his pony fell dead. The Friar's Bush in Ardnawark, County Donegal, was used by Cromwellian soldiers to hang a Franciscan brother; and in Carrick Na Horna, also County Donegal, the spirit of a priest was said to haunt the blackthorn upon which he died.[16]

Folk memories of landlordism and suppressive laws against Catholics surface in tales of Irish youths hanged by cruel landlords for minor offences. Particularly widespread were tales and ballads telling the fate of young Irishmen who broke some twigs or branches from trees that grew on the land or in the demesne of castles. As an act of retribution in these stories, the landlords have the young men hanged from the trees from which they took the branches. One such story linked an infamous hanging tree with Lord Lisgar of Bailieborough in County Cavan. Ballads and tales have kept alive the memory of the hanged boy's mother and her curses. She demanded that the sun never again shine on the castle door; that the birds were never to sing in the demesne; that no leaves were to grow on the tree; and that no heir was to be born to Lord Lisgar. 'Seven curses she did give, and on him they did fall', ends a popular ballad about Lisgar's Hanging Tree. Indeed, Lisgar's Castle has long since fallen into decay, and today it is but a memory.[17]

The Rebellion of 1798 – prominently linked with Liberty Trees, which are described in the next chapter – was also associated with hanging trees. Around 1798, several people were hanged from trees near Blackstaff's Chair in Iniskeen, County Monaghan, a place notorious for executions since the 1690s. On an ancient tree that overshadowed St John's Well in Talbotstown in County Wicklow, an Irish rebel was hanged; later, when a storm brought the tree down and it was used for firewood, it is said that the branch upon which the man died exploded in the fire. Three Wexford boys died on the Hanging Tree in Hacketstown in County Carlow; consequently, the tree never flourished again and withered away.[18]

Liberty Trees

It is a branch. Of what? Of the tree of liberty.
Where did it first grow? In America.
Where does it bloom? In France.
Where did the seeds fall? In Ireland.

United Irish Catechism (December 1797)[1]

From the times of the Bronze Age, when metalworking developed and allowed the production of sophisticated weapons, a new class of people emerged in societies throughout Europe: the class of warriors. Finds of sacrificed armoury and weaponry, historical accounts of oracles considered prior to important battles, offerings made to martial deities, and sagas of great mythical battles testify to the sacred character of warfare in ancient European cultures, and Celtic societies were no exception.

The Roman historian Tacitus described a sacred grove on the Isle of Mona, today Anglesey off the coast of Wales, where Celtic druids performed oracular rites, and made human sacrifice to please the gods before the Roman attack in AD 60. Cassius Dio, another Roman historian, related how, at about the same time in the east of Britannia, a Celtic tribe led by Queen Boudicca, sacrificed female prisoners in a forest sacred to Andraste, a goddess of war and victory. Hoards consisting of weapons, chariot-fittings and trumpets of war are material evidence of the sacred nature of warfare in areas of Celtic settlement in Ireland and abroad.[2]

We can assume that anciently, warriors would have gathered ceremonially at sacred places for the performance of rituals before marching into battle. In Ireland, the earliest references to military assemblies date from the Christian period. By then, the Irish term used to describe a mustering or meeting which could also have military connotations was *dál*. Historical sources do not explicitly refer to sacred trees in the context of martial conventions, but medieval Irish literature suggests that the sacred trees of a tribe or territory were also looked upon as channels of strength and symbols of victory.

The description of the Battle of Magh Rátha refers to a *bile buada*, a tree of victory that grew close to the battle field. Trees of victory or triumph are mentioned in several medieval tales, though their exact functions remain uncertain. Poems in the *Dindshenchas* reveal that some of the 'mythical' trees of ancient Ireland had martial associations: at the Craeb Uisnigh, 'troops did dwell', Eó Mugna could shelter some thousand warriors and Eó Rossa is called 'vigour of victory' and 'champion's cover'. A further unidentified Bile Tarbgha apparently gave strength to those who stroked it.[3]

In more recent history, trees linked to war, battle and conflict were – and still are – seen as living witnesses to significant events and people, as opposed to transmitters of mystic strength and power. Their names typically reflect the individuals, principles and battles they stand for.

Several trees and bushes with military associations were at one time regarded as memorials to combatants who died near them. The Soldier's Bush in Dillagh in County Cavan is so-called after the death of an English soldier at the spot; the Whiteboy's Bush in Mogeely parish in County Cork was said to grow where a local member of the secret agrarian society died from his wounds. Other trees were remembered as former vantage points and shelters, used as watch-posts for approaching enemies.[4] Trees of local significance are only vaguely remembered today, particularly when the trees themselves are gone, but the trees that commemorate the big battles and rebellions of Irish history are still renowned as legendary historical monuments, even though some of them have long decayed or are now reduced to dead stumps.

A venerable yew tree in a garden at Castle Avenue in Clontarf, County Dublin, was linked with the Battle of Clontarf in 1014, when a victorious Irish army under the lead of Brian Boru ended Viking power and dominance in Ireland. Brian Boru himself was killed by Vikings fleeing the battlefield, and it is locally held that he was slain under a mighty yew, which was hence popularly known as the Brian Boru Yew. Unfortunately, the tree fell in 1993, and shortly afterwards its remains were cut up and removed.[5]

The Council Bush, Clontibret, County Monaghan

A crossroads at Gallagh Bog, outside the village of Clontibret, County Monaghan, is still popularly known as the Council Bush. The name recalls the landmark thorn where the Irish officers, led by Hugh O'Neill, assembled to hold council prior to the 1595 Battle of Clontibret. Today, the spot is marked by a memorial stone, some decorative shrubs and three mature sycamore trees.[6]

The Council Bush, with its link to the great Aodh Ó Néill and the Battle of Clontibret of 1595, is also lost but well remembered. Aodh Ó Néill, anglicised Hugh O'Neill, Earl of Tyrone, was a man of great military experience who fought initially for Queen Elizabeth I. A supporter of Catholicism and of the Gaelic system of chieftainism, O'Neill rebelled in 1594 against the ongoing anglicisation of the province. The rebellion spread, and O'Neill led a confederacy of Ulster chieftains in several battles against Elizabeth's forces, one of them taking place in 1595 at Gallagh Bog near Clontibret. The battle ended with an Irish defeat, and so did the entire rebellion. When the leaders of the uprising left Ireland in the so-called Flight of the Earls in 1607, the old Gaelic ways of life came to an end, and the large-scale plantation of Ulster with 'loyal' Protestant settlers from England and Scotland began.

In 1685, James II – a Catholic and great grandson of Mary Stuart – became King of England, Scotland and Ireland. When English Protestants called for William of Orange, later King William III, to expel James from the throne, James had the support of Irish Catholics. In spring 1689, reinforced by French troops, James arrived in Ireland to win back the crown. The decisive battle between James II and William of Orange was fought on 12 July 1690 at the River Boyne.

A number of trees, some of them still preserved, are very prominently linked with the Battle of the Boyne. These memorial trees almost invariably became important symbols for the victory of King William III and his followers. One of the scarce references to King James II was made in a story told in the 1940s in County Donegal; it relates how James, fleeing from Derry southwards towards the Boyne, took a rest somewhere along the way under a sycamore tree and was about to dine there, when he noticed that William of Orange was already after him. James hastily resumed his flight, and the tree became popularly known as King William's Tree after the triumphant pursuer.[7] The exact location of the sycamore is not mentioned in the story, but it is possible that it is the same tree as King William's Tree in the grounds of Scarva House in County Down, which is a splendid Spanish or sweet chestnut sometimes erroneously described as a sycamore.

King William is also associated with the Big Tree in the Malone district of Belfast, where he supposedly sheltered from heavy rain, and with William's Tree in Legacorry near Richhill, County Armagh. The latter was a huge beech tree, revered because the king reportedly tied his horse to its trunk and slept in the shade of its branches. The beech has decayed, but the stump remained in place at least into the nineteenth century.[8]

King William's Tree, Scarva, County Down

The magnificent Spanish chestnut tree is certainly one of the best known historic trees in the north of Ireland, and one of the most impressive. Some of its major branches are hollow and need the support of timber poles, but despite its age, the tree still produces a good crop of chestnuts.

In June 1690, the Williamite army of around thirty thousand men camped at Scarva for training before marching to victory at the Battle of the Boyne. During his stay, William reputedly tied his horse to the chestnut tree and pitched his tent in its shade. An annual re-enactment of the Battle of the Boyne takes place at Scarva in July.[9]

William's Tree or the Big Tree, Malone, Belfast

William of Orange, so it is told, took breakfast in Belfast before heading south towards the Boyne. When he had travelled a short distance, a heavy shower of rain forced him to take shelter under a massive chestnut tree by the roadside, until the owner of the nearby residence asked him in. In remembrance of the big tree, *an crann mór*, the owner named his home Cranmore House. When the original Crann Mór was blown down in a storm, another was chosen as a memorial to William's short rest; and when the substitute fell, a third tree was planted. Today two old chestnut trees in front of ruined Cranmore House are pointed out as William's Trees, and it is said that he tied his horse to one of them, and took shelter under the other.[10]

The Schomberg Tree, Bangor, County Down

In the ground of Bangor Castle, a dead tree stump is preserved, supported by metal bars and concrete. A plaque informs us that the Duke of Schomberg, an ally of William III of Orange, pitched his headquarters under the ancient tree in August 1689 when he arrived in Ireland. From Bangor, the duke and field-marshal marched northwards and took Carrickfergus. The following year, Duke Schomberg joined forces with William III, and fell at the Battle of the Boyne.[11]

the 1798 Rebellion and the Tree of Liberty

In Ireland, the name 'Liberty Tree' is invariably linked with the Rebellion of 1798. The tree as a symbol of liberty, equal rights and resistance had its origin in America and was first used by the Sons of Liberty, a secret society of colonists who joined together in protest against British impositions on America's economic freedom.[12]

From August 1765, the Sons of Liberty held rallies in Boston Commons under a particularly large, dominant elm tree, which they dubbed Liberty Tree. When British authorities cut it down, the Sons of Liberty erected a pole to replace it. Soon, the practice of holding politically motivated meetings under trees spread throughout the American colonies that objected to British control. The conflict between the colonies and Britain escalated and ended in the American War of Independence (1776–1783), during which the Tree of Liberty as a symbol of resistance was born.

1789 marked the year of the French Revolution, which brought an end to monarchy in France and precipitated enormous political change throughout Europe. In 1793, the fall of the Bastille, and the death of former King of France, Louis XVI and his wife Marie Antoinette on the guillotine, were potent international symbols of the definitive collapse of the old regime. In the same year, the idea of a Tree of Liberty surfaced again, taken up by French revolutionaries.

In Ireland, Theobald Wolfe Tone and the United Irishmen welcomed the French revolution as 'the morning star of liberty' and began to organise an Irish rebellion modelled on French revolutionary notions of liberty and equality.[13]

The Society of United Irishmen, founded in 1791 in Belfast by Wolfe Tone, was a group of Catholic and Protestant radicals, who agitated for the creation of an independent and democratic republic of Ireland, with a parliament open to all Irish men irrespective of rank or religion. Clearly non-sectarian and non-denominational, their programme aimed to eradicate the old divisions between Protestants, Catholics and Dissenters, and to bring about a common Irish identity by gaining national independence.

Following the French model, the United Irishmen adopted the Tree of Liberty as a populist emblem of their movement. In August 1795, *Finn's Leinster Journal* reported that soldiers were called out from Cork to Blarney 'to prevent the planting of a tree of liberty, adorned with ribbons and mounted with the red cap by Irish *carmagnoles.*' The tree was a finely grown birch tree, and its planting was accompanied by the playing of 'The Marseillaise' and other French tunes of revolution.[14]

When France offered support to any people who were ready to rise against their

The Liberty Tree, Carlow Town, County Carlow

In 1998, Trees of Liberty were planted and monuments erected throughout Ireland to mark the bicentenary of the 1798 Rebellion. This particularly outstanding Liberty Tree, designed by John Behan, stands in the centre of Carlow Town.

government, the Society of United Irishmen was declared illegal and administering its oath became a capital offence. Early in 1798, the British government responded to ongoing United Irishmen recruitment, activities and surprise attacks by increasing the area under martial law. On 23 May 1978, the rebellion against British rule broke out openly, with risings in Counties Meath, Carlow, Kildare, Wicklow and Dublin in the east, Antrim and Down in the north and Mayo in the west.[15]

The beginning of the uprising held promise. At the end of May, an army of about 15,000 United Irishmen took the town of Wexford and celebrated the establishment of the first Irish Republic. Houses were decorated with green flags and leafy branches and twigs.[16]

The Tree of Liberty, Bull-Ring, Wexford, County Wexford

The Bull-Ring, right in the centre of Wexford Town, is renowned for having been a sort of open-air factory for the production of pikes for the revolutionaries of 1798. The place is distinguished by a memorial to the 'pike-men' and plaques explaining the concept of Liberty Trees. On 31 May 1998, a Tree of Liberty, a young oak, was planted by President Mary McAleese as part of the bicentennial commemorations of the Rebellion.[17]

The Liberty Tree, Roughfort, County Antrim

Prior to the Battle of Antrim on 7 June 1798, Henry Joy McCracken assembled twenty-five regiments of United Irishmen at the medieval motte of Roughfort, west of Newtownabbey. A prosperous young Presbyterian from Belfast, McCracken had joined the United Irishmen soon after their foundation. A strong advocate of liberty and equality and a fierce fighter for social justice, he had established the first Sunday School in Belfast open to students of all religious denominations. As commander-in-chief of the Antrim rebels, he led his men from Roughfort into Antrim Town. With their plans possibly betrayed by traitors from their own ranks, the United Irishmen were defeated by loyal troops. McCracken went into hiding, but was captured and executed in Belfast in July. The Liberty Tree in the field opposite Roughfort Motte is a grand solitary oak. It may have been planted in 1798 or 1799.[18]

In June, the rebels suffered their first disastrous defeats in Antrim Town and on Vinegar Hill near Enniscorthy in County Wexford. The Battle of Vinegar Hill was led by Father John Murphy (1753–98), who was initially opposed to the activities of the United Irishmen, but joined them after the outbreak of the rebellion in Wexford. At their camp on Vinegar Hill, the rebels erected a Liberty Tree prior to the battle on 21 June. Following their defeat, Father Murphy led his column into County Kilkenny; after several fights, he was separated from his troops on the march back, captured by the British in County Carlow and executed on 2 July 1798.[19]

On 22 August, the French General Jean Joseph A. Humbert (1755–1823) arrived with a thousand-strong invasion force in Killala Bay in County Mayo. They soon occupied Killala, Ballina and Castlebar, and planted Liberty Trees in Castlebar and Newport to celebrate their victory. Humbert's troops won another fight at Coolooney, but were defeated at Ballinamuck in County Longford on 8 September.[20]

Remnant of the Cotton Tree, Enniscorthy, County Wexford

The Cotton Tree, a black poplar, was closely associated with the Battle of Vinegar Hill in 1798. On 21 June, just before the decisive battle, while Father John Murphy and his patriots were camping on Vinegar Hill, the British troops gathered under the Cotton Tree by the old Slaney Bridge in Enniscorthy. They tied their horses to its branches and waited to receive instructions for the fight. In 1991 during road works, tree surgeons surveyed the Cotton Tree and found that the trunk was decaying. Consequently, the tree was taken down. A ring of its trunk is preserved in the dungeon of Enniscorthy Castle Museum; the rest was used by a local craftsman to carve souvenirs.[21]

Early in October, the Rebellion came to an end with the capture of Theobald Wolfe Tone. About six months after its outbreak, the Irish Rebellion was crushed by the British, and the results were devastating. About 30,000 people lost their lives in the rebellion. The majority of the dead were peasants who had fought with the United Irishmen, inadequately armed with pikes and pitch forks. Many Catholic civilians also died. Apart from their leaders, the Irish rebels were predominantly Catholic, and since the British forces had the support of Irish Protestants, the sectarian divide only deepened, ending Wolfe Tone's dream of a common Irish identity.

In 1998, the bicentenary of the Rebellion, the efforts and aims of the United Irishmen and their followers were commemorated during nationwide celebrations, which often involved the planting of Trees of Liberty.

Festival Trees

When every parish had its spot and held its patron day
Thousands came from every part this glorious sight to see.
Horse racing and cock-fighting and every other spree,
Pipers, fiddlers and dancers came to the Bush of Ardleney.

Anonymous, *The Bush of Ardleney* (c. 1162)[1]

Aeinach and *óenach* were old Irish names for meetings, conducted primarily for commerce, which also regularly involved a communal celebration of games and seasonal festivals. Assemblies of this type were traditionally linked with fixed dates, often around the harvest festival of Lughnasa at the turn from July to August. They were usually held at long-established assembly places, many of them distinguished by conspicuous stone monuments or venerable trees.

When Christianity transformed the religious parts of the festivals into pilgrimages, the commercial aspect of the *aeinach* continued in the shape of big market days, and the old name of the assembly survived in the Irish word *aonach* for a fair. Fairs are still held at fixed dates, usually at movable feast days such as Easter or Whitsunday, or else on the feast days of local patron saints. When set on the latter, fairs became linked with the pattern or patron day, the devotional celebration of the local patron saint.

Both fairs and pattern days retained a strong pagan aura. Aside from their official functions – which were commerce and religious devotion, respectively – fairs and patterns played an important social role. They were valued occasions for meeting and socialising. Hawkers and entertainers set up stalls, pipers and fiddlers provided music for dancers, and there were sporting contests and fights. The big fairs and the major pilgrimage sites attracted people from across the country and many pattern days have expanded beyond their religious origins into annual outdoor rural festivals.

The Great Ash of Leix, Emo, County Laois

The Great Ash of Leix was a well-known landmark and meeting point for the local community. In 1792, Samuel Hayes measured the enormous tree for his *Practical Treatise on Trees* and noted that its widest girth was some 12 m. The tree died in the nineteenth century, and its memory is preserved in the woodcut that Hayes used to illustrate his study.[2]

The medieval poem on the celebrated Bile Tortan is the earliest reference of a venerated tree standing at the centre of fairs and communal gatherings. Into the sixteenth century, fairs were held at the old traditional assembly places, often known as 'fair hills'. It was only from the time of the Plantations in the late sixteenth and early seventeenth century – when towns with wide main streets or central squares were deliberately established throughout Ireland – that the commercial parts of fairs shifted gradually from the fair hills into the more convenient towns. Folk memory, popular traditions and place names show that into the early twentieth century, the social aspects of fairs – such as sporting and fighting contests, music, games, dancing and matchmaking – continued to take place at the old assembly sites in the shade of designated trees.

The Dancing Bush or Sceichín a' Rince was a landmark in that part of Munster where the Counties Tipperary, Limerick and Cork meet. It gave its name to the County Tipperary townland of Skeheenarinky, and links back to the custom of outdoor dances. Well into the twentieth century, crossroads were a favourite site for the popular past-time of open-air dances. After a short decline, the custom has been revived in recent

The Dancing Tree, Cloncurry, County Kildare

The Norman motte by the old main road from Enfield to Dublin, adjoining Cloncurry graveyard and church, is dominated by an old ash tree growing on its top. The ash is popularly known as the Dancing Tree, and was reputedly planted around 1900 by the local parish priest. It must have had a predecessor, or else be much older than estimated, because in 1875, Canon O'Hanlon gave a description of Cloncurry, noting that: 'A remarkable moat or aboriginal earthwork adjoins the cemetery and on its summit rises a well-grown tree, which presents a very picturesque object from all approaches.'[3]

decades, and today open-air dances are often organised as part of local music events or family festivals. Dancing trees and bushes, however, have lost their former role as focal points of these events. Remembered into the early twentieth century, but since then utterly lost and forgotten, is the tradition of the countless 'fiddlers' bushes' throughout Ireland, which were named after the musicians who played their tunes at fairs and crossroad dances.[4]

The Ardleney Bush in County Cavan was once widely known and celebrated in ballads. Before it was blown down in a storm it 1894, it had been a local landmark and a strategic meeting point for the local division of the United Irishmen, and an assembly point for games and entertainment associated with the patron day of Ardleney.[5] Famous meeting points for the local communities were also the Great Ash of Leix in Emo, County Laois; the Ash of Duniry in County Galway; and the Spreading Hawthorn Tree of Lissoy in County Westmeath. In the early nineteenth century, this ancient thorn on the hill right behind the village pub of Lissoy was the favourite spot for locals to meet and socialise. In 1770, in his poem 'The Deserted Village', Oliver Goldsmith celebrated 'The hawthorn bush, with seats beneath the shade, for talking age and whisp'ring lovers made'. By the 1840s the Spreading Hawthorn of Lissoy had decayed, but its protective wall remained intact and was still pointed out as the last remnant of the landmark tree.[6]

Besides acting as focal points for fairs and patterns, conveniently sited or unusual trees were very popular places for general socialising. Banty's Bush in the townland of Ballindarragh outside Markethill in County Armagh was one such landmark and popular meeting point. It fell about 1950, but is still well remembered for its wishing chairs, which were three curved branches that people would sit on while making a wish.[7] The Big Tree at the crossroads in Termonfeckin in County Louth was a much used meeting point for many years. In 1836, the Ordnance Survey noted the antiquity of the venerable tree. When it died, the dead stump was allowed to remain in place for well over a hundred years. There are no traces left of the tree today, but its memory is still alive.[8]

Historically, well-sited bushes or trees were often chosen as begging spots, shelters or meeting points by people looking for alms. They were frequently hawthorn trees. Such trees were once popularly known as 'beggars' bushes', and could be found throughout Ireland, in cities and towns as well as in the countryside. The best known example was certainly the one that gave its name to a whole district in Dublin City, Beggar's Bush. All the passengers arriving by boat from England into the old port of Ringsend had to pass 'the beggar's bush' on their way into Dublin, making it an ideal place for begging. The bush grew at this spot until about 1900.[9]

YEW-TREE OF CROM.

The Twin Yews of Crom, Crom Castle, County Fermanagh

Also known as the Great Yew, the Twin Yews of Crom Castle in County Fermanagh are a fantastic pair of mature yew trees – a younger male and a larger, older female – whose intermingling crowns give the appearance of one tree when seen from a distance. Local tradition holds the Great Yew of Crom to be the oldest yew tree in Ireland, claiming that the tree pre-dates the arrival of Christianity. Early in the seventeenth century, following the failed rebellion against Elizabeth I, Hugh O'Neill, Earl of Tyrone, reputedly bid farewell to his love in the shade of the 'old yew tree' at Crom before leaving for Spain.

The age of the trees cannot be established with certainty, but there is reason to believe that they were planted around 1610, when Crom Castle was built for Lord Erne. When they were described in 1739, the trees must have been an impressive sight, with the branches trained horizontally, supported by circles of wooden pillars, the leaves forming a tightly woven roof through which no rain could penetrate. In the nineteenth century, a hedge was planted around the tree, and the branches of the female yew were strapped down to brick and stone pillars, to create a summer house for Lord Erne's guests. By 1845, the brick pillars had been replaced by oak posts, and the tree was said to resemble an enormous green mushroom. It covered an area of roughly 23 m across, under which some two hundred guests could sit and dine. The summer house was eventually abandoned, the pillars rotted away, and the trees have since begun to grow back into a more natural shape.[10]

Mass Trees

With reference to the Christian associations of the hawthorn, which I take to be a transfer of the Thorn cult from paganism, it should be noted that in more than one Irish county some Thorn Trees, known as 'Mass Bushes', were the marks of assembly for Roman Catholic congregations during the persecutions of the seventeenth and eighteenth centuries.

Vaughan Cornish, *Historic Thorn Trees in the British Isles* (1941)[1]

Cromwell's conquest of Ireland in 1649 was followed by ruthless persecution of the Catholic clergy, the destruction of churches and monasteries, the deportation of bishops and regulars, and the prohibition of the Catholic Mass. Catholic worship became a secret affair, celebrated by fugitive priests in private homes or in the open air, often in secluded places marked by stones or trees, which became popularly known as Mass rocks and Mass trees.

The short period of relative religious tolerance after Cromwell's death came to an end with the defeat of the Catholic King James II at the Battle of the Boyne in 1690, after which the Protestant parliament introduced a comprehensive body of suppressive laws, aimed at further diminishing the rights of the Catholic population of Ireland. The laws were known as Penal Laws, and the secret places of Catholic worship came to be called Penal sites.[2]

Penal altar and Mass tree, Gougane Barra, County Cork (opposite)

During Penal times, Mass was often celebrated outdoors at old places of Christian worship, such as holy wells and bullaun stones, or at the ruins of early monastic sites. Many of these were ancient places of pagan worship. Reinterpreted in the light of Christianity, they became firmly associated with local patron saints and with legends of their missionary works and miracles. The beautiful shrine of Gougane Barra is linked with sixth-century Saint Finbarr of Cork.[3]

Mass tree, Killarney, County Kerry (left)

In Killarney, a remote spot on the edge of the woods that surround Knockreer House is pointed out as a Mass site from the Penal times. The landmark for the secret religious assemblies was Cloch Mochoda, a bullaun stone in the shade of an ancient oak tree. The place is named after St Coda from Inisfallen; local lore relates that the saint knelt on the rock in prayer and left the imprints of his knees in the stone. Both the stone and the tree continued to be objects of veneration after the Penal era; visitors would hammer nails and coins into the bark of the oak as a token of good faith.[4]

Mass trees and bushes, often with their accompanying stone altars, occur in almost every county of Ireland, but are particularly common in the west and the north.[5] Huge concentrations of Mass rocks in some parishes have led to the suggestion that many Penal sites owe their reputation to folklore rather than to historical fact. However, given the accounts from both folklore and historical records of the dangers faced by priests who delivered Mass in secret, it is very possible that the density of Penal sites in some parishes is a result of frequent changes of Mass sites, as a precautionary measure against being caught or spied upon.[6]

Secret religious services were predominantly held at secluded places of early Christian significance, or in old or disused burial places. Old Stranmillis Graveyard in Belfast, for example, is still popularly known as Friar's Bush, named after the hawthorn tree where a priest was reputedly killed while saying Mass in the Penal times.[7] Besides being held at sites with religious connotations, during the times of Catholic repression Mass was also celebrated in isolated sheltered fields and remote glens and hollows. The Mass stones and trees in these locations are usually unattached to the lore of saints, and one can assume that they served primarily as landmarks for the community to identify the designated place at which to assemble for Mass.

Mass bushes were generally whitethorn or holly trees. The well-known and still highly revered Altar Bush of Ballylurgan in the Toome district of County Antrim is a carefully preserved cluster of whitethorn and blackthorn trees in a hedge alongside the road. Local traditions of religious services being offered here during the Penal times are supported by a reference in the Ordnance Survey Memoirs, which noted in the 1830s that Mass was said at an ancient hawthorn in Ballylurgan before the local church was built.[8]

Mass trees were usually old oaks. Hollow trees were particularly valued as hiding places for the bells and chalices used in the celebration of Mass. In County Down, chilling stories were once told of the mysterious ringing of an invisible bell in Kilbroney churchyard. In 1885, a storm felled a venerable oak in the churchyard, and the workers who chopped up the tree discovered an old bronze bell in the hollow fork of two branches. The bell turned out to be the lost bell of sixth-century St Bronach, founder of Kilbroney Church. It had been hidden in the tree during the troubled times of Cromwellian persecution and Penal Laws. The story of strange music and tinkling bells

Mass bush, Killinaspick, County Kilkenny

A single whitethorn grows at a junction in the townland of Tubrid, not far from Killinaspick Church. The spot is an excellent vantage point and on a clear day allows great views into Counties Kilkenny, Waterford, Tipperary and Wexford. During the time of religious persecution, the thorn was often used as an assembly point for the celebration of Mass. The memory of this tradition is fading, but locals do remember that until fairly recently, people fixed ribbons to the thorn for luck.[9]

was also told of Mullandoy graveyard near Castleblayney in County Monaghan, though no carefully concealed bell has yet come to light in its trees.[10]

The Fighting Tree outside Castleshane in County Monaghan was another Mass tree with a hollow trunk which was used to store the blessed vessels for Mass. Local tradition has it that a troop of Cromwell's soldiers happened to pass one night while Mass was being celebrated under the tree. Noticing the light of a candle, the soldiers came closer and shot the priest. A fight over the chalice and cups ensued, but the congregation could not prevent the soldiers from seizing the precious vessels.[11]

After Catholic Emancipation in 1829, when reforms strengthened and modernised the Catholic Church in Ireland, Mass was supposed to be celebrated exclusively in the newly erected church buildings, and outdoor devotion was no longer considered compatible with devout Christianity. However, despite the stance of the official Church, the majority of people continued to regard Penal sites – with their stones, wells and trees – as sacred, and any interference with them was considered unlucky and perilous. As late as 1942, the fate of a young man who incurred such misfortune was recalled in Drumintee in County Armagh. The story goes that the man asked the local parish priest whether it was wise to clear away a Mass bush in the nearby glen. Advised that if he was a true Christian, he would not believe that cutting a tree could bring about harm, he removed the bush; but when his beloved died soon afterwards and other misfortunes occurred, he blamed his troubles on foolishly meddling with the sacred tree.[12]

The hostility of the Anglican Church towards Catholicism – based on and fuelled by issues of power and supremacy – was notorious, and has left its marks on Irish folk memory. Less grave but still considerable was the unsympathetic and hostile attitude of Anglicanism towards other confessions, including Protestant factions. Around 1738 John Wesley and his younger brother Charles, the founding fathers of the Methodist Church, began preaching their religious message of love, faith and repentance in Britain and Ireland. This did not find acceptance with the established Anglican Church of the time, and the brothers were forced to conduct their meetings out of doors.[13]

John Wesley travelled tirelessly on horseback to spread his message, often preaching in the shade of trees, which subsequently became known as Wesley Trees. In 1756, he visited County Limerick, and preached under an old ash tree near the ruined Franciscan friary in Adare. The ash has decayed, but a stone still marks its site. In 1775 and in 1778, while on a mission in the Belfast area, Wesley spent some time at Derryaghy House in Lisburn. During his second visit, he addressed a large congregation in the garden of Derryaghy House under an old venerable yew tree, known since as the Wesley Yew.[14]

The Wesley Beeches, Ballyskeagh, County Antrim

In 1787, when John Wesley, the founding father of the Methodist Church, was on a mission to the industrial estates on the outskirts of Lisburn, he stayed with friends at their home on nearby Chrome Hill. Tradition has it that during this visit, Wesley joined a pair of young beech trees together to symbolise the unity of the Methodist and the Anglican Churches.

PART III

Trees of
Otherworld Experiences

Trees of
Life and Death

*Near Kennity Church in the King's County is an ash celebrated for
its dimensions, and for certain religious ceremonies which have for
many years been observed with respect to this tree, close to which the
lower class of people when passing by with a funeral, lay the corpse
down for a few minutes, say a prayer, and then throw a stone to
increase the number, which have been accumulating for years round
the root.*

Samuel Hayes, *A Practical Treatise on Planting and
the Management of Woods and Coppices* (1794)[1]

The Tree of Life in Early Irish Literature

With its roots reaching deeply into the ground, the world tree was thought to link the world of the living with the realm beyond, the otherworld, or the world of the dead. In medieval Ireland, the otherworld was firmly associated with the mythical race of the Tuatha Dé Danann, the ancient Celtic deities represented in literature.

When Celtic people began to filter into Ireland during the last five or six centuries BC, they found the landscape dotted with megalithic structures from previous cultures – massive burial chambers and cairns from the Neolithic, and arrangements of pillar stones, burial mounds and barrows from the Bronze Age. Acknowledging their spiritual significance, they linked these structures with the pantheon of their own deities.

The tales of the Mythological Cycle – today regarded as fictional, but until about 1700 accepted as historical fact – provide us with detailed information on the spiritual world of the Celts and the Tuatha Dé Danann, the People of the Goddess Danu. The tales were written by monks from the medieval Christian point of view, which interpreted the deities of old as a mythical race of aristocrats and heroic warriors, who had ruled Ireland prior to the arrival of the first Celtic invaders, the Sons of Míl. Following their defeat, the Tuatha Dé Danann reached an agreement with the Celts and were allowed to retreat to the otherworld, represented by the tumuli and cairns of Ireland. Echoing the native pre-Christian belief that the spirits of the dead formed communities who continued to live in their burial chambers, the Tuatha Dé Danann were thought to exist in a world parallel to the world of mortals. This world reflected Celtic lifestyles, customs and beliefs, and included the veneration of sacred trees.

The Tuatha Dé Danann were said to reside in magnificent palaces or in underworld realms, with haunting names such as Tír fá Thonn or the Land beneath the Waves, Tír na nÓg or the Land of Youth, Tír na mBeo or the Land of the Living, or Eamhain Abhlach, the Region of Apples. These places were often understood to represent other-world islands and gardens, where in the shade of marvellous, life-prolonging trees, all mortals would dwell after death.

The concept of Trees of Life, growing in paradise gardens which were also the last retreats for the souls of the dead, and bearing fruit eaten by the gods to make them immortal, existed in several ancient cultures around the world. The trees were usually believed to be apple trees, and were frequently guarded by snakes or dragons.[2]

The Trees of Life in medieval Irish literature belong to the world of the Tuatha Dé Danann. An episode in the twelfth-century romance, 'The Pursuit of Diarmaid and

(Clockwise from top left)
Trees of Knowledge on Drumcliff High Cross, County Sligo; on Ardmore Cathedral, County Waterford; and on Moone High Cross, County Kildare

Christianity readily adopted the ancient motif of the Tree of Life, linking it with the concept of the Tree of Knowledge. In Ireland, carvings representing the Biblical lore of Adam and Eve giving in to temptation and eating an apple from the Tree of Life, are frequently found on high crosses and masonry in and around old burial grounds. Ancient religious scriptures refer very vaguely to a 'forbidden fruit'; in the first century in Gaul, the fruit was for the first time interpreted as an apple.[3]

Gráinne', deals with the Quicken Tree of Dubhros, a miraculous rowan tree in the northwest of Ireland. According to the tale, the Tuatha Dé Danann lived on crimson nuts, arbutus apples and scarlet quicken berries, which they brought from the other-world, the Land of Promise. On one of their journeys, as they passed through Dubhros in the northwest of Ireland, a single quicken berry dropped down to the earth. From this berry, a rowan sprang up which inherited all the secret magical qualities of the original tree in the Land of Promise. The berries had the sweet taste of honey, and were intoxicating like wine or mead; more importantly, they were so life-giving and rejuvenating that the consumption of three berries was enough to ward off any disease, and could even return a hundred-year-old man to the age of thirty. To guard the precious fruit from the mortals, the Tuatha Dé Danann employed an ogre called Searbhán. Searbhán successfully protected the rowan for a long time, until Diarmaid slew him to obtain some berries for the pregnant Gráinne, who desperately craved them.[4]

Another marvellous rowan tree is mentioned in the romance recalling 'The Cattle Raid of Froech'. The hero, Froech, loves Findabair, the beautiful daughter of the royal Connacht couple Meadhbh and Ailill. Plotting the death of their daughter's suitor, they ask Froech to bring them a branch from the magical tree that stood on an island in a particular lake, which was guarded by a *péist* or snake coiled about its roots. Every month the tree bore berries, the juice of which could prolong life and heal illness. The 'Lays of Fionn' also mention magical berries, claiming that five berries from the Rowan Tree of Clonfert, taken in a sip of water, sustained the warrior Iollan for almost one week.[5]

The medieval genre of tales known as *imrama* abounds with references to life-giving or life-prolonging fruit. Literally meaning 'rowing' but commonly translated as 'voyages', the *imrama* deal essentially with the journeys of mythical kings and heroes to otherworld islands.

Several versions exist of the *imram* of Maol Dúin, a fictional character who set out

Rowan berries

Crann a Ghrá, or Tree of Love, Kilbaha, County Clare (left)

The tale of Diarmaid and Gráinne is very popular in Clare folklore, and numerous places are associated with the couple's flight from furious Fionn mac Cumhaill. West Clare sculptors Jim and Seamus Connolly have linked local traditions with the motif of the Tree of Dubhros, creating a modern interpretation of the theme from figures cast in bronze, and the trunk of a tree, found in a bog in west Clare and estimated to be about five thousand years old.[6]

in his boat to revenge his father's death. His quest became an extended voyage to a number of mythical islands, among them the Island of the Wonderful Apple Tree. Maol Dúin took several apples from the tree, and each apple sustained him and his men with food and drink for forty nights. Soon afterwards, on another island, the voyagers noticed fiery swine feeding on the fruit of a golden apple tree. On the Island of the Hermit and the Ancient Eagle, also known as the Island of the Mystic Lake, the men watched an old bird carrying one massive branch of a tree. It was covered with fresh leaves and laden with clusters of red fruit which resembled enormous grapes. The bird ate the fruit, then threw its stones and some of the pulp into the nearby lake, until the water turned red like wine. It then took a bath in the lake, emerging rejuvenated and invigorated.[7]

'Imram Brain', 'The Voyage of Bran', was written in the seventh or eighth century in the east of Ulster and is the earliest surviving text of the *imrama* type. The tale relates that Bran was lulled to sleep by sweet music, emitted by a silver branch from the unique apple tree of Eamhain Abhlach, the Region of Apples. The island of Eamhain Abhlach was said be supported by 'four legs of white silver', which is most likely a literary echo of the great oak-pole and timber stakes that were anciently built into the ceremonial site of Eamhain Mhacha in County Armagh.[8]

In a twelfth-century text, Manannán mac Lir visits Cormac mac Airt, High-King of Ireland. Cormac was probably a mythical character, though medieval historians date his reign in the third century AD. Manannán appeared to Cormac as a finely clad stranger on the Hill of Tara. On his shoulder he carried a branch with three golden apples. The sweet music that the branch emitted could soothe the wounded and the sick to sleep. Cormac desired the branch, and the stranger lured him to Tír Tairngire, where he introduced himself as Manannán mac Lir and revealed to the king the nature of true wisdom.[9]

A close ally of Cormac mac Airt was the fictional Munster nobleman, Tadhg mac Céin. A fourteenth-century description of Tadhg's voyage to several otherworld islands relates that on one island he met beautiful Cessair, the daughter or granddaughter of the Biblical Noah. She told him that her home was the otherworld paradise where the people of Ireland went to dwell after they left the world of mortals.

Cessair's island was also understood to be the home of the apple tree whose magic fruit lured Connla, a son of mythical King Con Céadchathach, away from his home and family. A medieval tale relates that Connla was walking on the Hill of Uisneach when a fine-looking lady from Magh Meall, the Plain of Delights, approached him. She handed him an apple, and for one month, Connla lived from this apple and did not partake of any other food. After this period, the lady reappeared, and Connla followed her to Magh Meall, never to return.[10]

Apple blossom

The island of Eamhain Abhlach was believed to be the realm of the deity Manannán mac Lir, who was also linked with Tír Tairngire, the Land of Promise. Both islands represent the Celtic idea of paradise, an orchard with one particularly sacred apple tree whose fruit symbolises immortality. The Welsh equivalent is Avalon, the paradisiacal island of apples in the Arthurian romance.

Official Christian doctrines of the souls of the dead being bound for heaven, purgatory or hell have gradually replaced the concept of otherworld islands as the last resorts of the dead. However, the idea of a Tree of Life in the centre of a paradise garden survived the change of religious perception. From medieval times, Christian interpretations of the tree appear carved in stone in architecture and on coffin lids. The custom of planting trees in cemeteries was recorded for the first time in the twelfth century. In the following centuries, this tradition developed into marking individual graves with trees.

Island of the Living, Monaincha, County Tipperary (left)

In medieval Ireland, the religious settlement of Monaincha was known as Mainistir Inse Na mBeo, the Monastery of the Island of the Living. Latin texts refer to Insula Viventium, the Island of the Living. The monastery – popularly linked with sixth-century Saint Canice of Aghaboe and eighth-century Saint Elair or Hilary – is mentioned in Giraldus Cambrensis' twelfth-century description of Ireland, and in the Book of Ballymote, a fourteenth-century compilation of earlier manuscripts. The texts described Monaincha as the thirty-first wonder of the world and claimed that no man ever died on the island. Women and female animals, however, passed away as soon as they set foot on Monaincha. In the eighteenth century, the land around the monastery was drained, and the beech trees on the perimeter of the sacred mound were probably planted shortly afterwards.[11]

Tree of Life, Strade Abbey, County Mayo (top)

From late medieval times, stylised trees appeared carved in relief on stone coffin lids. They represented the Tree of Life in its Christian understanding, and were usually deciduous trees. Deciduous trees are by their nature powerful symbols of the perpetual cycle of life, death and rebirth, as they shed their leaves in autumn, appear to die in winter, and come to life again in spring.

Ancestral Trees and the Return of the Soul

In 1902, the scholar William Gregory Wood-Martin was the first to write about the Celtic belief that the first man came from an alder tree, the first woman from a rowan. Unfortunately, since he does not give his sources, it is not possible to correlate his statement with any particular area or time of Celtic culture.[12]

The concept of an arboreal origin of the human race – the idea that trees were the ancestors of the first humans, or that men and women were created from trees – was widespread in pre-industrial societies throughout the world, and emerges also in the creation myths of Indo-European peoples. Tales from Greek mythology, for example, describe the oak as the maternal ancestor of mankind, or relate how Zeus formed the human race from ash trees. Ancient Roman beliefs surface in Virgil's *Aeneid* when the text refers to 'savage men who took their birth from trunks of trees and stubborn oaks.' The introduction to the Edda – a compilation of Norse mythology, written down around AD 1000 – provides an insight into Scandinavian creation myths and relates how Odin, Hönir and Lodur created the first man from *ask*, the ash, and the first woman from *embla*, the elm tree.[13]

In a Celtic context, the belief in the arboreal origin of men is apparent in the names of several ancient tribes or individuals who called themselves after trees. The Dervones in northern Italy were the 'oak people'; in Gaul, the Lemovices were the 'conquerors of the elm', while the Eburones and Eburovices translate as 'yew people' and 'conquerors of the yew' respectively. The tribal ancestor titles *Vernogenos* and *Viduogenos*, recorded in Wales, translate as 'the alder conceived' and 'the tree conceived', and the male name Guerngen, from the Welsh term *gwern* for alder, means 'son of alder'.[14]

In Ireland, the *fear bile* or 'men of the sacred tree' – associated with Craeb Dháithí, one of five mythical trees described in medieval literature – gave their name to Farbill in present-day County Westmeath.[15] Ogham inscriptions mention Ivogeni, 'the yew

'Adam and Eve', Dunloe, County Kerry (right)

Yew trees are renowned for their incredibly long lifespan. The oldest European example, the Fortingall Yew in Scotland, is thought to be over five thousand years old. In Ireland, several yews are estimated to be over one thousand years old. A veteran yew tree couple, one female, the other male, stand in the gardens of Dunloe Castle outside Killarney. They are affectionately called Adam and Eve.[16]

conceived', Maqi Crattinn, 'son of rowan', and Maqi Qoli, 'son of hazel'. Modern family names such as MacDara, MacCairthin or MacIbair translate literally as 'son of the oak', 'son of the rowan' and 'son of the yew' respectively.

The ancient sagas also contain some allusions to an arboreal origin for humanity. Ibar or 'yew tree' was the name of Conchobhar mac Nessa's charioteer in the tale concerning the *Táin Bó Cuailnge* or *The Cattle Raid of Cooley*; while according to the *Leabhar Gabhála*, the man who led the first Celts to Ireland was called Bile, meaning 'sacred tree'. The Craeb Ruad or Red Branch Knights of ancient Ulster, however, often popu-

Clochabhile, Stone of the Sacred Tree, Lough Gur, County Limerick

Clochabhile, the Stone of the Sacred Tree, stands in an area traditionally linked to the mythical ancestors of the mighty Eóganacht sept, Áine, Fer Í, Eogabal and Eoghan. It is possible that the pillar formerly adjoined a yew considered sacred to the Eóganacht, but its name might also reflect the memory of Fer Í and his mysterious 'Yew of the Disputing Sons'. According to the medieval poem of this name, this yew 'is not a tree but a fairy vision, its kind does not exist: that trunk is not of wood.' Local folklore relates that in olden times Lough Gur used to dry up every seven years to reveal a magic sacred tree at its bottom.[17]

King Oak, Tullamore, County Offaly

The King Oak in the grounds of Charleville Castle is a popular gathering place for the young people of Tullamore. It is one of the oldest and largest oaks in Ireland, and was probably growing before the estate was established around 1600. Local tradition claims that the tree is about eight hundred years old, while botanists estimate an age of four hundred and fifty to five hundred years. Around 1800, when William Bury, Earl of Charleville, built a castle in the demesne, the King Oak had already been described as an impressive giant.

Today, the tree reaches a height of about 21 m, and its widest girth is 7 m. The oak's most stunning features are its branches, the longest of them measuring about 23 m from the bole. Some of the lower branches touch the ground; others are supported by wooden props. Tradition links the King Oak with the fortune of the Hutton-Bury family, and it is still believed that if a major branch of the oak falls, a member of the family will die. In 1963, lightning splintered the main trunk from top to bottom; the tree survived, but Colonel Charles Howard-Bury, head of the family, died a few weeks later.[18]

larly linked with a sacred alder tree or with the red alder poles that supported their headquarters at Eamhain Mhacha, actually owe their name and its link to a tree to a misinterpretation of their original old name.[19]

In Munster, the old Eóganacht sept was intimately linked with yew trees. The tribal name is probably a derivation from a sept known as Ivogeni, or 'the yew conceived'; convention holds that the name is based on the old terms for a yew tree, *eó* or *í*. A poem entitled 'Ibar mac n-angciss' or 'Yew of the Disputing Sons', preserved in the Book of Leinster and attributed to the tenth-century king and bishop of Cashel, Cormac mac Culennáin, refers to the mythical otherworld ancestors of the Eóganacht dynasty, Eogabal, Fer Í and Eoghan.[20]

The poem describes the outrage of the divine Fer Í, literally 'son' or 'man of yew', when he found his father Eogabal slain and his sister Áine raped by Ailill Ólom, King of Munster.

To avenge Ailill's crime, Fer Í provoked a dispute between Ailill's son Eoghan and his half-brother Lugais mac Con. One version has Fer Í sitting in a beautiful yew tree and playing his harp. The argument started when Eoghan and Lugais discovered Fer Í and both claimed ownership over the yew. In another version of the text, Eoghan and two half-brothers argued over the ownership of a wondrous yew tree created by Fer Í. In both cases, Ailill was asked for judgement and awarded Eoghan with the tree. In the battle that followed his decision, the seven sons of Ailill fell.[21] Áine, who was in fact a land goddess and represented sovereignty, had a son by Ailill, and from this connection the Eóganacht dynasty claimed their descent and the justification to control Munster.

With this close relation between Celtic septs and trees, one would expect to find a widespread and lively tradition of so-called 'family' trees, individual trees whose fortunes were bound up intimately with the fate of particular clans. But the concept of family trees is scarcely found in Ireland, and was in all likelihood introduced from England, where it is quite common.

The Twining Branches

Linked to the notion of arboreal ancestors is the belief that the souls of the dead entered trees, thereby returning to their origins. The widespread practice of planting trees on graves, and the ancient custom of burying people in hollowed-out tree trunks are probably reflections of this spiritual concept. Tree trunk burial existed amongst several indigenous peoples of Australia and North America. A well-documented example from Bronze Age Europe is the Loose Howe tree trunk burial in Yorkshire, England.[22]

The idea that trees reflect the soul of those buried beneath them occurs frequently in Irish popular tradition. In local legends, graveyard trees were said to mirror the personality of the person buried beneath. One such story concerns an ancient ash tree that was said to grow at one time over the grave of Seán Na Sagart in the graveyard of Ballintubber, County Mayo. Seán was a notorious priest-hunter during the times of Catholic perse-cution, and the twisted, distorted ash tree over his grave was commonly looked upon as a mirror image of Seán's spiteful and ruthless personality.[23]

A romantic and tragic manifestation of graveyard trees and their link with the dead are Irish interpretations of the international 'doomed lovers' story, in which the young people die of broken hearts when their feuding parents oppose their union. After the lovers are buried in the same graveyard, a tree grows from each grave and their branches intertwine overhead.

Variants of the tale existed in Asia and in Europe. The central motif is widely known as the Romeo and Juliet theme, or, in a Celtic context, the Tristan and Iseult motif. In Ireland, the plot of twining trees was popular in folklore as well as in medieval literature. Around a hundred versions of the tale have been recorded, predominantly in Connacht and Munster. The earliest version is the eleventh-century 'Scél Baile Binnbérlaig', which tells of the unfortunate love between the Ulster youth, Baile mac Buain, and Aillinn, a Leinster princess. When the spite and malevolence of their families brought the lovers to their deaths, a yew with the shape of Baile's head grew out of his grave, while from Aillinn's grave grew an apple tree which resembled the princess' head. Years later, the trees were cut down and the poets of Ulster and Leinster crafted them into writing tablets on which to record the tales and traditions of their respective provinces. During a feast at Tara, when the tablets were placed close to one another, they immediately sprang together, twined and could never be separated again.[24]

Storytellers have also attached the motif of the twining branches to the medieval romance 'Longes mac nUislenn' or 'The Exile of the Sons of Uisliu'. The ninth-century tale from the Ulster Cycle of Tales is based on handsome Naoise, the youngest son of Uisliu, competing with the aging Ulster king, Conchobhar mac Nessa, for the love of beautiful Deirdre. It culminates in Conchobhar's men treacherously murdering Naoise, and Deirdre being forced to live with the king for one year. When at the end of this period, Conchobhar prepares to make Deirdre live with the murderer of Naoise, the desperate young woman dashes her head to pieces against a rock. The literary version of the romance ends here, but oral tradition frequently added that Deirdre and Naoise were buried in the same graveyard, and that the branches of the trees growing out of their graves entwined.[25]

Occasionally, historical characters and their romances have become linked with the twining trees theme. In the eighteenth century, wrestling champion Strong Thomas Costello and Una MacDermott, the daughter of a rich and influential family, fell in love. When her parents refused to let them marry, Una died from grief. Thomas composed a well-known love song, 'Una Bháin', and passed away soon after his beloved. Connacht lore told that when Una and Thomas were buried – in adjoining graves on Trinity Island on Lough Key in County Roscommon – the trees that grew from each of their graves entwined, uniting the lovers at last.[26]

**'Twining Branches',
Aghadoe, County Kerry**

Peig Sayers, the great story-teller from the Blasket Islands, had her own version of the tragic romance of a young couple who die from broken hearts when their parents refuse to let them marry. Peig did not reveal the names of the families involved, but ends her story with two trees growing from the youngsters' graves and twining together, remarking that as proof to the truth of her tale, these trees were plainly to be seen in the graveyard of Aghadoe outside Killarney. Aghadoe is no longer popularly associated with the romance, but in the old section of the cemetery, a couple of ancient yew trees leaning towards each other stand guard over two weathered gravestones.[27]

the Churchyard Yew and Immortality

From the nineteenth century, scholars have suggested that venerable yews may have existed in places of druidical worship, and that their presence and spiritual significance caused early Christian missionaries to establish cells and monasteries near the trees, as part of their drive to reinterpret old traditions in the light of the new faith.[28]

Yew trees were considered sacred in ancient Greece and Rome. In areas of Celtic settlement abroad, votive offerings were carved from yew. Yews are also among the trees mentioned in Lucan's descriptions of the sacred Celtic forest at Massilia. Medieval Irish literature relates that druids crafted magic wands from yews, and that one of the five 'mythical' trees of Ireland was a yew. Yew was also the most prominent tree species in terms of arboreal names for septs and individuals.[29]

In the context of death and burial, however, yew trees are first mentioned in chronicles and historical accounts from the eleventh century, and are firmly and exclusively linked with early Christian sites. Writing in 1188, the historian Giraldus Cambrensis remarked

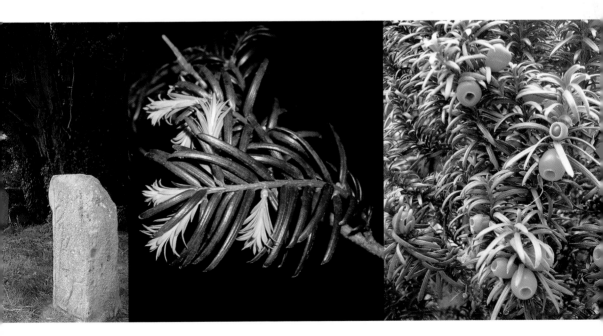

Graveyard Yew, Killadeas, County Fermanagh

Yew trees, often very old ones, are a familiar sight around the country in graveyards beside ancient churches. According to local belief, some of these yews are at least as old as the churches, while others are considerably older.

that yew trees 'are more frequently to be found in this country than in any we have visited; but you will see them in ancient graveyards and sacred places, planted long ago by the hands of holy men, to add to their decoration and ornament.' Cambrensis also referred explicitly to the yews and other trees at Finglas, just outside present-day Dublin, which were planted by the abbot and other holy men in the cemetery to beautify the church.[30]

Today, it is impossible to establish with certainty whether Giraldus Cambrensis was right when he said that graveyard yews were planted merely for the sake of beauty and ornament. Their origin and purpose remains obscure, and is a matter of scholarly dispute and controversy. Consequently, a variety of possible explanations have been offered.

The link between ancient yews and early Christian sites, combined with the fact that Christian ideas reached Ireland through contact with the Roman world – where coniferous trees and yews in particular are a common feature in old and modern cemeteries – has led to suggestions that the practice of graveyard yew-planting reached Ireland along with Christianity. Yet curiously, medieval biographies of saints contain no references to saints planting yews at sacred places.[31]

It is possible that graveyard yews served practical purposes. Since yew leaves are poisonous to livestock – with the exception of deer – the trees may have been planted to keep animals out of graveyards, where the rich grass would be particularly inviting. The Irish tradition of substituting fronds of yew for palm leaves

Palmerstown Yew, County Dublin

From the custom of adorning churches and chapels on Palm Sunday with yew branches, yew trees are in many parts of Ireland commonly known as palm trees. The village of Palmerstown in County Dublin was probably named after its celebrated 'palm' tree, an ancient yew that once grew beside the church. In the nineteenth century, antiquaries claimed that the yew was one of the oldest in Ireland. Unfortunately its roots were damaged by grave-digging, and in the 1880s the Palmerstown Yew was blown over in a storm.[32]

has led to the suggestion that yews were planted at monastic sites to provide fronds with which to decorate churches on Palm Sunday.[33]

Spiritually, yew trees may have been understood as a means of protecting and purifying the dead. In Brittany, it was said that each graveyard yew extended a root to the mouth of every corpse buried in the cemetery. Celtic tree calendars – a relatively modern tradition of assigning tree species to the months of the year – almost invariably place the yew at Samhain, which starts at Halloween. Samhain marked the beginning of the dark half of the year, and was considered to be a threshold, when the doors to the otherworld were thought be open. Today it is celebrated as the feast of All Saints and All Souls.

Graveyard tree, Adare, County Limerick (left)

The small chapel dedicated to St Nicholas of Myra, built on the far side of the River Maguire, was once the church of Adare Manor. The church ruins are now surrounded by a golf club, but the graveyard adjacent to the ruins has retained its peaceful atmosphere, with old yew trees growing on several graves, and three mature beeches that have joined together and closed around a nineteenth-century gravestone.[34]

Bedell's Tree, Kilmore, County Cavan (right)

William Bedell (1571–1642), a Protestant Bishop of Kilmore, is remembered for his translation of the Old Testament into the Irish language. In 1632, according to local tradition, the bishop brought the first ever sycamore trees to Ireland and planted a small grove of them at Kilmore. One of these trees, though hollow and battered, has survived; it stands close to the bishop's tomb behind the graveyard walls, and is popularly known as Bedell's Tree.[35]

Graveyard tree, Castlerahan, County Cavan (left)

The majority of the grave slabs in Old Castlerahan Cemetery date from the seventeenth and eighteenth centuries. The ivy-clad church ruins and a lone sycamore tree add to the captivating atmosphere of the place.[36]

The yew has become a symbol of death, but it can at the same time be interpreted as a symbol of eternity or immortality. The evergreen conifer holds onto its leaves even during the hardest winters; its timber is immensely tough and long-lasting; and above all, the tree itself is renowned for its almost incredibly long life span. A sequence in the fifteenth-century Book of Lismore gives us a sense of the medieval concept of the yew's longevity. Based on the multiplication factor of three, it states that men could reach an age of 81 years, stags an age of 243 years, black birds 729 years, eagles 2,187 years, salmon 6,561 years, yew trees 19,683 years, and the world 59,049 years. A Welsh poem from the fourteenth century contains a similar list. While these judgements of the yew's possible age are certainly overestimated, yews do have the longest life span of European trees.[37]

With their close association to immortality, yews are the most common and characteristic graveyard trees in Ireland. From the seventeenth century onwards, when new species of trees were introduced from England, it became fashionable to plant non-native trees, such as sycamores and beeches, in graveyards. Unlike the graveyard yews, however, these new species undoubtedly served the purpose of ornament and decoration as opposed to being 'trees of life'.[38]

Gentle Bushes on Ireland's Unofficial Burial Grounds

Early in the fifth century, St Augustine was the first to elaborate the concepts of sin and penance, purgatory, damnation and salvation. He introduced the dogma of 'original sin' into Christian doctrine. This holds that we are all born in a state of sin, which will prevent us from entering heaven unless we are cleansed by being baptised into a state of grace. It was claimed that the souls of righteous but unbaptised adults, and of children who died before being christened, lingered on the edge of heaven in 'limbo', a term which derives from the Latin word *limbus* for fringe or border. To avert this fate, the original custom of baptising people as adults was dropped, and baptising children became the norm.[39]

From the eleventh century, the Church on the Continent underwent significant structural and methodical reforms, largely based on the rules and teachings of St Augustine. Among these changes, new emphasis was placed on the importance of the sacraments and of burial in consecrated ground. Between 1205 and 1215, Canon Law adopted strict regulations around who was and who was not to be buried in ground consecrated for Christian burial. It was only during the second Vatican Council (1962–1965) that the Church reviewed her attitude towards burial restrictions, and eventually abolished the practice of separate burial for unbaptised children and 'unsanctified' adults.[40]

In Canon Law, non-Christians and 'unsanctified' Christians – meaning people who did not die in a state of grace – were to be explicitly excluded from burial in consecrated cemeteries. Considered 'unsanctified' were murderers and people who took their own lives; people who died while excommunicate or unrepentant; victims of battle or murder, because it was possible that they had not been absolved of their sins before death; mentally ill people who were not given the last rites; and strangers whose state of sanctification could not be established with certainty. Also excluded from Christian burial were women who died in childbirth; 'unchurched' women who had not received the ritual cleansing in church after having given birth; and stillborn infants and children who died before baptism. All of these people had to be buried in a place set apart from the official graveyard, and the law even ordered their exhumation if interred in consecrated ground through ignorance or mistake.

These Church regulations were officially issued for the whole of Christendom, and must have reached Ireland with monastic orders from the Continent from the twelfth century. Curiously, the scholar Susan Leigh Fry – who has surveyed written sources on burial in medieval Ireland – found no evidence for the separate burial of suicides, excommunicate people or unchurched women for the period from AD 900 to 1500. There is no reliable data for burial practices in the centuries that followed; but from the mid-nineteenth century, historical and folklore accounts relating to separate burial abound, indicating that the practice was widespread by then. It seems reasonable, therefore, to suggest that separate burial was initially alien to the philosophy of the Celtic Church, and only became compulsory in Ireland after Catholic Emancipation in 1828, when the Catholic Church gained sufficient power to enforce the strict rules of Rome.[41]

The separate burial places for stillborn or unbaptised children and unsanctified adults were sometimes on the boundary between two townlands, or in ancient mounds or ring forts. Most often these people were buried in earth that was at least considered blessed, such as in grounds on the perimeter of official graveyards, or to the north side of a church, or in the vicinity of holy wells or ruined monasteries and churches. The

St Berrihert's Kyle or Kilberrihert, Ardane, County Tipperary

This small plot, adjacent to the ruins of a monastic site founded by seventh-century St Berrihert, was for decades used as a burial place for unbaptised infants. In the 1940s, a stone enclosure was built around the burial place, and cross slabs from the monastery were incorporated into the wall. The area is beautifully sheltered by mature oak trees and holly bushes. People tie pieces of cloth and ribbons to the trees as part of a pilgrimage to the nearby healing well.[42]

most common names for unofficial burial places are 'killeen' or 'kyle', which are both anglicised forms of the Irish word *cíllin*. *Cíllin* means literally 'little church' or 'cell', and strictly speaking applies to the church enclosures or cemeteries of the very early Christian period in Ireland. Killeens were typically roughly circular or oval in shape, and enclosed by an earthen bank and ditch or a wall. Especially in the southwest and west, early Christian killeens were the preferred places for unsanctified burials.[43]

Mondrehid Cemetery, County Laois (above)

In the 1870s, nothing remained of the ancient burial place at Mondrehid but a few unadorned stones and a cluster of hawthorn trees. The place was considered haunted, and locals reported sightings of strange apparitions as forebodings of death and misfortune.[44]

Killeen, Mountbrigid, Buttevant, County Cork (right)

'Hic jacent sancti innocenti', reads an inscription on the stone wall: 'Here lie the innocent saints.' The lone whitethorn in a field close to St Brigid's Well marks the site of a fifth-century monastery, linked to St Brigid and St Colman. Because of this association, the plot was chosen in the nineteenth century as a blessed though unsanctified burial place for those not admitted into consecrated ground. From the late 1990s, several killeens in Ireland have been officially blessed in recognition of the souls that were denied a Christian burial; the killeen at Mountbrigid was thus acknowledged in 2001.[45]

The individual graves of the unsanctified dead were typically unmarked by gravestones, though in a few cases, small undecorated stones indicate the presence of a burial. Common features at these sad places, however, were trees, usually a single whitethorn or an ash tree, less frequently a cluster of trees. Popular tradition has sometimes tried to link these tree grave-markers with the concept of purgatory. In County Kerry, it was claimed that unfortunate souls suffered purgatory under thorn bushes. In County Laois it was believed that an unbaptised child's soul did twenty-one years of purgatory

in a tree: seven years between the bark and the wood on the windy side, seven years on the sunny side, and seven years in the heart of the tree.[46]

The names 'grave bush' or 'monument bush' were usually applied to distinguish the thorns marking the site of unsanctified burial. Sometimes they were known as 'gentle bushes' or 'fairy trees', and the tradition of the souls of the dead was mixed with motifs from fairy lore. In east Cavan, south Armagh and south Monaghan, for example, it was the custom to spill corpse-water, or the water used to wash a corpse, under lone bushes or fairy trees.[47]

Generally, trees and thorns in non-consecrated burial grounds were said to be haunted by the souls of unbaptised children, desperately seeking the baptism which would allow them to enter heaven. The taboo against interfering with these trees, accepted by all

The Grave of Caillemote, Oldbridge, County Meath

Caillemote was a French Protestant who joined the side of William of Orange. He fell in the Battle of the Boyne in 1690, and was buried on a slightly elevated mound, close to the gate lodge of Oldbridge House. His final resting place, known as the General's Grave, was marked by a pair of fine elm trees. The trees no longer exist, nor does any recollection of them.[48]

religious persuasions, is well-illustrated in reports of involuntary profanations. The killeen of Dereny near Whitegate in east Clare, so the legend goes, was once sheltered by two majestic ash trees. One of them died eventually from natural causes, fell into the adjoining river and was carried downstream. A carpenter came across the tree and, unaware of its provenance, made a coffin out of its timber – only to become the very person buried in it.[49]

With regards to killeens and other specified plots for multiple non-consecrated burials, historical and folklore accounts almost exclusively refer to unbaptised or stillborn children, the dead of the Famine, and occasionally strangers.[50] The remaining groups of 'unsanctified' dead as identified by Canon Law are not mentioned in historical or folklore accounts regarding separate burial. There are, however, folklore accounts from all parts of Ireland recalling trees, predominantly whitethorns, being planted in these places in remembrance of individuals who died suddenly. Some of the dead were victims of accidents or murder, others fell in battle. Since the sources do not always state explicitly whether the dead were also actually buried under these trees, it is impossible to say whether the trees were intended as memorials of death or grave-markers.[51]

Funerary Trees

Into the early decades of the twentieth century, great care was taken to assure that the spirit of the deceased left the corpse, and did not return to it again. The scholar Estyn Evans recalled a previously common practice to bring about this goal: 'With the idea no doubt of deceiving the spirit of the dead, the coffin was carried to the graveyard by the longest route, preferably a disused track, and the procession made a sunwise circle around some place or object on the way, a cross, a church-site, a lone thorn tree or a crossroads.'[52]

Descriptions of funerary customs in Ireland show that the trees involved in this ritual journey were mostly ash trees or thorns, popularly referred to as 'monument trees', 'coffin trees' or 'mile bushes'. Some of them were well-placed existing trees, while others were planted deliberately to mark the traditional stopping places of funerals. Occasionally, a whole line of trees were planted along the route to the graveyard.[53]

In Counties Kilkenny, Longford and Westmeath, coffins were placed on the ground at funerary trees and prayers were recited before the procession moved on. Funerals in Chapelizod, Palmerstown and Rathcoole, all in County Dublin, used to circle the local

Mile Bush, Hoodsgrove, County Kilkenny

From ancient times, crossroads were regarded as thresholds or transitional places between the human and spirit worlds. In many parts of Ireland, there were renowned monument trees at crossroads en route to burial grounds, which funeral processions used to circle.[54] This veteran hawthorn, popularly known as the Mile Bush, stands at a crossroads on the New Ross to Mullennakill Road, protected from damage by a low stone wall. County Kilkenny has a well-documented tradition of funerary trees, and the Mile Bush, although no longer associated with funerals, may have been one such tree.

monument tree before continuing on to the graveyard. In 1838, the Ordnance Survey for County Meath noted that this ritual was performed at the Red Cross Tree in Ratoath, at the Monument Bush in Lismahon, and at the Big Tree in Rathregan. In parts of Counties Cavan, Galway, Offaly and Laois it was customary to stop, lay the corpse down for a few minutes, pray and leave stones at the foot of the monument tree or bush. In some places, considerable heaps and cairns built up over the years.[55]

Elsewhere, small timber crosses were left in or beneath the trees. In Cong, County Mayo, the relatives of the deceased placed small crosses on a wall under the funerary ash on the road to the graveyard. An account from County Wexford, written in 1894, relates how the pieces of wood left over after making a coffin were cut into small crosses, and continues: 'At the crossroad nearest to the cemetery there is always a hawthorn tree, at the foot of which the procession pauses, and the cross-bearers lift the crosses to its branches, where they fix them. In some places the tree has fallen beneath its weight of crosses, but its root remains or at all events the memory of the place where it grew.'[56]

Until about 1900, funerary trees were revered in many parts of Ireland. From the 1930s, folklore surveys indicate that these old customs had been abandoned, and that their history had begun to fade. Today, the tradition of funerary trees is almost entirely lost. The majority of the old monument trees have decayed and their trunks, though preserved in some places into fairly recent times, have often since fallen victim to road works.

St Canice's Bush, Aghaboe, County Laois

The sixth-century founder of Aghaboe, St Canice, is according to local tradition buried in the so-called Cross Field close to the monastery. At the bottom of the field, adjacent to an old lane leading towards Aghaboe, stand the remains of a once highly venerated thorn, St Canice's Bush. When funerals passed the tree on the way to the graveyard, the procession stopped to lower the coffin, say a prayer and place a stone beside the thorn before moving on. Early in the twentieth century, St Canice's Bush decayed, and the memory of its former funerary associations began to fade, but to this day the stump of the tree is treated with respect.[57]

Fairy Trees
and Gentle Bushes

The white-thorn was considered a sacred tree. When it grows alone near the banks of streams, or on forts, it is considered to be the haunt and peculiar abode of the fairies, and as such is not to be disturbed without risk, sooner or later, of personal danger to the person so offending.

William Gregory Wood-Martin, *Traces of the Elder Faiths in Ireland* (1902)[1]

Fairies, Angels and the Tuatha Dé Danann

An ancient belief in the existence of another order of beings that lived in a world parallel to that of mortals can be traced to every part of the world. It was generally believed that these otherworld dwellers – thought to be invisible most of the time – had the ability to appear at will and interact with mortals, often presenting generous gifts to those who met them with respect, and severely punishing those who did not. While this notion has almost entirely disappeared from much of the Continent, it has persisted until the present day on the southeastern and western fringes of Europe.

The Christian Church, eager to interpret otherworld beings in an acceptable context, established a Biblical origin for them. The notion that otherworld beings were in fact fallen angels reached Ireland by the fifteenth century and has since become the most popular explanation for the origin of the fairies.[2] Folklore explanations claim that at Lucifer's revolt, God expelled from heaven those angels who were uncertain about which side to take. God softened as he saw the angels falling down to hell, and allowed

Fairy Thorn, Donaghmore, County Tyrone (left)

Since fairies are believed to be fallen angels, folklore sees no contradiction in linking fairy trees with places of Christian devotion. The religious settlement of Donaghmore, famous for its early medieval high cross, was according to legend founded by St Patrick, who left it in the care of St Colmcille. In the old cemetery a mature thorn grows beside a bullaun or basin stone, and is revered and respected as a fairy tree.[3]

Lone Bush, Kiltartan, County Galway (right)

Thorn trees growing over large boulders are considered protected or inhabited by the fairies. This lovely specimen thrives in County Galway, where fairy trees were usually referred to as 'lone bushes'.

them to remain where they were at that point. Those who had already reached hell stayed there and became malevolent; others continued to live in the air, or under water; but most of them reached earth and settled in prehistoric monuments, which were therefore known as fairy forts, fairy mounts and fairy hills.

The roots of the fairy belief, however, reach down to earlier pre-Christian times and concepts. In Ireland, fairy belief grew from an amalgamation of the ancient idea of communities of the dead living on in their burial chambers,[4] and the medieval tradition of the Tuatha Dé Danann as mythical heroes and aristocrats residing in magnificent underworld palaces. When the literary tradition filtered into folklore, some stories retained their original flavour and survived as popular renditions of heroes' tales and romances. But the motifs and plots were also transported from their originally aristo-cratic backgrounds into the everyday lives of ordinary people, and in this context, the otherworld dwellers became the fairies of oral lore and local legend.

Into the early decades of the twentieth century there was a strong reluctance to refer to the otherworld dwellers by their name. The English term 'fairy' and the Irish word *sí* with its diminutive form, *sióg,* were usually avoided in oral lore. Instead, people would refer to 'them', or more explicitly to *na daoine maithe* or 'the good people', or *na daoine uaisle,* 'the noble people' or 'the gentry'. In certain parts of Ireland, where fairies were thought to be smaller than the human race, people called them *na daoine beaga,* 'the little people' or 'the wee folk'.

As well as avoiding calling the fairies by their name, people eschewed using the term 'fairy tree' when referring to trees and bushes linked with the otherworld society. Common circumlocutions were 'noble bush', 'gentle bush' or 'gentry bush'. References to a 'shoemaker's tree' or a 'cobbler's bush' indicated a link with the leprechaun, a solitary otherworld dweller and guardian of hidden treasures, said to be the shoemaker of the fairies. The most popular and widespread names for fairy trees were the terms 'lone bush' or 'lonely bush', referring to such a tree's typically solitary growth, or the Irish word *sceach* for a thorn, with its regionally differing anglicised versions such as skeag, skeog, skea, skeagh or skagh. Only in the mid-twentieth century did the reluctance to mention the fairies and their trees by name decrease significantly.[5]

The trees linked with the world of the fairies are almost invariably thorns, especial-ly whitethorns or hawthorns. Occasionally blackthorns, rowans, hollies or gnarled old oaks have associations with the supernatural. Hawthorn was from ancient times linked with protective powers and fertility, and ancient laws list the tree among the 'Commoners of the Wood'. Oral fairy traditions adopted thorn trees as the counterparts to the marvellous sacred trees of gold and silver from the literary otherworld aristocracy.

the Bile of the Rath and the Fairy Tree in the Fort

Recurrent references to *bile rátha*, 'sacred tree of the fort', in early Irish sources and place names from all over Ireland indicate that sacred trees were once a common feature at enclosed dwelling places. The perceived lifestyle of otherworld communities usually mirrored the customs and habits of the real world. Accordingly, the authors of medieval literature assigned sacred trees to the dwellings of mythical characters, although they generally ascribed these otherworld trees with magical powers and appearances, qualities that distinguished them from real *biledha*. Magical trees occur particularly in tales of the 'adventure' type, which deal with the otherworld experiences of the great mythical kings and heroes of ancient Ireland.

Several otherworld trees are mentioned in the eighth-century text, 'Serglige Con Culainn', or 'The Wasting Sickness of Cúchulainn'. There is a short reference to a magic tree called *bile buada*, 'the tree of power' or 'of victory', and a slightly more elaborate description of the wondrous trees at the otherworld fort of Manannán mac Lir's wife, Fand. It reads: 'Before the entrance to the east, three trees of purple glass, in which the birds sing softly, unceasing, to the children from the royal fort. There is a tree at the entrance of the enclosure – it were well to match its music. A silver tree on which the sun shines, like gold is its brilliance.'[6]

Fairy Fort (Speaking Stones), Farranglogh, County Meath

An early medieval text describes how Mongán – a seventh-century prince of the Dál nAraidhe sept in east Ulster – paid a dream-visit to an otherworld fort with ancient trees growing at its entrance.[7] The motif of a dream-visit or vision also appears in the medieval account of an adventure of fictional King Conn Céadchathach. It describes how the king lost his way in a magic mist and found himself at the palace of the god Lugh, 'a kingly rath with a golden bile at its door.'[8]

A popular oral version of this tale is 'The Story of Conn-Eda, or The Golden Apples of Lough Erne'. It relates how young Conn Céadchathach, here called Conn-Eda, won three golden apples from a tree that grew by a castle of the Fir Bolg at the bottom of Lough Erne. He planted them in his own garden, and a great tree sprang up, which caused the province of Connacht to produce an abundance of crops and fruit. Also popular was a folktale from the Fionn lore, which merges the traditions of otherworld communities with the lore of the Vikings and tells how Míodhach, a Scandinavian prince, magically entrapped Fionn mac Cumhaill in the otherworld Bruidhean Chaorthainn or the Palace of the Quicken Tree, a fort surrounded by marvellous trees bearing clusters of scarlet berries.[9]

The underworld palaces lived in or visited by the leading characters of medieval literature and popular hero tales are usually the massive burial tumuli and cairns from the Neolithic. The fairies of oral tradition, on the other hand, are traditionally linked with later types of monuments. These include burial structures, such as wedge tombs from the early Bronze Age; ring barrows – often circular and situated on hilltops – which date to the transitional period between the late Bronze Age and the early Iron Age; Iron Age hill forts, which sometimes enclose Bronze Age burial mounds and may have been ancient assembly places; and occasionally mottes, the conspicuous fortifications from the Norman invasion of the twelfth century. Any of these structures may be pointed out as fairy dwellings.

In 1842, the German traveller Johann Kohl gave an account of his visit to the motte of Lisserdowling near Edgeworthstown in County Longford. He wrote:

> The popular tradition, I was told, assigned the moate as a dwelling-place to an ancient Irish chief of the name Naghten O'Donnell . . . [the] hill stands in fine repute throughout the country and is a favourite resort on fine after-noons, when hundreds may be seen sitting and lying on its sides; but not one of these visitors remains after dark, when the Moate of Lisserdowling, and the lane leading to it, are abandoned to the fairies or 'good people', as they are called in Ireland. Nor will anyone touch a stone or a stick on the

Fairy Thorn, Loughmacrory, County Tyrone

The Carrickmore-Creggan area of County Tyrone is rich in megalithic sites from the Bronze Age. Several of them feature a single thorn tree, usually old and weatherbeaten. This particularly impressive specimen grows from the well-preserved wedge tomb in the townland of Loughmacrory.

hill, 'unless they have a dream' and have had a commission from the good people. I observed at the side of the mount the stump of an old thorn bush. My guide informed me that the bush itself had been blown down one windy night, many years ago, and had been left to rot on the ground where it fell, no one daring to touch it . . . even people used to take any burnable thing. Young trees they will steal with very little remorse, but wood growing on one of these fairy mounts is almost always secure from their depredations.[10]

The most common archaeological monuments considered to be fairy dwelling places are the circular earthwork forts of early medieval Ireland. This type of monument is known as a *ráth* or ring fort, *dún* or fort and *lios* or enclosure. Archaeologists use the collective term 'ring forts' for these structures. Numbering at about 45,000, ring forts are the most numerous type of archaeological monument in Ireland. Most date from the early seventh to the end of the ninth century. They consist of one or more banks and an outer ditch, and were used as farms and homesteads.[11]

In late medieval times, when the origin of ring forts was no longer remembered, the construction of the enclosures became attributed to the fairies or, particularly in the north, to the Vikings, known as 'Danes' in popular tradition. The lore around Fionn mac Cumhaill in particular has assimilated the Danes to the fairies, and combined traits and characteristics of the Tuatha Dé Danann tradition with elements from Viking lore. William Butler Yeats plausibly suggested that the name 'Danes' arose from a misinterpretation or mistranslation of the Irish word 'Danann', and that places associated with the 'Danes' belonged initially to the divine Tuatha Dé Danann.[12]

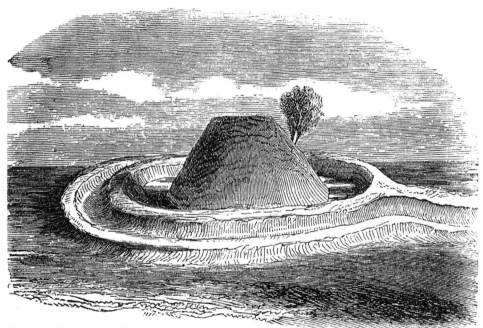

The Fairy Mound, Louth, County Louth

Mottes are medieval fortifications, constructed by the Normans in the early phase of conquering Ireland. Typically they consist of a mound of earth, flattened on top, and crowned by a wooden tower. From the nineteenth century onwards, when their original purpose was no longer understood, folklore began to interpret them as the homes or meeting places of the fairy folk.[13]

Ballymahon Fairy Mound, County Longford

Throughout Ireland, it is generally considered very unlucky to meddle with the dwelling places of the fairies. The trees growing within a ring fort or on its surrounding banks are regarded as the property of the otherworld dwellers, and swift retribution is thought to follow any interference with them.

Lone Bushes and Fairy Assemblies

Like the trees and thorns that grow on the banks of fairy forts, solitary whitethorn trees – often old, gnarled and bent by the wind – are also strongly associated with the fairies, and thus treated with great respect. Throughout Ireland, these lone fairy trees are a common sight standing in the middle of cultivated farmland cautiously left alone, often despite considerable inconvenience to the farmer.

The fact that these thorns – from the time that they began to sprout from seed – have survived the grazing of livestock, periods of drought and flood, and the work of plough and spade, is seen as evidence of some kind of protective magic. From the nineteenth century, visitors to Ireland and observers working for the Ordnance Survey took note of isolated fairy trees and the widely held belief that these trees were either specially chosen or deliberately planted by the fairies for their own purposes.

Aside from having solitary positions, fairy trees were often thought to be distinguishable from ordinary bushes by their appearance. Their physical traits tend to vary regionally. In some parts of Ireland, fairy trees are said to have more thorns than normal whitethorn bushes; elsewhere they are said to have no thorns at all; and in some districts, it was believed that fairy trees never bore blossom. Other fairy trees are discernible by their unusual formation, such as a long trunk with branches starting higher up, a flat top, or being mushroom- or umbrella-shaped.

Fairy bushes and trees are often considered indestructible. Stories were told of particular fairy bushes continuing to grow after they had been uprooted; of cut-off branches reappearing on the bush the next day; and of bushes seemingly on fire at night, yet standing unharmed in the morning.[14]

The lone bushes of Ireland are generally thought to mark the assembly places of otherworld communities. Local traditions recall occasions when people have noticed enchanted music and lights around particular fairy trees at nighttime. An old oak tree at the foot of Lissard in Killeaden, County Mayo, was said to stand at a place of seasonal fairy conventions. It was here the poet Antoine Ó Reachtabhra or Anthony Raftery is believed to have been given the gift of poetry by the fairies.[15]

Fairy Tree, Fore, County Westmeath

Solitary thorn trees growing by the banks of rivers are also popularly linked with the world of the fairies. This example stands beside the path leading to Fore Abbey. Visitors to the abbey have begun a custom of throwing small denomination coins into the river at the foot of the thorn for luck.

Latoon Fairy Thorn, Latoon, County Clare

In the 1980s, Eddie Lenihan recorded the tale of a lone whitethorn bush in a field near Newmarket-on-Fergus, where the fairies from Munster would gather before travelling northwards to fight the fairies of Connacht. Returning from the battle, they would again assemble at the bush, before parting for their homes all across the province. One several occasions, the owner of the field noted a greenish substance around the bush, which he took to be the blood of fairies wounded in those battles.[16]

The mythological tradition, based on the *Leabhar Gabhála Éireann*, describes various battles between the Tuatha Dé Danann and other population groups of prehistoric Ireland. Folklore transformed these battles into tales of different groups of fairies waging war against each other. In the 1840s, the German traveller Johann Kohl noted the belief that the fairies of two adjoining counties had regular faction fights, as did the mortal inhabitants. The most famous fairy assembly place with martial connections is the Latoon Thorn in County Clare. Here the fairies of Munster are said to convene prior to and after their battles against the fairies of Connacht.[17] In 1999, when the construction of the new Ennis relief road was in progress, it became obvious that the plan was to destroy the thorn for the sake of traffic lanes. Mr Eddie Lenihan, a well-known folklorist and collector of folk tales in County Clare, campaigned on behalf of the Latoon Thorn, writing letters of protest and warning of the consequences, such as road accidents, which would inevitably follow the destruction of the bush. As a result, Clare County Council and the National Roads Authority agreed to spare the thorn and change the route of the road.

In August 2002, the Latoon fairy bush appeared once more in Irish newspapers, when someone deliberately cut off every single branch, leaving the trunk standing bare. Living up to the lore of fairy bush indestructibility, the thorn survived the attack. The identity of the offender was never revealed, but people in the Latoon area have expressed strong doubts regarding the well-being of the person. That serious consequences for the offender are expected is not surprising, given the strong and widespread tradition in Ireland of the fairies never suffering the destruction of their property without a response, even though years may pass before the debt is inevitably paid.

The Bleeding Bush
and the Fairies' Warning

Although belief in fairies and otherworld spirits has diminished considerably in modern Ireland, lone bushes are still regarded with a mixture of awe and respect. For fear of dire consequences, people are very reluctant to interfere with fairy trees, often to the point that they will not even touch dead branches and twigs lying on the ground around them.

There is apparently a very strong bond between the fairies and their thorns. Numerous stories tell of people hearing fairies mourning, crying and wailing when their trees were destroyed. Occasionally fairies are said to have been seen pulling cut-off branches from carts or from fires, and reports exist of fairy trees marked to be cut disappearing mysteriously, secreted away by the fairies. Fairies are also said to have evacuated whole areas following the destruction of their homes or trees. A lovely story, recorded in the 1930s on Inishowen Head in County Donegal, tells of a man who intended to cut a fairy bush because some of the branches were blocking his way. When he next approached the bush, he found that the fairies had removed all the offending branches to save their beloved tree-home from destruction.[18]

To avoid unwittingly interfering with a fairy tree, caution was taken to ascertain whether or not a particular bush could be removed without consequences. In the north, it was customary to leave a stone at the foot of the bush in question overnight. If the stone was gone in the morning, it was taken as a sign that the bush was owned by the fairies; if the stone was still there, the plant was an ordinary as opposed to a fairy bush. Certain signs and sightings at lone bushes and trees were also regarded as an indication of the fairies' involvement. These included music or frightening noises emerging from under a bush; strange lights; unusual animals, such as large numbers of white mice or featherless birds; and voices ordering that the bush be left alone.[19]

Early in the eighteenth century, a farmer in Killeaden in County Mayo was widening a lane on his land, when he suddenly became ill as he came close to a particular thorn. When the man had recovered a couple of days later, he went to resume his work on the lane, this time starting from the other side; but as soon as he got near the bush, he felt ill again and was forced to stop. It took the man a few more failed attempts before he realised that a little thorn was the cause of his troubles. From then on he left the tree alone, and stopped other people if they tried to interfere with it.[20]

An unmistakable and dramatic warning sign was a bleeding tree. In Ireland it was generally believed that certain trees or bushes bleed when cut, fairy bushes in particular. Folklore stories from townlands all around the country tell of fairy bushes that shed blood the moment a hatchet or saw was set to them.

Fairy Tree, Ballyshannon, County Donegal

A bleeding fairy tree was seen as the ultimate warning signal to stop cutting immediately. It was believed that disregarding the sign would sooner or later be answered with death. Near Ballyshannon in County Donegal, local history tells of a man who ignored the blood spurting from a fairy thorn and carried on cutting. Soon after the tree was cut, the man went mad and died.[21]

In 1929, *Ireland's Own* reported that a stream of blood had come from a holly bush in County Mayo when cut by a local man. Returning to his farm, the man found one of his animals choked in the byre. In County Monaghan, a man reportedly ignored the bleeding of a fairy tree in a fort, and a strange voice that warned him against felling the bush. He died when the top of his hatchet fell off and split his skull. In the 1950s, during road works in north Clare, a foreman threatened to sack one of his labourers if he did not cut a conspicuous but obstructing thorn; reluctantly the labourer began to saw, but when blood spurted from the bush, he could not be persuaded to continue his task.[22]

In the 1950s in Forkill, County Armagh, locals splattered a bush with blood when the man who was about to cut it went for his break. It is not told whether they did this to protect the tree or to play a practical joke on the man. Needless to say, however, the tree was left uncut.[23]

the Fairies' Vengeance

Sometimes, humorous stories are told about the fairies taking revenge by playing practical jokes on people who interfered with lone bushes. In the 1940s, a tale was current around Hilltown in County Down of a woman who broke some twigs from a fairy bush for firewood, in order to bake bread on the griddle in the open fireplace. When the bread was almost done, she turned to check it, only to find fairies dancing around the fire, eating her bread.[24]

The fairies' retributions were usually serious affairs, and reports of their vengeance have a distinct lack of jest. Innumerable stories attribute the accidents and injuries sustained while cutting a particular bush to instantaneous supernatural retribution. There are tales of twigs damaging the eyes of meddlers and eventually causing blindness or death; of hatchets slipping, and seriously or fatally wounding the people using them; of falling bushes that hurt or kill the feller; and of injuries leading to blood poisoning, often resulting in the amputation of fingers or limbs, or, again, in death.

Some people were said to have disappeared while meddling with a fairy bush, apparently abducted by the fairy folk. Samuel Ferguson's poem, 'The Fairy Thorn', recalls the fate of a group of young girls who went one evening to dance around a hawthorn in a fairy fort. Suddenly, fear and panic befell the girls, and when they recovered, they found that one of them had vanished, never to be seen again. Her friends pined away and died within a year.[25]

Twigs from a Fairy Tree

Very popular and still told in various parts of Ireland are stories of sharp thorns being deposited by enraged fairies into the beds of people who meddle with lone bushes. In County Kerry, a man removed some thorns or briars from the churchyard in Cill Rialaigh, and another man took bushes from Mainistir graveyard. Night after night the fairies tormented these men, until they finally returned the thorns to their original places in the graveyards.[26]

The fairies' reprisal usually took effect the night following interference with the tree. Local traditions abound with stories of people who went to sleep in perfect health and woke up seriously ill, struck with terrible pain, or fully paralysed. Others have awoken to find that their faces have been disfigured by partial paralysis, or that their hair has turned white overnight or fallen out entirely. Very rare indeed are the cases of health being restored when an offender returned cut-off branches to a fairy tree and offered an apology to the good people.

In some stories of fairy retribution, people have ended up in mental hospitals or asylums because of their interference with lone hawthorn trees. Around 1950, a story was current of two men who cut down an old hawthorn tree at the creamery in Omagh, County

Tyrone; soon afterwards, both had to be sent to a mental home. Local lore in County Down had it that when a mentally disabled girl chopped down a fairy thorn near Tuber Doney, her malady quickly reached such a stage that she had to be confined to an institution.[27]

Accounts are numerous of retribution in the form of previously healthy people suddenly dying through accident or illness. These stories are known in all parts of Ireland, and characteristically involve a man who has ignored all warnings to leave a particular bush alone. In 1936 in County Galway, a story was told of a man who bought land from a woman and paid no attention to her advice not to interfere with a fairy tree on the plot. He felled the thorn and died shortly afterwards. Similarly, a man in Dungiven in County Derry who bought land with a gentle bush on it, failed to heed his wife's warnings and cut the tree down. Soon after, he took to his bed and died.

Sometimes it took days or even years before the debt was paid to the fairies. In 2000 in County Meath, it was recalled how a local man who had once cut a lone bush died two years later while he was cutting an apparently ordinary tree, which fell in an unfortunate way and killed him.[28]

Frequently, a chain of personal tragedies or economic misfortunes are blamed on interference with fairy trees. Among the consequences mentioned are sudden illnesses, accidents or deaths of the culprits' relatives, and the loss of money, livestock and property.

Fairy Mound, Clontarf, County Dublin

Fairy Tree, Ballyward, County Down

This lovely thorn in a field by the main road is protected from grazing sheep and cattle by a low wall. Great care is usually taken to protect lone trees from accidental damage. In the 1940s, however, the story was current in County Down of a Newtown man who attempted to con the fairies. Afraid to cut a lone tree on his land, he built a trench around a fairy tree in his field to expose it to the wind. Sure enough, the tree fell in stormy weather, but the man did not enjoy his victory for long, as soon he had to mourn his wife, his children and the loss of his cattle.[29]

Only when a fairy tree was cut or damaged involuntarily, or by reluctant workers threatened with being laid off if they refused to follow orders, would the fairies show mercy to offenders. Around 1940, the story was told of several Cavan men thus threatened by their employer. Before they followed his order to cut the bush, they knelt down in front of it, begging that misfortune should not befall on them, but on the one who gave the order. And so it came to pass. The men cut the tree, and that same night their boss suffered a stroke from which he never recovered.[30]

The fairies' vengeance usually hurt the individual who cut their tree, but often an additional curse was said to linger on the land where the tree stood. If a thorn in a field was cut down because it was thought to be in the way, bad luck was predicted for the farmer whose land it had been on. Tales recall horses and cattle that died without any apparent reason, or fell mad with fits; and of cows that suddenly gave bloody milk or no more milk at all. In local Mayo tradition, a curiously shaped thorn tree that once grew on the bank of Lissard fort was famed and respected as a fairy tree. In 1854, the owner of nearby Killeaden House desired the tree for his own garden, but no one would touch it for fear of the consequences. The man eventually dug up the thorn with his own hands, and moved it to the front garden of Killeaden House. The tree thrived in its new site, but the owner suffered a chain of troubles for several years and lost money and stock. Misfortunes continued to plague the family, all blamed on the removal of the tree, and in the 1950s there were proposals to return the thorn to its original location. But the tree remained at Killeaden House, until it decayed at the end of the twentieth century.[31]

When fairy trees are cut down to build or extend enterprises, the common belief is that the projects will not prosper. When lone trees have to make way for roads, those roads are said to become particularly treacherous. In about 1920, the priest of Kiltimagh in County Mayo organised the construction of a small hospital for his parish, for which a field was bought at the eastern end of town. There were two lone bushes on the field, and no matter how they tried, it was impossible to fit the hospital between them. The parish priest and the architect, who both dismissed belief in fairies as mere superstition, insisted that one of the trees be cut down. When they could not find a local man for the job, a workman was hired from outside the town. He laughed off the warnings of dire consequences and duly cut the tree. That very night, he suffered a bad stroke from which he died about a year later. The hospital was built, but obstacle after obstacle hindered its opening, until eventually the project was abandoned.[32]

In the late 1970s, two prestigious enterprises were closed down in Ireland after a chain of misfortunes. In both instances, interference with fairy trees was blamed. The bush that reportedly brought down the Ferenka Company – a wire factory that in the 1970s was the biggest employer in Limerick – stood at the entrance to the plant. Considered an obstruction, attempts were made to move the bush, but for no apparent reason the machines stalled. This warning sign was not heeded, and the tree was eventually shifted to another location. Soon afterwards, severe problems started to rock Ferenka. In 1975 the managing director was kidnapped, but later released. Prolonged strikes followed, and inter-union disputes led to such mayhem, that all efforts to save the company failed and it was closed down in 1977.[33]

A similar fate hit the DeLorean Motor Company in Dunmurry on the outskirts of Belfast. In the early 1970s, American-born John Zachary DeLorean bought the Dunmurry site, on which to build the most advanced car factory of his time. A lone hawthorn was growing on the plot, and since it was firmly believed to be linked with the 'wee folk', workmen preparing the land for the construction of the factory made sure to leave the tree alone. They resolutely refused orders to cut it, but one day, the tree was gone, and people said that from then on the enterprise was cursed. In 1981, soon after the proto-type of the DeLorean sports car had received a very positive response and the first series of cars was produced, the dire predictions started to come true. The plant was badly damaged in riots, and DeLorean came under pressure to pay back the loan he had taken out to build the factory. The following year, he was arrested for involvement in money laundering and drug trafficking, and the factory was closed down for good.[34]

Decisions to leave a fairy tree alone are sometimes said to be rewarded by its other-world owners. A farmer who heeded the warning not to build on a fairy circle was advised to build between a certain pair of whitethorns instead. As he dug the foundations he found a pot of gold. In County Donegal, a man went to cut the lone bush that was growing in the middle of his potato field. Suddenly feeling uncomfortable about his plans, he decided to leave the bush alone. Next morning he found a pipe beneath the thorn, and some ounces of tobacco, which he firmly believed had been left for him by the fairies in gratitude. Traditionally, the gold or coins left by grateful fairies are thought to originate from the riches and treasure that lie buried under fairy trees and bushes.[35]

Fairy Trees and the Crock of Gold

The belief that immense riches were hidden under particular trees or lone bushes was once widespread in Ireland. Place names such as Skeaghanore or 'thorn of the gold' in County Cork, and Skeanarget or 'thorn of the silver' in County Tyrone, are possibly based on this belief. Folk memories indicate that rumours of hidden treasure were taken very seriously. However, the frequent attempts made to retrieve that treasure were usually unsuccessful.[36]

The source of buried treasure was in some areas attributed to monks from early Christian monasteries, or to the chieftains of wealthy clans. The theory is that they buried their valuables to protect them from plundering invaders, planting a bush to mark the spot – to which they never got the chance to return.[37] More widespread was the belief that gold, precious stones and golden vessels were hidden in forts and barrows by the Vikings or Danes, who, when expelled from Ireland in the aftermath of the

Furze and whitethorn blossom

In popular oral tradition, the hidden riches buried under a solitary thorn or furze are collectively envisaged as a 'crock of gold', or in Irish, próca (an) óir. Innumerable local legends from all over the country, as well as Irish adaptations of international folktales, tell of the origin of these treasures, the hunts and searches for them, and the other-worldly guardians who watch over them.

Battle of Clontarf in 1014, did not have an opportunity to retrieve their valuables. The historical fact that the Vikings introduced the first coinage to Ireland, combined with the legendary medieval tradition of a massive, secretly hidden Norse treasure-hoard known as the Rhinegold, certainly gave rise to the idea of hidden Viking riches in Ireland.

Irrespective of the presumed origin of hidden treasures, they became popularly regarded as owned, guarded and protected by otherworld dwellers. The most prominent otherworld guardian of treasure buried under bushes and in forts is the tiny solitary leprechaun. The name leprechaun, Irish *luprachán*, derives from the medieval word

Fairy shoemaker under the whitethorn bush

The leprechaun is also known by regional variants of his name, such as lúracán, clúracán, luchramán and their anglicised versions. Popular oral traditions describe him as the shoemaker of the fairies. This idea seems to derive from the earliest literary reference to a leprechaun in an eighth-century text, who presents Leinster King Fearghus mac Léide with a pair of magical shoes.

luchorpán for a small body, and his character seems to be an Irish adaptation of lore of dwarf-communities from abroad.[38]

When the leprechaun appears in tales of hidden treasure, he frequently finds himself caught by a treasure-hunter and forced to reveal the hiding place of a crock of gold. But the little man is always capable of fooling his captor. Outside Templeport in County Cavan, a man reportedly got hold of a leprechaun, who duly pointed out a particular bush as the hiding place of a crock of gold. The man let go of the leprechaun and marked the precious bush with a red rag, but when he returned the next day with a spade to dig up the treasure, he found that all the bushes in the field had been decorated with red rags.[39]

Digging for riches under lone bushes was almost always unsuccessful, and because of the general taboo, regarded as extremely risky. Treasure-hunters have reportedly been frightened off by strange animals and unusual noises, sudden ailments and accidents, or by the untimely and sudden deaths of their relatives. From the mid-nineteenth century, the Church tried to counteract these beliefs, which it deemed as purely superstitious. But the reluctance to interfere with fairy property was firmly rooted in the people's minds, and even when assured by local priests that there were no supernatural retributions to fear, only a very few dared to dig for gold at the roots of a fairy tree.[40]

Exceptions were cases in which a person had recurring dreams, encouraging him to find hidden treasure at a particular place. These dreams were regarded as a commission from the 'good people' to avail of their property, and consequently allowed the dreamer to dig for gold successfully and without fatal consequences.[41]

The Dream of the Treasure at Home

Folktales of dreams leading to the discovery of riches are told in several parts of the world and usually belong to an international tale-type commonly called 'The Dream of the Treasure at Home'.[42]

International variants of this story belong largely to the 'once upon a time' type of tales, which may have happened any place, any time, and were essentially taken as invented. Irish variants, in contrast, were characteristically told as local legends, set in a definite place and time and involving real people and events, or so it was generally believed. Influenced by the native popular belief in gold buried under lone bushes, 'The Dream of the Treasure at Home' would often lead the treasure-hunter to a particular tree or bush.

The tale always followed the same story line. A lovely example from Ulster was recorded in the Drumgoon area in County Cavan in 1941 by the Irish Folklore Commission. Over a hundred years ago, so the story goes, a poor man from Drumgoon dreamt for three consecutive nights that he would find a crock of gold under a particular tree in Newcastle in County Meath. He duly travelled towards Newcastle, but half way there he had to shelter from a fierce storm. He was soon joined by a stranger, and to pass the time, the Drumgoon man revealed to the stranger his dreams and his intention to look for the treasure under the designated tree. To his amazement, the stranger recognised a tree on his own land in Newcastle in the man's description. He revealed that he, in turn, had dreamt three nights in succession of a crock of gold under a particular tree in Drumgoon and was on his way to look for it. Now it was the turn of the man from Drumgoon to hear his own field and tree described by a stranger. Each returned to their respective homes and discovered the riches at the spot indicated in the other man's dream.[43]

Some three hundred variants of this tale-type are known from Ireland, the majority of them recorded in Connacht and Munster. Shortened versions were also very common, which told of a certain person who dreamt for three consecutive nights of gold under a particular bush, until he dug and actually found it. Since a successful find of treasure under a bush is rather atypical for local legends, the derivation of these stories from the international tale is obvious. Elsewhere, storytellers have added distinctive motifs from the native Irish tradition. Most common is the motif of an Ogham-inscribed flagstone incorporated into local renderings of the tale. A typical example of such an elaborate variant was current in the townland of Skaghvickencrow or 'MacEnchroe's Hawthorn' in west Clare. The storyteller followed the international line of the tale up to the part

Fairy Trees, Kingscourt, County Cavan (left)

where the man returns home to dig for the crock of gold under the thorn on his land. Instead of the expected gold, however, he comes upon a flagstone with an old inscription that no one can decipher. Only when a wandering schoolmaster translates the cryptic words as 'one side is more lucky than the other' does the man know exactly where to dig, eventually finding the promised riches.[44]

Conclusion:

Sacred Trees and Tree Monuments
in Modern Ireland

From pagan times into the early twentieth century, designated trees and groves played an important role in the everyday lives of people. Cherished for their historical, social or spiritual value, and usually protected from wilful damage by commonly acknowledged taboos, tales and legends around these trees were passed on from generation to generation. When old venerable trees died, their stumps were left untouched. New trees were often allowed to grow in their place, or substitutes were planted. The contexts and rituals in which trees were honoured may have changed due to political and religious developments, but the high regard and reverence for trees persevered.

The industrialisation and rapid modernisation of Irish society, together with the strict organisation of the Catholic Church, brought about a significant change in people's attitudes towards old customs and traditions. Popular religious observances at the old places of worship lost their appeal; sanctuaries became neglected, and devotional practices that are at least as old as the Celtic Church were abandoned. Interest in the ancient myths, tales and legends declined, and so did respect for nature and the environment. Modernity and economic growth have no time for sacred landscapes, and often the profit motive lies behind decisions as to whether or not these special places are preserved. As a result, while major sites of pilgrimage or trees of national cultural importance are usually protected, sites of local significance are easily obliterated when they stand in the way of 'progress'.

Fortunately, a new awareness of the spiritual significance of nature began to arise just as modern lifestyles were taking a serious toll on sacred landscapes. From the last decade of the twentieth century, renewed interest in the natural history and folklore of trees has been mirrored in numerous publications on these subjects. The concept of a Celtic tree calendar in particular, first proposed by the scholar Robert Graves in 1946, has gained enormous popularity. Celtic tree calendars assign a different tree species to each month, with minor variants amongst the various calendars in the selection of the species. Tree calendars are an absolutely beautiful way to express love and respect for trees and nature; it should be mentioned, however, that there is no basis for a Celtic origin of the link between trees and the months of the year. The Gaulish Calendar of

Lourdes Grotto, Mount Melleray, County Waterford (right)

In 1833, Melleray Abbey was founded by Cistercian monks on the slopes of the Knockmealdown Mountains. On 16 August 1985, a teenage girl was praying with her mother and brothers in the grove at Lourdes Grotto near the abbey, when to her amazement, she noticed the statue of Mary moving among the trees of the sanctuary. For a period of nine days, several visitors witnessed the Virgin moving about; some of them also heard her reveal visions of the future and speak messages of peace and love. The Lourdes Grotto still attracts considerable numbers of pilgrims; particularly popular are the all-night vigils in summer.[1]

Coligny, the only surviving complete Celtic calendar, contains no reference at all to trees.

In recent decades, the open-air celebration of Mass at sacred places such as holy wells and groves, the ruins of early Christian monasteries, killeens or Penal sites has experienced a revival, and consequently, many sites that were neglected and almost inaccessible for years are now well cared for again. While these religious events do not attract the large crowds that attended pilgrimages and patterns in earlier centuries, the number of devotees is still considerable. Popular dates for these official open-air celebrations at sacred sites are the time around the ancient harvest festival of Lughnasa, or the feast days of parish patron saints.

Rag Tree, Knockmealdown Mountains, County Waterford (left), **and St Fintan's Money Tree, Clonenagh, County Laois** (right)

An old route of pilgrimage from Ardmore in County Waterford to Cashel in County Tipperary leads through the Knockmealdown Mountains. A lone whitethorn at the top of the road is adorned with the usual mixture of white rags, pieces of clothing and underwear and small personal items left by pilgrims on their way to nearby Melleray Grotto. The plastic bags tied to the sacred tree are a peculiar interpretation of an appropriate offering to the spirit of a place.

St Fintan's Tree in Clonenagh in County Laois has decayed from metal-poisoning. The stump is still a popular wishing tree, and drivers on the main Dublin to Limerick road frequently stop to press a coin into the rotten wood for luck.

The legends that initially linked the sacred trees at these sites with saints and miracles are often entirely lost. The ritual veneration of sacred trees in the context of pilgrimage – especially the practices of circumvention and votive offerings – declined from the mid-nineteenth century, but has regained popularity during the last decade. Trees covered with rags, religious objects and other offerings have become a common sight again.

Many shrines attributed with the power to heal or to grant wishes today attract a constant flow of visitors, who attend the communal celebrations or call by individually whenever the need arises. Wishing trees are visited for good luck, or for requesting

Tree of Life, St Peter's Church, Clonroche, County Wexford

In 2006, the artist Denis O'Connor organised a workshop for the pupils of St Aidan's National School in Clonroche, County Wexford. As part of the project, the pupils designed the 'leaves' of the steel oak, adding a very individual and personal touch to this stunning modern interpretation of the Tree of Life.

The Spirit of Trees

Neo-Druidism and Wicca are the most popular Pagan movements in Ireland. Neo-Druids focus particularly on ancient Celtic spirituality and druidic wisdom. They are organised in Groves, and often choose trees as places for meditation and celebration. The Druidic path sees trees as channels of communication between different spheres of consciousness, echoing the ancient concept of world or cosmic trees.

Wicca or Witchcraft endorses the concepts of animated nature and the veneration of the Earth Mother. Wiccan practitioners communicate with trees through ritual and link them with the Earth Mother. Her potent symbol is the Tree of Life, which represents the perpetual cycle of life, death and rebirth.

support, consolation, peace and serenity in difficult situations. Healing shrines are popularly resorted to in addition to visits to the doctor, or in cases where conventional medicine has no help to offer.

An increasing number of people are rediscovering the spiritual energy of ancient places of worship with their wells, sacred trees and stones. Their individual religious experiences at these shrines do not necessarily centre on Christian devotion and the veneration of saints, but are often a reflection of older, nature-based spiritual concepts.

An immense respect for nature and an acknowledgement of its sanctity is a character-istic trait of the modern spiritual movement that is collectively known as Paganism or Neo-Paganism.[2] In Europe, modern Paganism has its roots in the 1960s and 1970s. Various independent Pagan organisations follow their own differing paths whilst holding several ideas in common, including the worship of nature.

Since Pagan movements have no fixed buildings for conventions and worship, their members tend to gather in the open, often at places of pre-Christian religious or magical significance and at megalithic stone monuments. Wells, trees and groves are also focal points for Pagan meetings and ceremonies.

Belief in otherworld existences forms part of modern Paganism. This notion has sur-vived since ancient times in Irish fairy lore. Today, it seems that belief in the existence of otherworld beings clashes with modern lifestyles, and non-Pagans often deny the existence of fairies, belittling the old traditions as 'pishogues' or superstitions. But throughout Ireland, fairy trees and forts stand largely unmolested, testifying to an ongoing reluctance to interfere with 'them'. Lone trees are still regarded with a mixture of fear and respect. Now and again a fairy tree is vandalised, but reports of maimed or destroyed fairy trees are outnumbered by reports of relatively recent accidents and mis-fortunes, brought about by people interfering with the fairies' property.

Threatened by foolish acts of vandalism, road works, building developments and pollution, but also by disease and old age, the sacred trees, thorns and groves of Ireland are a very vulnerable part of our heritage. Yet, apart from the Forestry Act of 1946, which prohibits the felling of any tree without a felling licence, there is no specific law to protect trees of historical or spiritual significance. The English Tree Preservation Order is stricter, but void if a tree is declared dead, dying or dangerous.

Given the lack of state protection, the preservation of sacred trees and tree monuments lies in people's own hands. But to be willing to engage on their behalf if necessary, people have to know these special trees, their stories and legends, and their sacred and historical value.

Nationally, non-governmental organisations such as the Tree Council of Ireland, established in 1985, play a crucial role in the promotion of tree awareness. The Tree Council organises national tree weeks and days, and supports initiatives to plant new and preserve old trees. Founded in 1986, Crann – another organisation devoted to protecting trees – works with the Tree Register of Ireland, a database of remarkable trees cherished for their historical significance, age or dimensions.[3] The Woodland Trust, the Ancient Tree Forum and the Tree Register of the British Isles protect tree heritage in the North. As well as caring for historical trees, these organisations work to preserve heritage trees beyond their natural life spans by propagating descendants from their seeds and cuttings.

On a local level, community groups throughout Ireland contribute significantly to the preservation of venerable trees. By collecting and publishing their folklore and history, these groups help to ensure that the fascinating stories and tales around our trees, groves and thorns are passed on to future generations, and that the old Celtic reverence for trees is kept alive. With Christian pilgrims and modern Pagans seeking the divine in the sacred landscape, and with communities and organisations determined to create a wider awareness of the historical, spiritual and ecological value of trees, we have a fair chance of saving our tree heritage, and with it, a precious part of our cultural identity.

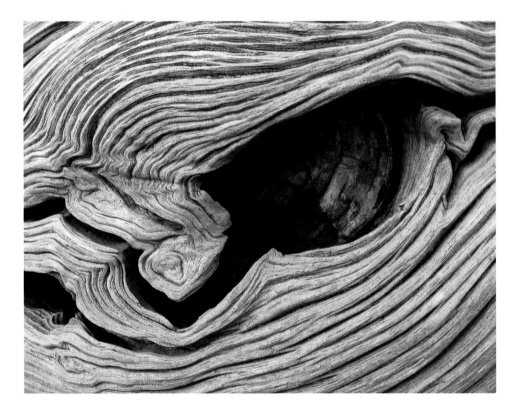

Lissoy Beech, Lissoy, County Donegal (above)

All over Ireland there are beautiful yet unrecorded trees that might once have played an important role for local communities. The magnificent beech in the village of Lissoy in County Donegal seems to be one of those. The half-rotten remains of a ladder and numerous initials carved long ago still distinguish the beech from adjoining trees. Unfortunately, there is no reliable data available on its former significance.

William's Tree, Scarva, County Down (left)

Notes and References

Introduction

1   D. A. Binchy, ed., 'An Archaic Legal Poem', in *Celtica* 9, (Dublin, 1971), pp. 152–168.

2   Tree worship is known from Egypt and the Middle East, Latin and North America, Africa, India, East Asia, ancient Greece and Rome, and the Nordic, Germanic and Celtic peoples. For a detailed international study see for instance Nathaniel Altman, *Sacred Trees: Spirituality, Wisdom and Well-Being* (New York, 2000) and James George Frazer, *The Golden Bough: A Study in Magic and Religion* (London, 1974).

3   For the history and development of Irish forests see especially Charles E. Nelson and Wendy F. Walsh, *Trees of Ireland: Native and Naturalized* (Dublin, 1992).

4   The role of different species of trees in Irish popular traditions is beautifully illustrated in Niall Mac Coitir, *Irish Trees: Myths, Legends and Folklore* (Cork, 2003).

5   On Celtic sanctuaries see for instance Miranda J. Green, *The Gods of the Celts* (Gloucester, 1986) and Fred Hageneder, *The Spirit of Trees: Science, Symbiosis and Inspiration* (Edinburgh, 2000), p. 65. During their period of use, several stone circles in Wales and England, such as Avesbury and Stonehenge, were adjoined by circles of wooden posts for ritual use.

6   P. W. Joyce, *Irish Names of Places I* (Dublin/Cork/Belfast, 1869), pp. 499–500; Dáithí Ó hÓgáin, 'Trees in Irish Lore', in *Journal of the Society of Irish Foresters*, vol. 60, (Dublin, 2003), pp. 46–60.

7   See Alwyn and Brinley Rees, *Celtic Heritage: Ancient Tradition in Ireland and Wales* (London, 1961), pp. 26–80 for a very detailed study of the Cycles.

8   Dáithí Ó hÓgáin, *Myth, Legend and Romance: An Encyclopaedia of the Irish Folk Tradition*, (London, 1990), pp. 312–313 on the Mythological Cycle. The earliest sections of the *Leabhar Gabhála Éireann* survived in a twelfth-century manuscript that was in turn based on a lost eighth-century text.

9   Ó hÓgáin (1990), op. cit., p. 318; Dáithí Ó hÓgáin, *The Sacred Isle: Belief and Religion in Pre-Christian Ireland* (Cork, 1999), p. 97; John R. Walsh and Thomas Bradley, *A History of the Irish Church 400–700 AD* (Dublin, 2003), p. 61. The survey was carried out from 1963–71 by archaeologists from Belfast University. Shortly after its completion, the structure was filled with stones, purposely burned and then covered with sods and earth. Tradition has it that Eamhain Macha was destroyed in 332 by the three Collas who broke the power

of the Ulaidh, but modern historians claim that it was not destroyed until the late 450s.

10 R. A. Stewart Macalister, ed., *Lebor Gabála Érenn 1–5* (London, 1941), pp. 61–62, 73; Thomas F. O'Rahilly, *Early Irish History and Mythology* (Dublin, 1946), pp. 154–172; Rees, op. cit., pp. 118–139; Geoffrey Keating, *Foras Feasa Ar Éirinn. The History of Ireland* (Dublin, 1901–13), vol. 1, pp. 156, 158, 162; vol. 2, p. 247. The seventeenth-century historian Keating links Bile with the deity Bel or Belenus and the festival Bealtaine, though his theories have long since been dismissed. The name Bealtaine means probably 'Fire of Bel' or Bright Fire; and it is possible that the customary May Day fires were initially lit in honour of the god Bel or Belenus. Celebrations of May festivals are still common in many parts of Europe, often linked with ceremonial fires and may poles or may bushes. For May Day celebrations in Europe see Frazer, op. cit., p. 157; for Bealtaine see Ó hÓgáin (1990), op. cit., pp. 402–403; for Belenus see Jan de Vries, *Keltische Religionen* (Stuttgart, 1961), p. 76.

11 Medieval sources refer to several other *biledha*. Bile mac Crúaich (or Macc Crúach), mentioned in the Book of Armagh, possibly stood at Narraghmore in County Kildare; Bile Bridam and Bile Cairne are today placed in County Offaly; Bile Methais is linked with County Laois; and Bile Tened with County Meath. Ó hÓgáin (1999), op. cit., p. 115.

12 Edward Gwynn, *The Metrical Dindshenchas 3* (Dublin, 1913), p. 148.

13 Fintan is alternatively called Fintan mac Bóchra. R. I. Best, ed., 'The Settling of the Manor of Tara', in *Ériu 4* 121–172 (Dublin/London, 1910), pp. 152–153.

14 Edward Gwynn, *The Metrical Dindshenchas 4* (Dublin, 1924), pp. 238–239, pp. 241–247; A. T. Lucas, 'The Sacred Trees of Ireland', in *JCHAS 68*, 16–54 (Cork, 1963), pp. 17–23; Whitley Stokes, ed., 'The Prose Tales of the Rennes Dindshenchas II. Extracts from the Book of Leinster', in *RC 16*, 269–310 (Paris, 1895), pp. 277–79; Gwynn (1913), op. cit., p. 148; Prof. Connellan, ed., *Transactions of the Ossianic Society for the Year 1857* (Dublin, 1860), p. 153. For Eó Rossa in hagiographical sources see John O'Hanlon, *Lives of the Irish Saints* (Dublin, 1875) vol. 4, p. 218; vol. 6, p. 702; Whitley Stokes, ed., 'The Birth and Life of St Moling', in *RC 27*, 257–312 (Paris, 1906), p. 281. On Craebh Dháithí see Lucas, op. cit., p. 18; on Bile Uisnigh see Best, op. cit., p. 151; on Uisneach and the Navel of Ireland see Christine Zucchelli, *Stones of Adoration* (Cork, 2007), pp. 9–12.

15 Stokes (1895), op. cit., pp. 278–279. The plain is named after St Ailbhe (died 527), the founder of Emly, anciently Imleach Iubhair or the Lakeside by the Yew in County Tipperary. Mugna was also the name of a goddess of sovereignty, linked with the Erainn people of Munster, but a link between the deity and the tree has not yet been established. The element Mugna survived in place names such as Cluain Mughna or Clonmona in County Tipperary, Bealach Mughna or Ballaghmoon in County Carlow, and Cill Mugna or Kilmoone in County Cork. On Mugna see Ó hÓgáin (1990), op. cit., pp. 269, 305.

16 Aodh Sláine or Aed Slane was a historical high king who reigned AD 565 to 604. His sons Diarmaid and Bláthmhac were joint kings of Ireland from 642 until they perished in the

plague in 664. Ó hÓgáin (1990), op. cit., pp. 36, 157. Whitley Stokes, ed., 'The Prose Tales of the Rennes Dindshenchas', in *RC 15*, 272–336; 418–484 (Paris, 1894), p. 420.

17 Edward Gwynn, *The Metrical Dindshenchas* 3 (Dublin, 1913), p. 144.

18 Connellan, op. cit., p. 152 quoting O'Flahertys *Ogygia*, vol. 2, pp. 207–208, claims that all five trees remained hidden until the birth of King Conn Céadchathach. Stokes (1895) op. cit., pp. 419–421.

19 The concept of cosmic trees was also known by the native people of South and North America and Russia, as well as by Babylonians and Sumerians. 'Irminsul' was the sacred world ash of the Saxons. For the cosmic tree in international contexts see particularly Altman, op. cit., p. 23. On Asvattha and its interpretation in Indian creation myth see for instance Hageneder, op. cit., pp. 70–72. The *Vedas*, written c. 900–500 BC, are the earliest religious scriptures of India. An inverted world tree occurs also in *The Kabala*, the ancient mythical lore of Judaism.

Trees of Sacred Knowledge

1 On *imbas forosna* see Fergus Kelly, *A Guide to Early Irish Law* (Dublin, 1988/1998), p. 44; Dáithí Ó hÓgáin, *Myth, Legend and Romance: An Encyclopaedia of the Irish Folk Tradition* (London, 1990), p. 169; Dáithí Ó hÓgáin, *The Sacred Isle: Belief and Religion in Pre-Christian Ireland* (Cork, 1999), p. 111; John O'Donovan, ed., *Annála Ríoghachta Éireann. Annals of the Kingdom of Ireland by the Four Masters from the Earliest Period to the Year 1616,* vol. 1 (Dublin, 1848), p. 90. Latin sources use the terms *magus*, plural *magi* for the Irish words *druid*, plural *drui*. The Irish name for a poet was *fili*, plural *filid*. For Amergin see Prof. Connellan, ed., *Transactions of the Ossianic Society for the Year 1857* (Dublin, 1860), p. xvi.

2 Gaius Plinius Secundus (Pliny), *Historia Naturalis*, XVI, 249. Pliny lived c. AD 23–79.

3 Eugene O'Curry, *Lectures on the Manuscript Materials of Ancient Irish History* (Dublin, 1873), p. 188.

4 Ó hÓgáin (1999), op. cit., pp. 71, 92–93; Miranda J. Green, *The Gods of the Celts* (Gloucester, 1986), p. 22. The interpretation became additionally difficult when the element *wid* for wisdom was confused with *vidu* for a wood.

Trees of Religious Manifestations

1 John O'Donovan, ed., *Annála Ríoghachta Éireann. Annals of the Kingdom of Ireland by the Four Masters from the Earliest Period to the Year 1616,* vols. 1–7 (Dublin, 1848–1851).

2 Deuteronomy, 33:16, Genesis, 18:1; Judges, 4:5; Genesis, 35:8, 35:19; Luke, 22:39; John, 18:2.

3 Nathaniel Altman, *Sacred Trees: Spirituality, Wisdom and Well-Being* (New York, 2000) has a detailed study of the influence of Christianity on nature worship.

4 Cary Meehan, *The Traveller's Guide to Sacred Ireland* (Glastonbury, 2002), pp. 243–244; information on site.

5 Anna Rackard and Liam O'Callaghan, *Fishstonewater: Holy Wells of Ireland* (Cork, 2001), p. 108; visit in February 2008.

6 Martin of Tours (c. 316–397) was the son of a Roman soldier from present-day Hungary; he converted to Christianity, founded the first ever monastery of Gaul in Ligugé, and was elected bishop of Tours in 371. Alexander Demandt, *Über allen Wipfeln. Der Baum in der Kulturgeschichte* (Köln, 2002/2005), pp. 142–145, 153–154.

7 In AD 723, St Boniface felled the Sacred Oak of Donar (Thor) in a sanctuary belonging to German Saxons in Geismar; in 772, Charlemagne destroyed the Irminsul in Westphalia, another Saxon tree sanctuary; in 789 he ordered the elimination of all kinds of nature worship in his empire. Orders to destroy sacred groves came c. 1000 from the Bishop of York, and a little later from the Bishop of Bremen; in 1093, the Prince of Bohemia burnt down the heathen groves and trees in his realm, and as late as 1386, the last pagan Grand Duke of Lithuania converted to Christianity and gave orders to fell the sacred groves in his country.

8 On the Continent significant reforms from the eighth century onwards brought about a well-organised Church under the sole authority of the Pope. The spiritual and structural independence of the Celtic Church with her ancient traditions and rituals was no longer compatible to the ideals of the Papacy. Calls for reorganisation and reform were answered in 1111 with the Synod of Cashel, the starting point for a rigorous reformatory initiative in Ireland. The system of independent monasteries was replaced by a diocesan system of parishes and bishoprics with centres in Armagh, Cashel, Dublin and Tuam. In 1142, the Cistercians were the first reformative order to arrive, soon followed by the Benedictines, Augustinians, Dominicans and Franciscans.

9 The term 'Green Man' was coined in 1939 by Lady Raglan to describe a type of carving previously known under a variety of local names such as Face in the Leaves, Jack in the Green, Green George and many others. The earliest example occurs on a second-century Roman column in Turkey; from the eleventh century, Green Man carvings appear in Europe, particularly in England, Scotland, Wales, Germany, France, Italy and the Netherlands. The carvings have been linked with Gawein, the Green Knight of the Arthurian tradition, or with the Knights Templar and images of the Tree of Life in the Temple of Solomon. So far, no survey of the Green Man has been conducted in Ireland.

10 For the distribution see Altman, op. cit., and James George Frazer, *The Golden Bough: A Study in Magic and Religion* (London, 1974), p. 145.

11 A number of Celtic wooden temples from pre-Roman times possibly existed on the Continent and in Britain.

12 Vernementon was near Lincoln, Nemetostatio in Devon, Aquae Arnemetiae at modern

Buxton in Peak District; Medionemeton near Edinburgh; see also Strabo, XII, 5, 1; Dáithí Ó hÓgáin, *Myth, Legend and Romance: An Encyclopaedia of the Irish Folk Tradition* (London, 1990), pp. 70–71; 92–93; Miranda J. Green, *The Gods of the Celts* (Gloucester, 1986), pp. 17–19, 21. Jan de Vries, *Keltische Religionen* (Stuttgart, 1961), pp. 60–61, 122. Inscriptions dedicated to Nemetona stem from Altripp near Spier and from the Mainz area in Germany, and from Bath in England; the Matres Nemetiales were apparently worshipped around modern Grenoble in France.

13 Máire MacNeill, *The Festival of Lughnasa* (Dublin, 1962/1982), pp. 153–155; NFC 891:431–437; 443–450; 455–457; 459–660; 486–491 (1942); NFC S 959:302; 308–310.

14 Lucan, *Civil War (Pharsalia)*, III, 399–450. Lucan lived AD 39–65.

15 Tacitus, *Annals*, XIV, 30. Tacitus, born c. AD 55, was a Latin writer, politician and historian; his *Annals* deal with time from AD 14 to the death of Nero in 68; Cassius Dio, LXII 7:3.

16 John O'Hanlon, *Lives of the Irish Saints* (Dublin, 1875), vol. 2, pp. 616–617; vol. 5, p. 517; vol. 7, p. 308.

17 Whitley Stokes, ed., 'O'Mulconry's Glossary', in *Archiv für Celtische Lexikographie*, Bd. 1 (Halle, 1900), p. 272; O'Donovan, op. cit., William M. Hennessy, ed., *Annals of Ulster* (Dublin, 1887).

18 O'Hanlon, op. cit., vol. 6, p. 296; Andrew O'Kelleher and Gertrude Schoepperle, eds., *Betha Colaim Chille. Life of Columcille by Manus O'Donnell (1532)* (Illinois, 1918), pp. 83–85.

19 Whitley Stokes, ed., *Lives of the Saints from the Book of Lismore* (Oxford, 1890), p. 305; Charles Plummer, ed., *Bethada Náem nÉrenn. Lives of Irish Saints* (Oxford, 1968), p. cliii; A. T. Lucas, 'The Sacred Trees of Ireland', in *JCHAS* 68 (Cork, 1963), pp. 29–30.

20 Peter Harbison, *Pilgrimage in Ireland. The Monuments and the People* (London, 1991), p. 125; Thomas Johnson Westropp, *A Folklore Survey of County Clare and County Clare Folk-Tales and Myths* (Dublin, 1910–1913), ed. Maureen Comber, CLASP (Ennis, 2000), p.20.

21 See also Lucas, op. cit., p. 27.

22 Lucan, op. cit., III, pp. 399–450; Alexander Demandt, *Über allen Wipfeln: Der Baum in der Kulturgeschichte* (Köln, 2002/2005), p. 138; At the time of Maximos' writing, the Celts of Gaul had long since depicted their gods in human form.

23 For Crann Greine and Eohy see Prof. Connellan, ed., *Transactions of the Ossianic Society for the Year 1857* (Dublin, 1860), p. 153.

24 Rudolf Thurneysen, ed., 'Der Mystische Baum', in *ZCP* 14, 16–17 (Halle, 1923), p. 16.

25 Whitley Stokes, 'The Voyage of Snedgus and Mac Riagla', in *RC* 9, 14–25 (Paris, 1888), p. 21; Whitley Stokes, ed., 'The Adventure of St Columba's Clerics', in *RC* 26, 130–170 (Paris, 1905), pp. 139–140; O'Kelleher and Schoepperle, op. cit., p. 391.

26 O'Hanlon, op. cit., vol. 1, frontispiece and vol. 7, pp. 107–108; Lucas, op. cit., p. 36; information leaflet; visit June 2008.

27 Craibhi-Laisre is probably Creevagh near Clonmacnoise. O'Hanlon, op. cit., vol. 1, p. 19.

28 Estyn Evans, *Irish Folk Ways* (London, 1957/1989), p. 298; Vaughan Cornish, *Historic Thorn Trees in the British Isles* (London, 1941), pp. 51–53.

29 J. H. Wilks, *Trees of the British Isles in History and Legend* (London, 1972), p. 109; visit May 2008.

30 MacNeill, op. cit., p. 632; NFC 889:11–14 (1942); local information, visits September 2007 and May 2008.

31 Liam de Paor, *Saint Patrick's World: The Christian Culture of Ireland's Apostolic Age* (Dublin, 1993), pp. 167–168.

32 In yet another version, the relics were hidden by a leper. Stokes (1890), op. cit., pp. 85, 111; Lucas, op. cit., p. 32. The exact location of St Kevin's original monastic foundation is a subject of scholarly dispute, with some claiming it was at the Upper Lake, others suggesting a site by the Lower Lake. Nineteenth-century tradition in the valley of Luggela claimed that the saint built his first oratory here when he retreated from public life. See O'Hanlon, op. cit., vol. 6, pp. 36, 39; Harbison (1991), op. cit., pp. 118–119.

33 NFC S 1091:16 (I); Stokes (1890), op. cit., p. 176. Decayed and forgotten are for instance St Ciarán's Ash at Errill Monastery, St Ciarán's Bush in Knockseera Graveyard and St Ciarán's Ash beside Monamonra Graveyard, all in County Laois.

34 For Rutland see Lucas, op. cit., p. 37; for Cullen see MacNeill, op. cit., pp. 268–275; NFC 466:283–284 (1934–1937); NFC 888:359–360; 528–539; 542–543 (1942).

35 Patrick Logan, *The Holy Wells of Ireland* (London, 1980), p. 23; local information, July 1999 and July 2008. Ciarán, the founder of Clonmacnoise, died c. 550.

36 Mr and Mrs Samuel Carter Hall, *Ireland: Its Scenery, Character etc.*, vols. 1–3 (London, 1841–1843); Samuel Hayes, *A Practical Treatise on Planting and the Management of Woods and Coppices* (Dublin, 1794), pp. 144–145; Ben Simon, 'A Review of Notable Yew Trees in Ireland', in *Arboricultural Journal*, vol. 24/2, 97–137 (Bicester, 2000), pp. 99–101.

37 John McVeagh, ed., *Richard Pococke's Irish Tours* (Dublin, 1995), p. 184; Arthur W. Hutton, ed., *Young, Arthur, A Tour in Ireland 1776–1779* (London 1780/Shannon 1970), p. 350; Johann G. Kohl, *Ireland, Scotland and England* (London, 1844), p. 81; Hall and Hall, op. cit., p. 220; W. H. Bartlett, *The Scenery and Antiquities of Ireland* (London, 1842), pp. 31–36. Muckross Friary was founded in 1448 by Donald McCarthy and enlarged in 1621. On the estimated age of the yew, see for instance Charles E. Nelson and Wendy F. Walsh, *Trees of Ireland: Native and Naturalized* (Dublin, 1992), p. 225.

38 Lucas, op. cit., p. 35; Charles Plummer, ed., *Vitae Sanctorum Hiberniae* (Oxford, 1910), vol. 2, p. 143.

39 O'Hanlon, op. cit., vol. 2, p. 547.

40 Dind Ríg lies south of Leighlinbridge in County Carlow. In Ptolemy's *Geography*, it appears under the name Dunon; see also Dáithí Ó hÓgáin, *The Sacred Isle: Belief and Religion in Pre-Christian Ireland* (Cork, 1999), p. 163.

41 For the episode in the biography of St Laserian and St Moling see O'Hanlon, op. cit., vol. 4, p. 218; vol. 6, p. 702; and Whitley Stokes, ed., 'The Birth and Life of St Moling', in *RC* 27, 257–312 (Paris, 1906), p. 281.

42 Whitley Stokes, ed., 'The Prose Tales of the Rennes Dindshenchas II. Extracts from the Book of Leinster', in *RC 16*, 269–310 (Paris, 1895), pp. 277–279; see also Edward Gwynn, *The Metrical Dindshenchas* 4 (Dublin, 1913), pp. 238–239. Banba is also the poetic name for Ireland. Prof. Connellan, ed., *Transactions of the Ossianic Society for the Year 1857* (Dublin, 1860), p. 153, establishes a link with druidism when he relates that Eohy the Druid made a shield of the wood of Eó Rossa for Hugh, King of Oriel.

43 In English tradition, 'walking sticks' – often the Sire's Walking Stick or similar – are usually linked with the tale of a small tree being pulled out for a walking stick. When it was stuck back into the ground because it was thought unsuitable, it grew again. For examples see Wilks, op. cit., p. 194. In Ireland, 'walking sticks' are usually linked with saints. Exceptions are O'Lawlor's Stick in Tinryland, County Carlow (NFC 462:322 [1938]) and the Sire's Walking Stick in Tullamore (Thomas Pakenham, *Meetings with Remarkable Trees* (London, 1996/2003), pp. 24–25); Altman, op. cit., p. 158; Nigel Pennick, *Celtic Sacred Landscapes* (London, 1996), pp. 33–34.

44 G. T. Stokes, ed., *Pococke's Tour in Ireland in 1752* (Dublin/London, 1891), p. 109; NFC 404:213–214 (1937). The AFM report for 1157 that Ruaidhri Ua Conchobhair plundered the country as far as Cuaille-Cianacht, but the entry does not refer to the aetiology of the tree.

45 St Mochoemóg, also known under the name of Pulcherius, was a nephew of St Ita, and abbot of Liathmor, today Leigh; he died in 656. O'Hanlon, op. cit., vol. 3, p. 349; for Thornback see James Graves, 'Proceedings', in *JRSAI* 16, 14–15 (Dublin, 1883); for Kilcorkey see H. T. Knox, 'Miscellanea', *JRSAI* 32, 188–189 (Dublin, 1902).

46 Francis Joseph Bigger, 'The Lake and Church of Kilmakilloge, the Ancient Church, Holy Well, and Bullán-stone of Temple Feaghna, and the Holy Well and Shrine of St Finan's, Co. Kerry', in *JRSAI* 28, 314–324 (Dublin, 1898); NFC 466:10–11 (1934); Hall and Hall, op. cit., vol. 1, p. 122.

47 William Shaw-Mason, *Parochial Survey of Ireland*. Vol. 3 (Dublin, 1819), p. 244; Canon William Murphy, 'The Pattern of Mullinakill', in *Old Kilkenny Review* Nr. 22, pp. 42–44 (Kilkenny, 1970). A pattern is held on the saint's feast day on 20 August.

48 OSL Waterford (1841), p. 84; E. Fitzgerald, 'Proceedings and Papers: St Colman's Tree and Holy Well', in *JRSAI* 4, 40–49 (Dublin, 1856), pp. 41–42.

49 Lucas, op. cit., p. 40; local information, www.irishmidlandsancestry.com.

50 Rhona Fogarty, *Rooted in Folklore: A Study of Native Tree Lore in Ireland* (unpubl. Dipl. Thesis, Department of Irish Folklore, University College Dublin, 2005), p. 29; Ó hÓgáin (1990), op. cit., p. 384; Stokes (1890), op. cit., pp. 57, 204. The tree on Inis Cathaigh is

alternatively described as a holly or a hazel. Daniel Mescal, *The Story of Inis Cathaigh* (Dublin, 1902), p. 65; Stokes (1890), pp. 71, 218; NFC S 630:196–199.

51 OSL Donegal (1835), p. 212; O'Kelleher and Schoepperle, op. cit., pp. 131–132; O'Hanlon, op. cit., vol. 6, p. 340; NFC 972:454(I:1941), NFC 991:221–363 (I:1941). In July 2007, the tree and its story were no longer remembered in Meenaneary.

52 OSL Meath (1836), pp. 122–123; MacNeill, op. cit., vol. 2, pp. 637–638; NFC 466:293 (1934–1927); NFC 468:218–219 (1934–1937) has a variant where the trees grew from the handles of the wheel-barrow in which the boy was brought to the well; local information, February 2008.

53 William Gregory Wood-Martin, *Traces of the Elder Faiths in Ireland: A Folklore Sketch. A Handbook of Irish Pre-Christian Traditions*, vol. 2 (London/New York/Bombay, 1902), p. 159. I made several visits to the area between 2003 and 2008, but failed to locate the tree and could not establish whether it still stands.

54 NFC S 968:414; NFC S 969:1–2; MacNeill, op. cit., pp. 117–118; OSL Fermanagh (1834), pp. 83–84; St Naile is also known under the name of St Natalis; O'Hanlon, op. cit., vol. 1, pp. 450–455.

55 For Derry see Patrick Logan, *The Holy Wells of Ireland* (London, 1980), pp. 52, 88; for Limerick, local information, August 2007.

56 John J. O'Meara, ed., *Topography of Ireland. Giraldus Cambrensis. Newly translated from the earliest Manuscript* (Dundalk, 1951), pp. 60–61.

57 O'Hanlon, op. cit., vol. 6, p. 58; for a present-day rendition of the tale see P. J. O'Núanáin, *Glendalough or the Seven Churches of St. Kevin* (Wicklow, 1984), pp. 28–29; Logan, op. cit., p. 92; Donncha Ó hAodha, *Bethu Brigte* (Dublin, 1978), p. 29; Mac Coitir, op. cit., p. 35.

58 O'Hanlon, op. cit., vol. 5, p. 251. St Carthage or Carthach is also known as St Mochuda of Lismore.

59 O'Hanlon, op. cit., vol. 6, p. 308.

60 Gerard Madden, *Holy Island. Jewel of the Lough* (n.p., n.y.), pp. 5–8; Mary Ryan D'Arcy, *The Saints of Ireland: A Chronological Account of the Lives and Works of Ireland's Saints and Missionaries at Home and Abroad* (St Paul/Minnesota, 1974/1985), p. 35; local information, May 2001.

61 O'Hanlon, op. cit., vol. 4, pp. 155–156, refers to *arbor tilia* and its sap having the taste of vine in Colgan's *Life of St Ruadhán*; Stokes (1890), op. cit., vol. 1, pp. 80, 227.

62 O'Hanlon, op. cit., vol. 3, p. 129.

63 NFC S 1113:285–286.

64 St Féichín lived c. 580 or 590 to c. 665. Dáithí Ó hÓgáin, *Myth, Legend and Romance: An Encyclopaedia of the Irish Folk Tradition* (London, 1990), pp. 197–198; information plaque on site.

Trees of Spiritual Transformation

1 John O'Hanlon, *Lives of the Irish Saints*, vol. 8 (Dublin, 1875), p. 228.

2 Nathaniel Altman, *Sacred Trees: Spirituality, Wisdom and Well-Being* (New York, 2000), pp. 114–115, supports the theory of a pagan origin of most shrines.

3 Seán J. Connolly, *Priests and People in Pre-Famine Ireland, 1780–1845* (Dublin, 2001), pp. 141–142.

4 Connolly, op. cit., pp. 142–143.

5 OSL Roscommon (1837), p. 64; OSL Mayo (1838); vol. 1, p. 98; vol. 2, pp. 142–143; Connolly, op. cit., p. 124. In 1942 (NFC 889:242, 257–258) it was well remembered that those who had sick cows brought a roll of butter and placed it beside the well, while others hung cow chains or ropes on the tree which grows over the well. Visits to the well took place until the late 1930s.

6 NFC 1786:137 (1971); NFC S 965:293–294.

7 Connolly, op. cit., pp. 141, 148; Joseph Lee, *The Modernisation of Irish Society 1848–1918* (Dublin, 1973), p. 43.

8 Lucas, op. cit., p. 37; Charles Plummer, ed., *Vitae Sanctorum Hiberniae* (Oxford, 1910), vol. 1, pp. 218–219.

9 NFC 145:142; http://archives.tcm.ie/westernpeople; local information, October 2007.

10 For Kilkee see Lucas, op. cit., p. 41; for Kilcrohan see OSL Kerry (1841), pp. 157–158; Máire MacNeill, *The Festival of Lughnasa* (Dublin, 1962/1982), pp. 648–649; local information, September 2007; NFC 453:258 (1934–1937), NFC 947:29–31.

11 For Ballyvourney see NFC 466:168 (1934–1937); for Carnagh see NFC S 988:12, 171; NFC S 973:160; NFC S 987:49.

12 O'Hanlon, op. cit., vol. 6, pp. 765–766.

13 Information plaque on site, visit July 2007.

14 Patrick Logan, *The Holy Wells of Ireland* (London, 1980), p. 68; visit July 2007.

15 NFC S 169:21, 25–27, 398; John Cowell, *Sligo – Land of Yeats' Desire. History, Literature, Folklore, Landscape* (Dublin, 1990), p. 26.

16 Information plaque on site; Peter Harbison, *Pilgrimage in Ireland: The Monuments and the People* (London, 1991), pp. 231–232, has a beautiful image of the tree. O'Hanlon, op. cit., vol. 2, pp. 578–579; John R. Walsh and Thomas Bradley, *A History of the Irish Church 400–700 AD* (Dublin, 2003), p. 87.

17 NFC 992:168 (1947; I), NFC 1034:277–278 (1946; I).

18 Cork: NFC 466:293 (1934–1937); Clare: NFC 466:135 (1934–1937); Laois: Lucas, op. cit., p. 41; Armagh: T. G. F. Paterson, 'The Cult of the Holy Well in County Armagh', in *UJA* 11, 127–130 (Belfast, 1948), p. 128; Antrim: Ben Simon, 'Tree Traditions and Folklore from Northeast Ireland', in *Arboricultural Journal*, vol. 24/1, 15–40 (Bicester, 2000), p. 29.

19 NFC S 962:21–26.

20 MacNeill, op. cit., pp. 626, 627; NFC 889:509, 527–528 (1942); OSL Galway 1 (1838), pp. 232–233; visit February 2008.

21 One of the ancient trees in Aghabog Churchyard in County Monaghan, cut down by the 1930s and long forgotten, held a tree well. It was said to never run dry and to have a cure for warts.

22 Jeanne Cooper-Foster, *Ulster Folklore* (Belfast, 1951), p. 113; Sheila St Clair, *Folklore of the Ulster People* (Cork, 1971), p. 67.

23 A. T. Lucas, 'The Sacred Trees of Ireland', in *JCHAS* 68, 16–54 (Cork, 1963), p. 36; local information, September 2007.

24 Connolly, op. cit., pp. 141–142. Apart from the religious aspect, patrons were valued as festive and social occasions. The major pilgrimage sites attracted people from far across the country, while less prominent ones were attended by people from the surrounding townlands.

25 Logan (1980), op. cit., pp. 118–119; local information, May 2008.

26 MacNeill, op. cit., p. 602; Dáithí Ó hÓgáin, *Myth, Legend and Romance: An Encyclopaedia of the Irish Folk Tradition* (London, 1990), pp. 194–196. Other popular designations mirror some of the festival customs and traditions which continued into the early decades of the twentieth century. The term Fraughan or Bilberry Sunday recalls communal berry gatherings; the name Garland Sunday, the practice of decorating stones at the assembly sites; Height Sunday reflects the custom to climb the highest hill or mountain in the area; and Lammas derives from the old English 'Loaf Mass'.

27 John Toland, *A History of the Celtic Religion and Learning Containing an Account of the Druids or the Priests and Judges* (Edinburgh, 1815), pp. 17–18; William Gregory Wood-Martin, *Traces of the Elder Faiths in Ireland: A Folklore Sketch. A Handbook of Irish Pre-Christian Traditions*, vol. 2 (London/New York/Bombay, 1902), p. 56.

28 MacNeill, op. cit., pp. 184, 254, 607–608. NFC 467:190 (1934–1937); NFC 889:47, 49–50, 160, 171, 175, 193 (1942); NFC 891:417 (1942); NFC S 176:182, 192; NFC S 177:59; NFC S 178:187; John Cowell, *Sligo – Land of Yeats' Desire. History, Literature, Folklore, Landscape* (Dublin, 1990), p. 121.

29 Harbison, op. cit., p. 231; Cary Meehan, *The Traveller's Guide to Sacred Ireland* (Glastonbury, 2002), p. 130; local information, June 2008.

30 Patron saint is eighth-century St Ciarán of Castlekeeran. O'Hanlon, op. cit., vol. 6, pp. 665–666; Máire MacNeill, op. cit., pp. 260, 283; NFC 468:250–252 (1934–1937); NFC 890: 61–64 (1942).

31 NFC S 945:153–154; NFC S 946:80, 212; NFC S 952:76; NFC S 956:13; NFC S 1002:134; NFC 467:59–60 (1934); visit March 1995.

32 Donegal: NFC S 1110:47, 247; Sligo: NFC S 169:21, 25–27, 398; Cowell, op. cit., p. 26; MacNeill, op. cit., p. 263.

33 Gertrude Schoepperle and Andrew O'Kelleher, eds., *Betha Colaim Chille. Life of Columcille by Manus O'Donnell (1532)* (Illinois, 1918), p. 39; NFC S 1073:98; for Mayo see Harbison, op. cit., p. 69.

34 For international examples see Altman, op. cit., pp. 79, 161, 164–165.

35 Life of St Brigid, composed by Animosus, c. AD 980; Latin text: Lucan, op. cit., p. 32; translation: Logan (1980), op. cit., p. 91.

36 Lucas, op. cit., pp. 32–33; *Pococke's Tour in Ireland in 1752*, ed. G. T. Stokes (Dublin/London, 1891), p. 109; NFC 404:213–214 (1937).

37 Kilkenny: Lucas, op. cit., p. 36; visit September 2007; Cork: Wood-Martin, op. cit., pp. 158–159; Clare: local information.

38 William Shaw-Mason, *Parochial Survey of Ireland*, vol. 3 (Dublin, 1819), p. 244; Canon William Murphy, 'The Pattern of Mullinakill', in *Old Kilkenny Review* Nr. 22 (1970); O'Hanlon, op. cit., vol. 6, p. 705; local information, October 2006.

39 NFC 404:213–214 (1937).

40 Dáithí Ó hÓgáin, *The Sacred Isle: Belief and Religion in Pre-Christian Ireland* (Cork, 1999), p. 42; Miranda J. Green, *The Gods of the Celts* (Gloucester, 1986), p. 21. Strabo mentions treasure of gold ingots at the sacred lake belonging to the Celtic Volcae Tectosages at Toulouse in 106 BC; Caesar describes the Celtic custom of dedicating weapons and booty heaped on the ground in honour of the god of the winning side.

41 Lucan, op. cit., I, 446; Demandt, op. cit., pp. 137–138 (quoting from P. M. Duval, *Les Dieux des Celtes* [Paris, 1957]); Scholiae to Lucan, I, 444: Hesus Mars sic placatur: homo in arbore sic suspenditur, usque donec per cruorem membra digesserit; Tacitus, *Annals*, XIV, 30; Cassius Dio, LXII, 7:3.

42 Local information, June 2008; Meehan, op. cit., pp. 203–204.

43 Among the finds, discovered in the nineteenth century mostly near the Nun's Church, were a c. tenth-century brooch, a crucifixion plaque from around 1100 and various pins. See also Harbison, op. cit., pp. 115–116.

44 Mr and Mrs Samuel Carter Hall, *Ireland: Its Scenery, Character etc.*, vol. 1 (London, 1841), p. 309.

45 Information sign at site, visit February 2008. For the biography of fifth-century saint Olcan see O'Hanlon, op. cit., vol. 2, pp. 643–648.

46 Shaw-Mason, op. cit., vol. 1, p. 328.

47 O'Hanlon, op. cit., vol. 3, p. 228; NCF 767:213 (1939).

48 Wood-Martin, op. cit., p. 156.

49 The belief that trees can take on diseases from people occurs for instance in the Bulgarian tradition of willows having a cure for fever, or the old German and Austrian tradition of fir trees taking on gout. Altman, op. cit., pp. 115–116.

50 Logan (1980), op. cit., p. 118; local information, Ballyvourney May 2004, Doon June 2008.

51 For examples from Cavan see NFC S 978:205; NFC S 990:34; NFC S 995:104; for Monaghan see NFC 1567:238–239 (1960); for Tyrone see Simon, op. cit., vol. 1, pp. 22–23. The tree at Beragh fell c. 1960; there are no remains left.

52 Wood-Martin, op. cit., vol. 2, p. 85; Altman, op. cit., pp. 116, 119; Logan (1980), op. cit., pp. 118–119; Nigel Pennick, *Celtic Sacred Landscapes* (London, 1996), p. 36.

53 In Rome, the offering was initially part of an annual festival; later, it was made in times of pestilence or as atonement for crime. Sidney Hartland, 'Pin Wells and Rag Bushes', in *Folklore* 4, 451–470 (London, 1893), p. 457. A prominent example in France was an old oak called Lapalud near Angers; in Austria, the remnant of a similar tree – Stock-im-Eisen – is still preserved in a glass case in the centre of Vienna; Timisoara in Romania has also an old tree trunk, covered with nails.

54 NFC S 936:166; NFC S 943:447; NFC S 944:47; visit February 2008.

55 Logan (1980), op. cit., pp. 113–114.

56 Local information, visits March 1995 and March 2008. The origin of a monastic settlement at Ardboe is attributed to sixth-century St Colman. Cooper-Foster, op. cit., p. 113; Estyn Evans, *Irish Folk Ways* (London, 1957/1989), p. 303; Simon, op. cit., vol. 1, p. 28; St Clair, op. cit., p. 67; NFC 1159:59, 70 (1948); NFC 891:245 (1942).

57 NFC S 248:314–316; Logan (1980), op. cit., pp. 24–25; local information, visits August 2004 and September 2007.

58 Paterson, op. cit., pp. 127–130; Simon, op. cit., vol. 1, p. 29. At several pin wells in Counties Antrim and Armagh which are not located within a tree, pins are deposited in the water of the well. Antrim: NFC 1361:146, 147 (1953); NFC 1413:356 (1956).

59 Giraldus Cambrensis, *Topographia Hibernica, chap. liv*; ed. James F. Dimock (London 1867), p. 135.

60 Charles Plummer, ed., *Bethada Náem nÉrenn. Lives of Irish Saints* (Oxford, 1968), p. cliii; O'Hanlon, op. cit., vol. 6, p. 316.

61 O'Hanlon, op. cit., vol. 6, p. 36.

62 Edward O'Toole, 'The Holy Wells of Co. Carlow', in *Béaloideas* 4/1 3–23; 107–130 (Dublin, 1933), p. 123; P. J. Hartnett, 'The Holy Wells of East Muskerry', in *Béaloideas* 10 103–130 (Dublin, 1940), pp. 110, 113; NFC 468:20–21 (1934–1937).

63 E. Fitzgerald, 'Proceedings and Papers: St Colman's Tree and Holy Well', in *JRSAI* 4, 40–49 (Dublin, 1856), pp. 41–42.

64 Cork: NFC 466:287 (1934); Kilkenny: NFC 468:115–116 (1934); Kildare: Walter Fitzpatrick, 'Corbally Hill', in *JKAS* 4 (1903–1905), pp. 370–371; Tipperary: Wood-Martin, op. cit., vol. 2, p. 159; Lucas, op. cit., pp. 40–41.

65 Lucas, op. cit., p. 37; Charles Plummer, ed., *Vitae Sanctorum Hiberniae* (Oxford, 1910), vol. 1, pp. 218–219.

66 O'Hanlon, op. cit., vol. 2, p. 206.

67 NFC 463:81–82 (1938).

68 Longford: local information, March 2008; OSL Longford (1838); Limerick: Lucas, op. cit., p. 40; for warning signs see for instance NFC S 945:257, NFC S 950:109.

69 O'Toole, op. cit., pp. 3–23, 107–130; Logan (1980), op. cit., p. 94.

70 NFC 132:130.

71 Anna Rackard and Liam O'Callaghan, *Fishstonewater. Holy Wells of Ireland* (Cork, 2001), p. 108.

Trees of Bardic Inspiration

1 MS of St Gall, in Whitley Stokes and John Strachan, eds., *Thesaurus Paleohibernicus: A Collection of Old-Irish Glosses, Scholia, Prose and Verse* (Cambridge, 1903), vol. 2, p. 290.

2 Dáithí Ó hÓgáin, *The Sacred Isle: Belief and Religion in Pre-Christian Ireland* (Cork, 1999), p. 111; John O'Donovan, *Annála Ríoghachta Éireann. Annals of the Kingdom of Ireland by the Four Masters from the Earlier Period to the Year 1616,* vol. 1 (Dublin, 1848), p. 90.

3 Edward Gwynn, *The Metrical Dindshenchas* 3 (Dublin, 1913), p. 158; Whitley Stokes, ed., 'The Prose Tales of the Rennes Dindshenchas', in *RC* 15 (Paris, 1894), p. 456; Michael Dames, *Mythic Ireland* (London, 1996/1992), pp. 169–170. A fourteenth-century text has King Cormac mac Airt seeking true wisdom at another Well of Segais in Tír Tairngire, the Land of Promise.

4 Dáithí Ó hÓgáin, *Myth, Legend and Romance. An Encyclopaedia of the Irish Folk Tradition* (London, 1990), pp. 326–327.

5 Ó hÓgáin (1990), op. cit., p. 216.

6 Ó hÓgáin (1990), op. cit., p. 115. Niall Mac Coitir, *Irish Trees. Myths, Legends and Folklore* (Cork, 2003), pp. 156–158, suggests a possible derivation from the Welsh word *gogam* for crooked, in reference to Ogham's unique characteristic of being written at angle to edge instead of on a flat surface. The *Auraicept na nEces* suggests a derivation of the script's name from *óg-uaim* for perfect alliteration, or alternatively from the god Oghma.

7 Mac Coitir, op. cit., p. 156.

8 Kuno Meyer, ed., 'Scél Baili Binnbérlaig', in *RC* 13, 220–225 (Paris, 1982), p. 220; a very detailed study of Ogham in Mac Coitir, op. cit., pp. 154–183.

9 Meyer (1982), op. cit., pp. 220–225. This eleventh-century rendition is a variant of the international folktale AD 970.

10 Nathaniel Altman, *Sacred Trees: Spirituality, Wisdom and Well-Being* (New York, 2000), p. 110; Caesar, *Bellum Gallicum*, I 50:4; Tacitus, *Germania*, 10; Alexander Demandt, *Über allen Wipfeln. Der Baum in der Kulturgeschichte* (Köln, 2002/2005), pp. 157–158.

11 John Healy, *Maynooth College. Its Centenary History 1795–1985* (Dublin, 1895); Ben Simon, 'A Review of Notable Yew Trees in Ireland', in *Arboricultural Journal*, vol. 24/2, 97–137 (Bicester, 2000), pp. 109–110.

12 Lady Augusta Gregory, *The Kiltartan Book. Comprising the Kiltartan Poetry, History, and Wonder Books by Lady Gregory* (Gerrards Cross, 1971), pp. 68–69. For the literary tradition see Ó hÓgáin (1990), op. cit., p. 268; Prof. Connellan, ed., 'The Origin of the Harp', in *Transactions of the Ossianic Society for the Year 1857*, 156–166 (Dublin, 1860), pp. 156–157.

13 Gerard Murphy, *Early Irish Lyrics* (Dublin, 1998), pp. 110–119 (translation by J. G. O'Keeffe).

14 Sir Walter Raleigh lived 1554–1618. In 1588 and 1589 he was Mayor of Youghal. In the reign of Elizabeth's son, James I, he was accused of high treason, imprisoned and beheaded. Myrtle Grove is closed to the public. Information plaque at the gates.

15 J. H. Wilks, *Trees of the British Isles in History and Legend* (London, 1972), p. 46, suggests that the tree was a hawthorn; local information, March 2008.

16 Standish Hayes O'Grady, *Silva Gadelica* 1 (London, 1892), pp. 238–252.

17 Ó hÓgáin (1990), op. cit., pp. 364–369.

18 The poem 'Raifterí dall agus an Sceach' or 'Blind Raftery and the Thorn Tree' consists of 99 four-line stanzas, and recounts Ireland's history from prehistoric myths to the Williamite War 1689/1690; full Irish version in Críostóir O'Flynn, *Irish Comic Poems* (Indreabhán Conamara, 1995), pp. 155–165. The exact year of Raftery's birth is uncertain, but was possibly 1779 or 1784; local information, July 2007.

19 Jonathan Swift (1667–1745); Simon, vol. 2, op. cit., pp. 108–109; local information, June 2008.

20 Ben Simon, 'Tree Traditions and Folklore from Northeast Ireland', in *Arboricultural Journal*, vol. 24/1, 15–40 (Bicester, 2000), p. 17.

21 Andrew Morton, *Tree Heritage of Britain and Ireland: A Guide to the Famous Trees of Britain and Ireland* (Ramsbury, Wiltshire, 1998/2004), pp. 190–191; Charles E. Nelson and Wendy F. Walsh, *Trees of Ireland: Native and Naturalized* (Dublin, 1992), p. 111; Gregory, op. cit., pp. 19, 38; local information, October 2003.

Trees of Assembly

1 Edward Gwynn, *The Metrical Dindshenchas* 4 (Dublin, 1924), pp. 241–247; A. T. Lucas, 'The Sacred Trees of Ireland', in *JCHAS* 68, 16–54 (Cork, 1963), pp. 17–23. Ardbraccan lies roughly at the centre of a triangle formed by the three great centres of early Ireland, Tara, Tlachtga and Tailtiu, and is named after St Braccan (Breacain) who died c. 650. When the Ordnance Survey visited Ardbraccan in the 1830s, they noted that local people had no memory at all of the former *bile* in their neighbourhood. OSL Meath (1836), p. 70. Ochann is identical with Faughan Hill, near Navan, County Meath, Tlachtga is modern-day Hill of Ward. Nath Í, or Dáithí, was a historical king who died c. 445; his name means literally 'nephew of yew', figuratively it stands for a champion. The Conaille are probably the sons of Conall mac Suibhne, who slew Aodh Sláine.

2 Elizabeth Fitzpatrick, *Royal Inauguration in Gaelic Ireland c. 1100–1600: A Cultural Landscape Study* (Woodbrigde, 2004), pp. 14–17; see also Estyn Evans, *Irish Folk Ways* (London, 1957/1989), p. 253.

Chieftain Trees and Royal Oaks

1 Edward Gwynn, *The Metrical Dindshenchas* 3 (Dublin, 1913), p. 145.

2 Dáithí Ó hÓgáin, *Myth, Legend and Romance: An Encyclopaedia of the Irish Folk Tradition* (London, 1990), p. 116; Prof. Connellan, ed., *Transactions of the Ossianic Society for the Year 1857* (Dublin, 1860), p. 152 quoting O'Flaherty, *Ogygia*, vol. 2, pp. 207–208.

3 Dáithí Ó hÓgáin, *The Sacred Isle: Belief and Religion in Pre-Christian Ireland* (Cork, 1999), p. 169.

4 Ó hÓgáin (1990), op. cit., pp. 76–77; Gwynn (1913), op. cit., vol. 3, p. 177.

5 A. Martin Freeman, ed., *Annála Connacht. Annals of Connacht* (Dublin, 1944). 'The Fate of the Children of Tuireann' is one of three sorrowful tales of Ireland. In the course of the tale, the brothers Brian, Iuchair and Iucharba have to bring back three apples from the gardens of the Hesperidians. Alwyn and Brinley Rees, *Celtic Heritage: Ancient Tradition in Ireland and Wales* (London, 1961), p. 130.

6 A. T. Lucas, 'The Sacred Trees of Ireland', in *JCHAS* 68, 16–54 (Cork, 1963), p. 20; Myles Dillon, ed., *Serglige Con Culainn* (Columbus/Ohio, 1941), pp. 15, 39.

7 Deirdre and Laurence Flanagan, *Irish Place Names* (Dublin, 1994/2002), pp. 31, 207.

8 The kingdom of Oriel consisted of present-day Counties Armagh and Monaghan, and parts of Counties Louth and Tyrone. Christine Zucchelli, *Stones of Adoration* (Cork, 2007), p. 104; local information, June 2006 and May 2008.

9 On the naming of Magh Adhair see Gwynn (1913), op. cit., vol. 3, p. 443 and Connellan, op. cit., p. 155; Whitley Stokes, ed., 'The Prose Tales of the Dindshenchas', in *RC* 15, 278–336; 418–484 (Paris, 1894), p. 481. On the association with the Dál gCais and O'Brien septs see Elizabeth Fitzpatrick, *Royal Inauguration in Gaelic Ireland c. 1100–1600: A Cultural Landscape Study* (Woodbrigde, 2004), pp. 52, 57–58. The AFM 981 report the destruction for 982, the Annals of Clonmacnoise for 976, the Chronicum Scotorum for 980. The second attack is dated by the Chronicum Scotorum to 1049, by the AFM to 1051.

10 The most significant monument on Crew Hill was a mound; it was levelled in 1981. In 1002, Brian Boru took the high-kingship from Mael Sechlainn. Fitzpatrick, op. cit., pp. 37–38; entries in the AFM, AU and Annals of Inisfallen for the year 1111.

11 Fitzpatrick, op. cit., p. 167 suggests that Clanrickard's Chair or Cathair na nIarla, in Dún Caillin (Dunkellin), County Galway, is possibly the enclosure where the sacred tree of the Uí Fhiachrach Aidhnethe once stood; Lucas, op. cit., p. 26 links the inauguration site with Reevehagh, between Kilcolgan and Ardrahan in County Galway.

12 Lucas, op. cit., p. 93; P. W. Joyce, *Origin and History of Irish Names of Places* (Dublin, 1871), p. 66; P. W. Joyce, *Irish Place Names Explained* (Dublin/London, 1923), p. 500.

13 Information board on site.

14 Charles Plummer, ed., *Bethada Náem nÉrenn. Lives of Irish Saint* (Oxford, 1968), vol. 1, p. 203, vol. 2, pp. 196–197; Fitzpatrick, op. cit., p. 58. In medieval Ireland, Bréifne consisted of modern-day Counties Leitrim, Cavan and parts of Sligo.

15 Mircea Eliade, *The Sacred and the Profane* (London, 1959), pp. 29–44; Fitzpatrick, op. cit., pp. 57–58; Ó hÓgáin (1990), op. cit., p. 172.

16 Painted shields as an aid to recognition in battle were almost certainly used by Celts in Ireland and abroad, but the pattern were not hereditary. In the first half of the twelfth century, knights in continental Europe first began to use markings on their shields to identify themselves in battles and tournaments; with the development of full-body plate armour and helmets, large, clearly identifiable patterns became essential to recognise friend or foe. Coats of arms became hereditary by the end of the thirteenth century. For detailed lists and descriptions of Irish coats of arms and their symbolism see for instance John Grenham, *Clans and Families of Ireland: The Heritage and Heraldry of Irish Clans and Families* (Dublin, 1993) or Micheál Ó Comáin, *The Poolbeg Book of Irish Heraldry* (Swords, 1991). Oak is linked with O'Boyle, O'Callaghan, O'Concannon, O'Conor and O'Connor, O'Donnellan, MacEnchroe (Crowe), O'Flanagan, MacGeraghty, O'Hegarty, Woulfe, Tobin, O'Gara and O'Molloy families. Holly is linked with the arms of O'Dowling, O'Mooney and O'Dunn families. Fruit trees appear on arms of O'Beirnes and O'Morchoes (Murphy). Several coats of arms feature stylised trees that are not identifiable.

17 Oaks can live for up to a thousand years and reach a height of 40 m.

18 Charles II (1630–1685) was King of England, Scotland and Ireland from 1660–1685; Royal Oak Day was formerly called Oak-Apple-Day.

19 Visits September 2007 and February 2008.

20 J. H. Wilks, *Trees of the British Isles in History and Legend* (London, 1972), pp. 164–165. Queen Victoria (1819–1901) reigned from 1837–1901; information by Cormac Foley, Office of Public Works, Killarney, and Frank Lewis, Killarney, August 2008.

Judgement Trees

1 John O'Hanlon, *Lives of the Irish Saints* (Dublin, 1875), vol. 2, p. 547.

2 On the Críth Gablach see D. A. Binchy, ed., 'An Archaic Legal Poem', in *Celtica* 9, 152–168 (Dublin, 1971), p. 152; on myths see Dáithí Ó hÓgáin, *Myth, Legend and Romance: An Encyclopaedia of the Irish Folk Tradition* (London, 1990), pp. 123–124; and Daragh Smyth, *A Guide to Irish Mythology* (Dublin, 1988/1996), pp. 146–147.

3 Fergus Kelly, *A Guide to Early Irish Law* (Dublin, 1988/1998), p. 197; Niall Mac Coitir,

Irish Trees: Myths, Legends and Folklore (Cork, 2003), p. 62.

4 The Annals of Ulster, for instance, report that in the year 745, six criminals were hanged for violating the sanctuary of Downpatrick; Kelly (1988/1998), op. cit., pp. 215–218.

5 Fergus Kelly, 'The Old Irish Tree-List', in *Celtica* 11, 107–124 (Dublin, 1976).

6 Kelly (1976), op. cit., p. 110.

7 Haws are described as food in the 'Dialog of King and Hermit', 21 (see Lucas, op. cit., p. 20) and in 'Buile Suibhne', 58 (see Gerard Murphy, *Early Irish Lyrics* (Dublin, 1998), pp. 110–119).

8 Medieval Wales had similar laws, established by King Howel Dda or Howel the Good and dating from around 1200, albeit without an explicit classification of the trees. Poetry and trees are linked in the Welsh 'Cad Goddeu' or 'Battle of Goddeu', a poetic battle between various letters in the form of trees. Mac Coitir, op. cit., p. 15.

9 Strabo, *Geography*, V, 12.5.1. Strabo lived c. 63 BC to AD 24.

10 '. . . *ibi sententiae capitales de robore proferuntur*.' Alexander Demandt, *Über allen Wipfeln: Der Baum in der Kulturgeschichte* (Köln, 2002/2005) p. 186, assigns the quote to Querolus I:2, Jan De Vries, *Keltische Religionen* (Stuttgart, 1961), p. 189, to the comedy *Aulularia*.

11 O'Hanlon, op. cit., vol. 2, p. 547. Rathin could not be located.

12 OSL Derry (1835/1927), p. 143; Elizabeth Fitzpatrick, *Royal Inauguration in Gaelic Ireland c. 1100–1600: A Cultural Landscape Study* (Woodbrigde, 2004), pp. 16–17; Estyn Evans, *Irish Folk Ways* (London, 1957/1989), p. 253. One of earliest descriptions of trees connected to justice dates back to early Hebrews. Judges 4:5 describes how the prophetess Deborah dwelled under a sacred palm tree when the children of Israel came to her for justice. In medieval France, Germany and Switzerland, trees – particularly oak, elm, linden, chestnut and plane trees – grew in public squares where meetings were held, rents and fees were paid and justice was delivered. Nathaniel Altman, *Sacred Trees: Spirituality, Wisdom and Well-Being* (New York, 2000), p. 145.

13 Edmund Spenser, *A View of the Present State of Ireland*, ed. W. L. Renwick (Oxford, 1970), p. 77.

14 NFC 1176:253–4 (1949); NFC S 1007:103–4; NFC S 1009:14–15, 17, 23; NFC S 1012:145; visit March 1995.

15 Wicklow: Walter Fitzpatrick, 'Corbally Hill', in *JKAS* 4, 370–371 (Kildare, 1903–1905), pp. 357–358; Derry: NFC 1800:362 (1973); Cavan: NFC S 963:311.

16 Cork: NFC 303:254 (1953); Donegal: NFC S 1028:21; NFC S 1035:182.

17 NFC 832:415–416, 457–459 (1942); NFC 922:224–227 (1943); NFC 1023:177 (1947); NFC 1762:326–328 (1969); NFC 1800:527–528 (1972); NFC S 1001:216; NFC S 1011:42; for a similar story from County Monaghan see NFC S 934:243.

18 Iniskeen: NFC S 932:108, 233–234; Wicklow: Edward O'Toole, 'The Holy Wells of Co. Carlow', in *Béaloideas* 4/1, 3–23; 107–130 (Dublin, 1933), p. 122; Carlow: NFC 265:78

(1938). A hanging tree in Killinagh, County Cavan, is named after an old woman who hung herself when she was evicted, NFC 1850:239–241 (1976).

Liberty Trees

1   Kevin Whelan, *The Tree of Liberty: Radicalism, Catholicism and the Construction of Irish Identity 1760–1830* (Cork, 1996), p. 57.

2   Tacitus (c. 55–115 AD), *Annals*, XIV, 30; Cassius Dio (c. 150–235 AD), LXII 7:3.

3   A. T. Lucas, 'The Sacred Trees of Ireland', in *JCHAS* 68, 16–54 (Cork, 1963), p. 19; Myles Dillon, ed., *Serglige Con Culainn* (Columbus/Ohio, 1941), p. *15*; Whitley Stokes, ed., 'The Prose Tales of the Rennes Dindshenchas', in *RC 15*, 272–336; 418–484 (Paris, 1894), pp. 471–472. Dumha-Selca, the Mound of Selc, is a Bronze Age tumulus, in the townland of Carns, not far from the inauguration mound of Carnfree.

4   Cavan: NFC S 991:185; Cork: NFC 651:391, 393 (1939). In the second half of the eighteenth century, common land had been enclosed by landlords; heavy tithes were imposed on potato crops, rents were prohibitive and evictions were a threat. Agrarian societies formed to engage in rural protest. The first of them were the Whiteboys, founded in 1761 in County Tipperary. Although condemned by the Church, agrarian protests spread quickly, and especially in Munster and Ulster, several local secret societies formed, dedicated to defending their members, usually the poorest tenants. See also James Lydon, *The Making of Ireland from Ancient Times to the Present* (London/New York, 1998), pp. 259–263. The Irish Volunteers kept watch for the Black and Tans in 1921 at a tree that stood in Tomiska, County Monaghan (NFC S 929:42). A group of trees near Knocknacarry, in the parish of Layd, County Antrim, reputedly made sounds to warn a group of men from the 'movement' that an RIC troop was approaching (NFC 1102:358 [1948]). A bush in Islandstown, lower Antrim, was used by highwaymen and Orangemen as an assembly point (NFC 1362:158 [1953]).

5   Ben Simon, 'A Review of Notable Yew Trees in Ireland', in *Arboricultural Journal*, vol. 24/2, 97–137 (Bicester, 2000), pp. 104–105.

6   NFC S 936:348, 397; visit February 2008.

7   NFC S 1100:111, told in Cavanacor, County Donegal.

8   Ben Simon, 'Tree Traditions and Folklore from Northeast Ireland', in *Arboricultural Journal*, vol. 24/1, 15–40 (Bicester, 2000), p. 16.

9   J. H. Wilks, *Trees of the British Isles in History and Legend* (London, 1972), p. 71; visit February 2008; the tree has a circumference of some 7 m.

10 Charles E. Nelson and Wendy F. Walsh, *Trees of Ireland: Native and Naturalized* (Dublin, 1992), p. 105; Trevor Carleton, 'Aspects of Local History in Malone, Belfast', in *UJA* 39, 62–67 (Belfast, 1976), p. 65; visit February 2008.

11 Simon, op. cit., vol. 1, p. 16; local information, June 2008.

12 The group fiercely opposed the Stamp Act of 1765 and the Tea Act 1773, which they saw as merely financing the British economy and warfare, and they organised the Boston Tea Party on 16 December 1773.

13 Whelan, op. cit., p. 100.

14 Whelan, op. cit., p. 85, quoting from *Finn's Leinster Journal*, 5–8 August 1795.

15 John Grenham, *Clans and Families of Ireland. The Heritage and Heraldry of Irish Clans and Families* (Dublin, 1993), p. 53.

16 Thomas Pakenham (abridged by Toby Buchan), *The Year of Liberty: The Great Irish Rebellion of 1798* (New York, 1997), p. 188.

17 Pakenham (1997), op. cit., p. 191.

18 Henry Joy McCracken (1767–1798); Ruán O'Donnell, *1798 Diary* (Dublin, 1998), p. 202; Pakenham (1997), op. cit., pp. 171–173.

19 Father John Murphy (1753–1798); O'Donnell, op. cit., p. 203; Pakenham (1997), op. cit., p. 193.

20 O'Donnell, op. cit., p. 201; Pakenham (1997), op. cit., pp. 317, 320.

21 The tree was a black poplar; this species is also known as 'cotton tree' because the seeds are borne on white down resembling cotton, or as *crann critheac* or 'quivering tree' because its leaves rustle in the slightest wind. The former Cotton Tree Pub, opposite where the tree once stood, has changed its name; visit September 2007. Morton, op. cit., pp. 185–186.

Festival Trees

1 NFC S 991:31–32.

2 Samuel Hayes, *A Practical Treatise on Planting and the Management of Woods and Coppices* (Dublin, 1794), p. 11; Andrew Morton, *Tree Heritage of Britain and Ireland: A Guide to the Famous Trees of Britain and Ireland* (Ramsbury, Wiltshire, 1998/2004), p. 196.

3 Morton, op. cit., p. 195; John O'Hanlon, *Lives of the Irish Saints* (Dublin, 1875), vol. 9, p. 399.

4 Remembered into the 1950s, but since lost are, for example, the Fiddler's Bush in the parish of Layd in County Antrim NFC 1387:102 (1955), and another outside Castleblayney in County Monaghan, where a fiddler reputedly sat and played at fair days. NFC S 936:348; NFC S 944:29; NFC S 957:166.

5 NFC S 978:272–273; NFC S 991:31–32, 86–91; NFC S 993:175–178; NFC S 994:235–237.

6 Mr and Mrs Samuel Carter Hall, *Ireland: Its Scenery, Character etc.*, vol. 3 (London, 1843), p. 284, place the village erroneously in County Longford. Charles E. Nelson and Wendy F. Walsh, *Trees of Ireland: Native and Naturalized* (Dublin, 1992), p. 173. In Goldsmith's poem, the village is referred to as Auburn.

7 Ben Simon, 'Tree Traditions and Folklore from Northeast Ireland', in *Arboricultural Journal*, vol. 24/1, 15–40 (Bicester, 2000), p. 22.

8 OSL Louth (1835–1836), pp. 47–48; local information, February 2007.

9 For the Beggar's Bush in Carnaghan, County Donegal, see NFC S 1110:124; for Lousybush in St Canice's Parish, County Wicklow, see Lucas, op. cit., p. 48; for Dublin see Nelson and Walsh, op. cit., p. 175.

10 Michael Dames, *Mythic Ireland* (London, 1996/1992), pp. 192–193; J. H. Wilks, *Trees of the British Isles in History and Legend* (London, 1972), p.200. Information leaflet on Crom Estate; estate open to the public April to September. The trees are English Yews (Taxus baccata) and have a combined circumference of 115 m, and a diameter of 35 m.

Mass Trees

1 Vaughan Cornish, *Historic Thorn Trees in the British Isles* (London, 1941), p. 55.

2 On the Catholic Church during the Cromwellian era, see James Lydon, *The Making of Ireland: From Ancient Times to the Present* (London/New York, 1998), pp. 193–194.

3 On monasteries of the early Celtic Church see Máire and Liam de Paor, *Early Christian Ireland* (London, 1958/1978), pp. 50–51.

4 Local information, June 1998.

5 Laois: A. T. Lucas, 'The Sacred Trees of Ireland', in *JCHAS* 68, 16–54 (Cork, 1963), p. 43; Monaghan: NFC S 933:36; NFC S 937:238; NFC S 948:137, 141; Fermanagh: NFC 1697:76, 206–207 (1966); Donegal: NFC S 1035:204; NFC S 1083:124; NFC S 1086:211; NFC S 1104:89; NFC 169:504–505 (1935); Antrim: NFC 1361:106 (1952); Armagh: NFC 1786:318–319 (1971); Cavan: NFC S 963:530; NFC S 968:144, 157; NFC S 975:243; NFC S 998:12; Kilkenny: J.H. Wilks, *Trees of the British Isles in History and Legend* (London, 1972), p. 108.

6 A. T. Lucas, 'The Sacred Trees of Ireland', in *JCHAS* 68, 16–54 (Cork, 1963), p. 43; Ben Simon, 'Tree Traditions and Folklore from Northeast Ireland', in *Arboricultural Journal*, vol. 24/1, 15–40 (Bicester, 2000), p. 20; Mary Ryan D'Arcy, *The Saints of Ireland: A Chronological Account of the Lives and Works of Ireland's Saints and Missionaries at Home and Abroad* (St Paul/Minnesota, 1974/1985), pp. 190–209; NFC S 953:293.

7 Simon, op. cit., vol. 1, p. 20.

8 Simon, op. cit., vol. 1, pp. 20–21.

9 Local information, visit June 2008.

10 D'Arcy, op. cit., p. 48; NFC S 943:447.

11 NFC S 938:108; NFC S 956;288–290.

12 NFC 974:39 (1942).

13 John Wesley lived 1703–1791, his younger brother Charles 1707–1788.

14 Ben Simon, 'A Review of Notable Yew Trees in Ireland', in *Arboricultural Journal*, vol. 24/2, 97–137 (Bicester, 2000), pp. 116–17; Jon Stokes and Donald Rodger, *The Heritage Trees of Britain and Northern Ireland* (London, 2004), pp. 72–73.

Trees of Life and Death

1   Samuel Hayes, *A Practical Treatise on Planting and the Management of Woods and Coppices* (Dublin, 1794), pp. 139–140. Kennity is modern Kinnitty in County Offaly.

2   The Hesperidins of Greek mythology lived on the Island of the Blessed. A sacred apple tree in their orchard bore golden fruit and was guarded by a serpent coiled around its roots. The Norse gods ate apples to retain their immortality. See also Nathaniel Altman, *Sacred Trees: Spirituality, Wisdom and Well-Being* (New York, 2000), p. 118.

3   Alexander Demandt, *Über allen Wipfeln. Der Baum in der Kulturgeschichte* (Köln, 2002/2005), p.22.

4   Dubhros lies in Hy Ficra, in the barony of Tireragh in County Sligo. The romance appears first in the Book of Leinster, written c. 1130. P. W. Joyce, *Old Celtic Romances, translated from the Gaelic* (Dublin, 1978), pp. 274–350; Dáithí Ó hÓgáin, *Myth, Legend and Romance: An Encyclopaedia of the Irish Folk Tradition* (London, 1990), p. 162.

5   Daragh Smyth, *A Guide to Irish Mythology* (Dublin, 1988/1996), pp. 74–75; Niall Mac Coitir, *Irish Trees: Myths, Legends and Folklore* (Cork, 2003), p. 31.

6   Information plaque on site.

7   Joyce (1978), op. cit., pp. 112–176; Alwyn and Brinley Rees, *Celtic Heritage: Ancient Tradition in Ireland and Wales* (London, 1961), pp. 157–163, 319, 322; Whitley Stokes, ed., 'The Voyage of Mael Dúin', in *RC* 10, 50–95 (Paris, 1889), pp. 72–79. The oldest version of the tale survived in the Book of the Dun Cow, written about 1100. On the literary tradition see Ó hÓgáin (1990), op. cit., pp. 290–291.

8   Ó hÓgáin (1990), op. cit., p. 286; Dáithí Ó hÓgáin, *The Sacred Isle: Belief and Religion in Pre-Christian Ireland* (Cork, 1999), p. 152; Rees, op. cit., pp. 324–325.

9   Ó hÓgáin (1990), op. cit., pp. 123–124; Smyth, op. cit., pp. 146–147.

10 Ó hÓgáin (1990), op. cit., pp. 118, 399; Smyth, op. cit., p. 147.

11 Information on site.

12 Niall Mac Coitir, *Irish Trees: Myths, Legends and Folklore* (Cork, 2003), p. 122; William Gregory Wood-Martin, *Traces of the Elder Faiths in Ireland: A Folklore Sketch. A Handbook of Irish Pre-Christian Traditions*, vols. 1–2 (London/New York/Bombay, 1902).

13 On arboreal origin see Altman, op.cit., pp. 65–66; for Greek examples see Diodorus Zonas (first century BC) and Hesiod, *Werke und Tage*, c. 145; for Roman examples see Virgil (70–19 BC), *Aeneid*, VIII 314–316; for Scandinavia see Demandt, op. cit., p. 154.

14 Rhona Fogarty, *Rooted in Folklore: A Study of Native Tree Lore in Ireland* (unpubl.) Dipl. Thesis, Department of Irish Folklore, University College Dublin, 2005), p. 10; Mac Coitir, op. cit., p. 38.

15 A. T. Lucas, 'The Sacred Trees of Ireland', in *JCHAS* 68, 16–54 (Cork, 1963), p. 279.

16 David Hickie and Mike O'Toole, *Native Trees and Forests of Ireland* (Dublin, 2002), p. 78.

17   Michael Dames, *Mythic Ireland* (London, 1996/1992), pp. 98–100; Myles Dillon, ed., 'The Yew of the Disputing Sons', in *Ériu* 14, pp. 154–165 (Dublin, 1946); local information.

18   Historical records of an oak forest reach back to c. 1600, when the lands of Tullamore were granted to Sir John Moore under the plantation of James I. Andrew Morton, *Tree Heritage of Britain and Ireland: A Guide to the Famous Trees of Britain and Ireland* (Ramsbury, Wiltshire, 1998/2004), pp. 192–193; Thomas Pakenham, *Meetings with Remarkable Trees* (London, 1996/2003), p. 27; visit March 2008.

19   The Ulaidh called themselves Rudhraighe. Early on, the name was misinterpreted as containing *ruadh* for red, hence the palace in Eamhain Mhacha was called An Chraobhruadh, meaning red-branches or red-poled edifice. Ó hÓgáin (1990), op. cit., p. 413.

20   Dillon, op. cit., pp. 154–165; Ó hÓgáin (1990), op. cit., pp. 20–21. The language of the poem assigns it to the twelfth century.

21   Dillon, op. cit., pp. 154–165.

22   Aubrey Burl, *Rites of the Gods* (London/Melbourne/Toronto, 1981), p. 206; Altman, op. cit., p. 70; Demandt, op. cit., p. 306 refers to tree burial in Celtic and Germanic societies, but does not give any further information.

23   In 1838, the ash was described by John O'Donovan in his Ordnance Survey letters relating to the County of Galway. It has long decayed since, and its memory is lost.

24   In the register of international tale-types, the narrative is listed under the number AT 970. Beautiful Iseult was married against her will to Mark, King of Cornwall. A potion meant to make her fall in love with her husband was drunk by Mark's nephew Tristan, and consequently Iseult and Tristan fell in love. The doomed lovers finally died in each other's arms, and were buried above Merlin's Cave at Tintagel Castle in Cornwall. Within a year, a tree sprouted from each grave and though Mark repeatedly cut the trees, they kept growing back, and they were eventually left alone. Soon the branches became so entwined that it was impossible to part them. Kuno Meyer, ed., 'Scél Baili Binnbérlaig, in *RC* 13, 220–225 (Paris, 1982), Ó hÓgáin (1990), op. cit., p. 43. Tradition has it that the tablets were destroyed when Tara was raided and burnt.

25   Vernam Hull, ed., *Longes mac n-Uislenn* (New York, 1949); Ó hÓgáin (1990), op. cit., pp. 155–156.

26   Ó hÓgáin (1990), op. cit., p. 392; John O'Hanlon, *Lives of the Irish Saints* (Dublin, 1875), vol. 9, pp. 474–475, refers to an ancient MacDermott castle on one of the islands on Lough Key.

27   NFC 911:282–288 (1943); Sean O'Sullivan, *The Folklore of Ireland* (London, 1974), pp. 83–86.

28   Prof. Connellan, ed., *Transactions of the Ossianic Society for the Year 1857* (Dublin, 1860), p. 154; Lucas, op. cit., p. 34.

29   Such offerings have been discovered in France, Switzerland and Britain. The most important find consists of some five thousand votive figurines and comes from a pagan sacred spring

near Les Roches in France. Altman, op. cit., p. 98. The Children of Lir were changed into swans by the touch of a wand made of yew.

30   Giraldus Cambrensis, *Topographia Hibernia,* ed. James F. Dimock (London 1867), pp. 135, 152.

31   Charles Plummer, ed., *Bethada Náem nÉrenn* (Oxford, 1968), p. ciii.

32   Wakeman (1892), op. cit., pp. 101–106.

33   Ben Simon, 'A Review of Notable Yew Trees in Ireland', in *Arboricultural Journal,* vol. 24/2, 97–137 (Bicester, 2000), pp. 123–124; W. F. Wakeman, 'Ante-Norman Churches in the County of Dublin', in *JRSAI* 22, 101–106 (Dublin, 1892).

34   Cary Meehan, *The Traveller's Guide to Sacred Ireland* (Glastonbury, 2002), p. 433; visit October 2007.

35   NFC S 982:334; NFC S 1005:25–26; Morton, op. cit., p. 193; information board on site.

36   Visit February 2008.

37   J. Weisweiler, 'Vorindogermanische Schichten der Irischen Heldensage', in *ZCP* 24; 165–197 (Tübingen, 1954), p. 172.

38   By the eighteenth century, landscaped parks and arboreta, or collections of impressive native and imported trees, had become status symbols of the gentry.

39   St Augustine (354–430) was Bishop of Hippo in North Africa and one of the four great fathers of Christendom.

40   The Councils of Trent (1545–1563) and Vatican I (1869–1870) stuck to the old, restrictive laws on burial in consecrated ground.

41   Susan Leigh Fry, *Burial in Medieval Ireland 900–1500: A Review of the Written Sources* (Dublin, 1999).

42   Máire MacNeill, *The Festival of Lughnasa* (Dublin, 1962/1982), pp. 642–643; OSL Tipp III, (1840), pp. 195–205; G. Nuttall Smith, 'Holy Well and Antiquities near Cahir, Co. Tipperary', in *JRSAI* 29, 258–259 (Dublin, 1899), p. 258. The shrine is still popularly visited between 18 and 26 February; local information, visits May 2004 and January 2008.

43   Estyn Evans, *Prehistoric and Early Christian Ireland: A Guide* (London, 1966), pp. 33–34; Charles Thomas, *Britain and Ireland in Early Christian Times. AD 400–800* (London, 1971), pp. 105–111. Early Christian cemeteries, usually small burial grounds for neighbourhoods and families, were often by the roadside, outside the settlements. From the seventh and eighth centuries onwards, small chapels of timber were added, and from 700 onwards, chapels of stone.

44   O'Hanlon, op. cit., vol. 9, pp. 413–414.

45   Information board on site.

46   Kerry: NFC 28:147 (1938); Laois: NFC 38:175–177.

47   Ó hÓgáin (1990), op. cit., p. 237.

48   Mr and Mrs Samuel Carter Hall, *Ireland: Its Scenery, Character etc.,* vol. 2 (London, 1842), pp. 439–440; visit June 2008.

49 Cushendun, County Antrim: NFC 1363:180 (1954); Lisnaskea, County Fermanagh: NFC 1697:206–207 (1966); Deirdre Ó Brien, *Children's Burial Grounds in East Clare: A Neglected Heritage. A study of the awareness and curation of Cillíns in East County Clare* (unpubl. thesis, Mayo Institute of Technology, Galway, 2003), pp. 36–37; Sliabh Aughty, 1991, p. 4.

50 O'Hanlon, op. cit., vol. 1, pp.220, 297–298; vol. 7, p. 47.

51 In Kiltober, in County Fermanagh (NFC 467:67 (1934); NFC S 947:339), monks planted a whitethorn bush to mark the spot where one of their brothers was killed by a collapsing wall. In County Laois (NFC 652:80–81, 84–88, 90–91, 98 [1939]), it was customary to mark the site of a fatal accident or a murder with a small 'monument tree'. The Whiteboy's Bush in County Cork (NFC 651:391, 393 [1939]), the Soldier's Bush near Ballintemple in County Cavan (NFC S 991:185), and memorial trees in Rosnakill in County Donegal (NFC S 1090:304) and in Gleagh, County Monaghan (NFC S 950:368) remember the victims of battles. Trees such as Dolly's Bush in Ballymoe, County Galway (NFC 653:520–521 [1939]) and Taylor's Bush near Glendun, County Antrim (NFC 1232:165 [1952]) recall the sudden deaths of locals.

52 Estyn Evans, *Irish Folk Ways* (London, 1957/1989), pp. 292–293.

53 A line of trees is reported to have existed but is long forgotten by most in Kilnaleck, County Cavan (NFC S 994:103, 250). Two ash trees, known as the Coffin Trees, at Ballyquin Cross near Mullinavat in County Kilkenny were conventional resting places for funeral processions. J. H. Wilks, *Trees of the British Isles in History and Legend* (London, 1972), p. 109.

54 Nigel Pennick, *Celtic Sacred Landscapes* (London, 1996), p. 135.

55 William Shaw-Mason, *Parochial Survey of Ireland* (Dublin, 1819), vol. 3, p. 515; Longford: NFC 652:294, 312–313 (1939); Westmeath: NFC 652:191 (1939), Dublin: Lucas, op. cit., p. 44; Meath: OSL Meath (1838), pp. 125, 290, 294. For cairns at funeral stops in County Galway see for instance NFC 652:73 (1939); NFC S 978:272; Bweeounagh: OSL Galway 1 (1838), pp. 81–82; Offaly: Morton, op. cit., p. 196; Samuel Hayes, *A Practical Treatise on Planting and the Management of Woods and Coppices* (Dublin, 1794), pp. 139–140; Laois: O'Hanlon, op. cit., vol. 9, p. 413; Mac Coitir, op. cit., p.124. Kennely is identical with Kinnitty. The venerated ash and the memory of its former significance are long lost.

56 Margaret Stokes, 'Funeral Customs in the Baronies of Bargy and Forth, County Wexford' in *JRSAI* 24, 380–385 (1894), p. 381; Lucas, op. cit., p. 44.

57 William Shaw-Mason, *Parochial Survey of Ireland* (Dublin, 1814), vol. 1, pp. 41–42; Vaughan Cornish, *Historic Thorn Trees in the British Isles* (London, 1941), pp. 53–54; local information, visit May 2007.

Fairy Trees and Gentle Bushes

1 William Gregory Wood-Martin, *Traces of the Elder Faiths in Ireland: A Folklore Sketch. A*

Handbook of Irish Pre-Christian Traditions, vols. 1–2 (London/New York/Bombay, 1902), vol. 2, p. 156.

2   In Scandinavian tradition, fairies are thought to have the same origin as humans, and therefore salvation is possible. A popular tale has a person passing a fairy mound and hearing the fairies sing songs of their hope for salvation. The person tells them that their salvation was as likely as the stick he was carrying bearing flowers and leaves. The following day, however, the miracle occurs, and the dry stick sprouts leaves and flowers. Reidar Th. Christiansen, 'Some Notes on the Fairies and the Fairy Faith', in *Béaloideas* 39–41, 95–111 (Dublin, 1975), pp. 100–101; see also Patrick Logan, *The Old Gods: The Facts about Irish Fairies* (Belfast, 1981), p. 16; Dáithí Ó hÓgáin, *Myth, Legend and Romance: An Encyclopaedia of the Irish Folk Tradition* (London, 1990), pp. 187–188.

3   Séamus Ó Duilearga, *Leabhair Shéan Uí Chonaill. Seán Ó Conaill's Book* (Dublin, 1948/1981), p. 312.

4   The lore of fairies is sometimes mixed with the lore of the ghosts and spirits of the dead. Ó hÓgáin (1990), op. cit., p. 237.

5   NFC 1743:42 (1966). Today, the term is sometimes loosely used to describe any old bush growing on its own, or marking a burial site, or standing at a holy well.

6   Myles Dillon, ed., *Serglige Con Culainn* (Columbus/Ohio, 1941), pp. 15–16, 39–40.

7   Ó hÓgáin (1990), op. cit., p. 302; Daragh Smyth, *A Guide to Irish Mythology* (Dublin, 1988/1996), pp. 121–122.

8   Mongán was killed in AD 624. Eugene O' Curry, *Lectures on the Manuscript Materials of Ancient Irish History* (Dublin, 1873), p. 621; Ó hÓgáin (1990), op. cit., p. 274. Lugh is said to have been reared in Eamhain Abhlach, the Region of Apples.

9   William Butler Yeats, *Fairy and Folk Tales of Ireland* (Gerrards Cross, 1973), pp. 275–285; Ó hÓgáin (1990), op. cit., p. 207; Yeats, op. cit., pp. 177–222.

10   Johann G. Kohl, *Ireland, Scotland and England* (London, 1844), pp. 16–17.

11   For a detailed study see for example Matthew Stout, *The Irish Ringfort* (Dublin 1997/2000). Early Irish laws indicate that large bivallete forts were the home of kings, while the smaller and simpler ones were built for the lesser ranks of society, and some were possibly merely cattle enclosures. Hill forts were apparently uninhabited for periods of time, and may have been assembly places.

12   The Viking period in Ireland began in 795 with the Norse raid of Lambeg Island in Dublin Bay and the plundering of the monastic settlements of Inishmurray and Inisbofin off the west coast. It ended in 1014 with the Battle of Clontarf. Yeats, op. cit., p. 288.

13   Peter Harbison, *Guide to National Monuments in Ireland* (Dublin, 1979), p. 25.

14   In 1968 in County Donegal, a proposed road from Ballintra to Rossnowlagh was realigned to bypass a tree that was locally revered as the Fairy Tree. According to local information, gathered in June 2008, the tree was recognisable as a fairy tree because it never blossomed.

J. H. Wilks, *Trees of the British Isles in History and Legend* (London, 1972), p. 109; local information, visit June 2008.

15 Dermot A. MacManus, *The Middle Kingdom: The Faerie World of Ireland* (Gerrards Cross, 1973), p. 32; local information, visit November 2007.

16 Eddie Lenihan and Carolyn Eve Green, *Meeting the Other Crowd: The Fairy Stories of Hidden Ireland* (Dublin, 2003); newspaper clippings in the archive of Clare Local Studies Centre, Ennis.

17 In the First Battle of Moytirra of Cong, the Tuatha Dé Danann fought the Fir Bolg, and in the Second Battle of Moytirra, they fought the demonic race of the Fomorians. Finally, several decisive battles between the Tuatha Dé Danann and the Sons of Míl brought about the beginning of Celtic rule in Ireland. Johann G. Kohl, *Ireland, Scotland and England* (London, 1844), p. 35.

18 NFC S 1110:180–181.

19 Tyrone: NFC 1221:39 (1951); Down: NFC 1567:88 (1960).

20 MacManus, op. cit., p. 61.

21 NFC S 1028:41.

22 *Ireland's Own* (1929), vol. 43, p. 14; catalogue of the NFC, Dublin; Monaghan: NFC S 929:51–52; Clare: Lenihan, op. cit., pp. 115–119.

23 NFC 1569:67 (1962). Nine years later, the joke was recalled as the story of a tree that actually bled when it was cut (NFC 1786:319 [1971]).

24 NFC 939:417 (1943) from Hilltown, County Down.

25 Yeats (1973), op. cit., pp. 41–43.

26 Lisbanlemneigh, County Tyrone: NFC 971:491 (1945); The Bay, County Antrim: NFC 1386:10 (1955); Miltown Malbay, County Clare: Lenihan, op. cit., p. 121, collected in 1999; Ó Duilearga, op. cit., pp. 273–274.

27 NFC 1215:135–136 (1949); W. S. Cordner, 'Some Old Wells in Antrim and Down', in *UJA* 5, 90–95 (Belfast, 1942), pp. 91–92.

28 NFC 257:236–237 (1936) from County Galway; for Derry see NFC 1220:340 (1951); for Meath (2000) see Lenihan, op. cit., p. 119.

29 Newtown, County Down: NFC 976:226 (1945).

30 Crossreagh, County Cavan: NFC S 973:129.

31 The fairies' wrath, however, seems to linger on the place, and Killeadan House has almost reached a state beyond repair. MacManus, op. cit., pp. 54–56; visit August 2007.

32 MacManus, op. cit., pp. 61–63.

33 Lenihan, op. cit., pp. 119–120. Local tradition.

34 The DeLorean sports car gained worldwide fame, however, in the *Back to the Future* movies. Plans to go back into production were made in 2007, and since 2008, updated customised versions of DeLorean cars are available from the plant in Houston. www.delorean-dmc12.co.uk.

35 Yeats, op. cit., pp. 307–308; NFC S 1031:296.

36 P. W. Joyce, *Origin and History of Irish Names of Places* (Dublin, 1871), p. 519.

37 Drumlane and Cloncovet, both in County Cavan: NFC S 972:7; NFC S 988:65, 142.

38 The derivation of the word *luprachán* from the Irish compound *leith bhrogan* for the 'one-shoemaker', as suggested by Douglas Hyde in William Butler Yeats, *Fairy and Folk Tales of Ireland* (Gerrards Cross, 1973), p. 75, is no longer accepted. An etymological relation with Lugh, who has some traditional link with shoemaking (MacNeill, op. cit., p. 665) is also questionable. For the derivation of the term see Ó hÓgáin (1990), op. cit., p. 270; Logan (1981), op. cit., p. 68.

39 Muineal, County Cavan: NFC S 966:352.

40 Scotstown, County Monaghan: NFC S 954:136.

41 Kohl, op. cit., pp. 16–17.

42 The tale is listed under the number AT 1645 in Antti Aarne and Stith Thompson, *The Types of the Folktale: A Classification and Bibliography* (Helsinki, 1973).

43 Drumgoon, County Cavan: NFC 791:144–146 (1941).

44 Thomas Johnson Westropp, *A Folklore Survey of County Clare and County Clare Folk-Tales and Myths* (Dublin, 1910–1913), ed. Maureen Comber, CLASP (Ennis, 2000), p. 76.

Conclusion: Sacred Trees and Tree Monuments in Modern Ireland

1 Local information, October 2007 and August 2008.

2 For a comprehensive study of modern Paganism, see for instance Ronald Hutton, *The Triumph of the Moon: A History of Modern Pagan Witchcraft* (Oxford, 1999).

3 www.crann.tcd.ie; www.treecouncil.ie; the Tree Register of Ireland was set up in 1999.

Glossary

Aetiological – 'explanatory'. From the Greek words *aitia* for cause and *logos* for word. Aetiological tales are stories that explain the origin of natural features.

Bile – old Irish term for a sacred tree, venerated for various reasons; plural *biledha*. In modern Irish the word is no longer used.

Bronze Age – began in Ireland c. 2500 BC with the introduction of metal work. The early phase of the Bronze Age overlapped with the late Neolithic and lasted until c. 2000 BC. During this time, metal gradually replaced stone as the major raw material. The Bronze Age may have lasted until c. 700 BC.

Bullaun – a stone with one or more oval or round depressions of artificial or natural origin.

Cairn – a heap or mound of stones covering a megalithic structure, or deposited at shrines, holy wells, mountain passes and funeral stopping places.

Celtic Church – common term for the early Christian Church in Ireland. Soon after the introduction of Christianity in the fifth century, the Celtic Church deviated from Roman principles and developed structurally and spiritually into a largely independent organisation.

Clootie tree – a sacred tree or bush that has offerings of mainly clothes and rags tied to its branches. Also known as rag tree.

Cosmic or world tree – mythical tree representing the universe and the perpetual cycle of life, death and recreation. Anciently known in many cultures around the world, the cosmic tree was understood to stand at the centre of the earth, linking the human world with the heavenly realms of the divine and the underground abodes of the dead.

Craobh – literally 'a branch'. Occurs in medieval Irish literature as an alternative for *bile* to denote a sacred tree.

Danes – term used in folklore to describe the Viking invaders of Ireland. The Viking period lasted from the late eighth century to the defeat of the Vikings in the Battle of Clontarf in 1014.

Dindshenchas – twelfth-century collection of older poems and prose tales which explain the place names of Ireland.

Fir Bolg – mythical inhabitants of Ireland, said to have come from Greece. They divided Ireland into provinces, marked the centre with the 'Stone of Division', and established the system of sacral kingship.

Gaelic – term used to distinguish the language and traditions of the Celtic inhabitants of Ireland from the culture of Anglo-Normans and English, who began their conquest of Ireland in the twelfth century.

Gothic – architectural style of the late twelfth century. Characteristics are pointed arches and elaborately decorated altar tombs.

Hill fort – stone enclosure of the Iron Age, encircling the summit of a hill. The original function of hill forts is not fully understood. They may have been assembly places. Since some hill forts enclose older Bronze Age burial mounds, it is possible that they were linked with earlier burial cults. Folklore often associates them with fairies.

Iron Age – began about 700-600 BC, when iron replaced bronze as raw material for tools and weaponry. Ended with the introduction of Christianity in the fifth century AD.

King's County – eighteenth-century name for County Offaly.

La Tène – ornamental style of the Continental Celts of the last five centuries BC. The style is named after a bay in Lake Neufchatel in Switzerland, where a great deposit of Celtic artefacts was discovered.

Leabhar Gabhála Éireann (Leabhar Gabhála) – the Book of Invasions of Ireland. A compilation of pseudo-historical texts which reconstruct the conquest of the country by successive groups of peoples.

Lughnasa – ancient harvest festival at the start of August.

Megalithic – from the Greek words *mega* for large and *lithos* for stone. Term to describe the massive stone monuments of the Neolithic and Bronze Age.

Milesians – also called Sons of Míl. The first Celtic settlers in Ireland, according to myth. They came from Asia Minor and had to defeat the divine race of the Tuatha Dé Danann to gain possession of the country.

Motte – Norman fortification. A high circular mound of earth with a flattened top, originally crowned by a wooden tower.

Neolithic – also called late Stone Age. From the Greek words *neo* for new and *lithos* for stone. The Neolithic may have lasted from c. 4000-2500 BC. In the last phase, the Neolithic overlapped with the early Bronze Age.

Ogham – earliest form of written Irish. Ogham was in use from about the fourth until the seventh or eighth century AD.

Pagan – 'pagan' in the text is used to denote pre-Christian religions, while 'Pagan' stands for the modern spiritual movement.

Pattern – a communal pilgrimage on a particular day. The term derives from the Irish word *pátrún* for patron saint.

Queen's County – eighteenth-century name for County Laois.

Ring barrow – burial mound of late Bronze and early Iron Age, often on hill tops. In folklore frequently described as fairy mound or fairy fort.

Ring fort – archaeological term for an early Christian enclosed farmstead or homestead, in Irish known as *rath* (fort), *dún* (fort) or *lios* (enclosure). Some 45,000 ring forts exist in Ireland; most of them date from the early seventh to the late ninth century. The circular or penannular enclosures were protected by one or two banks, or walls of earth or stone, and an outer ditch.

Romanesque – style of architecture of the early twelfth century. Characteristic features are rounded arches and elaborate carvings.

Rosary – a prayer series of five decades of 'Hail Marys', beginning with an 'Our Father' and ending with a 'Gloria'.

Round – (Irish *an turas*). Prescribed sacred journey, usually in clockwise direction, between the praying stations of a shrine. The phrase 'doing the rounds' stands for making a pilgrimage.

Stations – stages along a pilgrimage route or round. Typically marked by stones, trees or crosses, where people stop to pray and perform certain prescribed rites.

Tuatha Dé Danann – 'the People of the Goddess Danu'. Mythical divine inhabitants of prehistoric Ireland. They fought and defeated the Fir Bolg and the Fomorians, but were later forced to submit to the Celtic Milesians.

Turas – see 'Round'.

Abbreviations

AFM: Annals of the Four Masters

AT: Index of International Folktales by Antti Aarne and Stith Thompson

AU: Annals of Ulster

JCHAS: *Journal of the Cork Historical and Archaeological Society*

JKAS: *Journal of the Kildare Archaeological Society*

JRSAI: *Journal of the Royal Society of Antiquaries in Ireland*

NFC: National Folklore Collection (formerly Irish Folklore Collection) in the UCD Delargy Centre for Irish Folklore, University College Dublin

NFCS: National Folklore Collection's Schools' Manuscript Collection (compiled 1937–1938) in the UCD Delargy Centre for Irish Folklore, University College Dublin

OSL: Ordnance Survey Letters

OSM: Ordnance Survey Memoirs

PRIA: *Proceedings of the Royal Irish Academy*

RC: *Revue Celtique*

UFTM: Material from the Ulster Folk and Transport Museum Archive, Bangor, County Down

UJA: *Ulster Journal of Archaeology*

ZCP: *Zeitschrift für Celtische Philologie*

Picture Credits

The photographs on the cover and spine, and on pages 6, 18, 26, 63, 71, 112, 113, 125, 134, 140, 153, 183, 210, 214 are by Daniela Deutsch. All remaining photos are by the author.

The black and white drawings are taken from the following sources:

P. x   John O'Hanlon, *Lives of the Irish Saints*, vols. 1–9 (Dublin, 1875)

P. xvii   Anon, *Arboretum et Fructicetum* (London 1844)

P. 4   (Motte of Killeshin): John O'Hanlon, *Lives of the Irish Saints*, vols. 1–9 (Dublin, 1875)

P. 8   (Patrick's Ash, Tamlaght): John O'Hanlon, *Lives of the Irish Saints*, vols. 1–9 (Dublin, 1875)

P. 20   (Derryloran): John O'Hanlon, *Lives of the Irish Saints*, vols. 1–9 (Dublin, 1875)

P. 24   (Maelruan's): John O'Hanlon, *Lives of the Irish Saints*, vols. 1–9 (Dublin, 1875)

P. 34   (St Fiachna's, Garranes): Mr and Mrs Samuel Carter Hall, *Ireland: Its Scenery, Character, etc*, vols. 1–3 (London, 1841–1843)

P. 41   (Coppicing): Samuel Hayes, *A Practical Treatise on Planting and the Management of Woods and Coppices* (Dublin, 1794)

P. 52   (Toberara): John O'Hanlon, *Lives of the Irish Saints*, vols. 1–9 (Dublin, 1875)

P. 64   (Castelkieran): Wood-Martin, W. G., *Traces of the Elder Faiths in Ireland: A Folklore Sketch. A Handbook of Irish Pre-Christian Traditions*, vols. 1–2 (London/New York/Bombay, 1902)

P. 72   (Rag Tree, Tubber Grieve): Mr and Mrs Samuel Carter Hall, *Ireland: Its Scenery, Character, etc*, vols. 1–3 (London, 1841–1843)

P. 84   (Luggella): John O'Hanlon, *Lives of the Irish Saints*, vols. 1–9 (Dublin, 1875)

P. 85   (Borrisokane): Wood-Martin, W. G., *Traces of the Elder Faiths in Ireland: A Folklore Sketch. A Handbook of Irish Pre-Christian Traditions*, vols. 1–2 (London/New York/Bombay, 1902)

P. 96   (Raleigh): Mr and Mrs Samuel Carter Hall, *Ireland: Its Scenery, Character, etc*, vols. 1–3 (London, 1841–1843)

P. 114   (Magh Adhair): Thomas Johnson Westropp, *A Folklore Survey of County Clare and County Clare Folk-Tales and Myths* (Dublin, 1910–1913)

P. 150   (Ash of Leix): Samuel Hayes, *A Practical Treatise on Planting and the Management of Woods and Coppices* (Dublin, 1794)

P. 153   (Yews of Crom): Cavanensis, 'Ancient Yew' in *Gardeners' Chronicle* 12, (n.p., 1845)

P. 171   (rowan): Anon, *Arboretum et Fructicetum* (London 1844)

P. 184   (Palmerstown): W. F. Wakeman, 'Ante-Norman Churches in the County of Dublin', in *JRSAI* 22, 101–106 (Dublin, 1892).

P. 190   (Monadrehid): John O'Hanlon, *Lives of the Irish Saints*, vols. 1–9 (Dublin, 1875)

P. 192   (Caillemote's grave): Mr and Mrs Samuel Carter Hall, *Ireland: Its Scenery, Character, etc*, vols. 1–3 (London, 1841–1843)

P. 201   (Farranglogh): Eugene Conwell, *Discovery of the Tomb of Ollamh Fodhla* (Dublin, 1873)

P. 204   (Fairy Mound, Louth): John O'Hanlon, *Lives of the Irish Saints*, vols. 1–9 (Dublin, 1875)

P. 213   (Fairy Mound, Clontarf): John O'Hanlon, *Lives of the Irish Saints*, vols. 1–9 (Dublin, 1875)

P. 218   (Leprechaun): Mr and Mrs Samuel Carter Hall, *Ireland: Its Scenery, Character, etc*, vols. 1–3 (London, 1841–1843)

Bibliography

Aarne, Antti and Thompson, Stith, *The Types of the Folktale: A Classification and Bibliography* (Helsinki, 1973)

Altman, Nathaniel, *Sacred Trees: Spirituality, Wisdom & Well-Being* (New York, 2000)

Bartlett, William Henry, *The Scenery and Antiquities of Ireland* (London, 1842)

Best, R. I., ed., 'The Settling of the Manor of Tara', *Ériu* 4, 121–172 (Dublin/London, 1910)

Bigger, Francis Joseph, 'The Lake and Church of Kilmakilloge, the Ancient Church, Holy Well, and Bullán-stone of Temple Feaghna, and the Holy Well and Shrine of St Finan's, Co. Kerry', *JRSAI* 28, 314–324 (Dublin, 1898)

Bigger, Francis Joseph, 'Inis Clothrana (Inis Cleraun), Lough Ree: Its History and Antiquities', *JRSAI* 30, 69–90 (Dublin, 1900)

Binchy, D. A., ed., 'An Archaic Legal Poem', *Celtica* 9, 152–168 (Dublin, 1971)

Bradley, Thomas and Walsh, John R., *A History of the Irish Church 400–700 AD* (Dublin, 2003)

Brand, Susan H., ed., *Civil War (Pharsalia)* by Lucan (Oxford, 1992)

Burl, Aubrey, *Rites of the Gods* (London/Melbourne/Toronto, 1981)

Carleton, Trevor, 'Aspects of Local History in Malone, Belfast', *UJA* 39, 62–67 (Belfast, 1976)

Cavanensis, 'Ancient Yew' in *Gardeners' Chronicle* 12, 187 (n.p., 1845)

Christiansen, Reidar Th., 'Some Notes on the Fairies and the Fairy Faith', *Béaloideas* 39–41, 95–111 (Dublin, 1975)

Christiansen, Reidar Th. and Ó Súilleabhán, Seán, *The Types of the Irish Folk-Tale* (Helsinki, 1963)

Connellan, Prof., ed., *Transactions of the Ossianic Society for the Year 1857* (Dublin, 1860)

Connolly, Seán J., *Priests and People in Pre-Famine Ireland, 1780–1845* (Dublin, 1982/2001)

Cooper-Foster, Jeanne, *Ulster Folklore* (Belfast, 1951)

Cordner, W. S., 'Some Old Wells in Antrim and Down', *UJA* 5, 90–95 (Belfast, 1942)

Cornish, Vaughan, *Historic Thorn Trees in the British Isles* (London, 1941)

Cornish, Vaughan, *The Churchyard Yew and Immortality* (London, 1946)

Cowell, John, *Sligo – Land of Yeats' Desire: History, Literature, Folklore, Landscape* (Dublin, 1990)

Dames, Michael, *Mythic Ireland* (London, 1992/1996)

Danaher, Kevin, *The Year in Ireland: A Calendar* (Cork, 1972)

D'Arcy, Mary Ryan, *The Saints of Ireland: A Chronological Account of the Lives and Works of Ireland's Saints and Missionaries at Home and Abroad* (St Paul/Minnesota, 1974/1985)

Demandt, Alexander, *Über allen Wipfeln: Der Baum in der Kulturgeschichte* (Köln, 2002/2005)

de Paor, Liam, *Saint Patrick's World: The Christian Culture of Ireland's Apostolic Age* (Dublin, 1993)

de Paor, Máire and Liam, *Early Christian Ireland* (London, 1958/1978)

de Vries, Jan, *Keltische Religionen* (Stuttgart, 1961)

Dimock, James F., ed., *Giraldi Cambrensis Opera V. Giraldi Cambrensis Topographia Hibernica* (London, 1867)

Dillon, Myles, ed., *Serglige Con Culainn* (Columbus/Ohio, 1941)

Dillon, Myles, ed., 'The Yew of the Disputing Sons', *Ériu* 14, 154–165 (Dublin, 1946)

Dutton, Hely, *A Statistical Survey of the County of Clare* (Dublin, 1808)

Eliade, Mircea, *The Sacred and the Profane* (London, 1959)

Evans, Estyn, *Irish Folk Ways* (London, 1957/1989)

Evans, Estyn, *Prehistoric and Early Christian Ireland. A Guide* (London, 1966)

Feehan, John, 'The Spirit of Trees', *Releafing Ireland: Millenium Issue*, vol. 48, 15–21 (Banagher, 1999)

Ferguson, Samuel, 'On the Ceremonial Turn, called Desiul', in *PRIA* 1, 355–364 (Dublin, 1879)

Fitzgerald, E., 'Proceedings and Papers: St Colman's Tree and Holy Well', *JRSAI* 4, 40–49 (Dublin, 1856)

Fitzgerald, Walter, 'Miscellanea', *JRSAI* 22, 188, 307 (Dublin, 1892)

Fitzpatrick, Elizabeth, *Royal Inauguration in Gaelic Ireland c. 1100–1600: A Cultural Landscape Study* (Woodbridge, 2004)

Fitzpatrick, Walter, 'Corbally Hill', *JKAS* 4, 370–371 (Kildare, 1903–1905)

Flanagan, Deirdre and Laurence, *Irish Place Names* (Dublin, 1994/2002)

Fogarty, Rhona, *Rooted in Folklore: A Study of Native Tree Lore in Ireland* (unpubl. dipl. thesis, Department of Irish Folklore, University College Dublin, Dublin, 2005)

Frazer, James George, *The Golden Bough: A Study in Magic and Religion* (London, 1974)

Freeman, A. Martin, ed., *Annála Connacht. Annals of Connacht* (Dublin, 1944)

Fry, Susan Leigh, *Burial in Medieval Ireland 900–1500: A Review of the Written Sources* (Dublin, 1999)

Garvey, Seán and O'Reilly, Barry, *Legends of Hidden Treasures: A Preliminary Type Catalogue* (unpubl. typescript, DIF, Dublin, 1986)

Giraldus Cambrensis, *Topographia Hibernica,* ed. Dimock, James F. (London, 1867)

Gerald of Wales (Giraldus Cambrensis), *The History and Topography of Ireland*, ed. O'Meara, John J. (London, 1951/1982)

Glynn, Fiona, ed., *A Sense of Carlow: A Collection of Local Folklore and Myth* (Carlow, 1997)

Grant, Michael, ed., *The Annals of Imperial Rome* by Tacitus (London, 1996)

Graves, James, 'Proceedings', *JRSAI* 16, 14–15 (Dublin, 1883)

Green, Carolyn Eve and Lenihan, Eddie, *Meeting the Other Crowd: The Fairy Stories of Hidden Ireland* (Dublin, 2003)

Green, Miranda J., *The Gods of the Celts* (Gloucester, 1986)

Gregory, Lady Augusta, *The Kiltartan Book: Comprising the Kiltartan Poetry, History, and Wonder Books by Lady Gregory* (Gerrards Cross, 1971)

Grenham, John, *Clans and Families of Ireland: The Heritage and Herarldry of Irish Clans and Families* (Dublin, 1993)

Gwynn, Edward, *The Metrical Dindshenchas* 1–5 (Dublin, 1903, 1906, 1913, 1924, 1935)

Hall, Mr and Mrs Samuel Carter, *Ireland: Its Scenery, Character etc.*, vols. 1–3 (London, 1841–1843)

Hageneder, Fred, *The Spirit of Trees: Science, Symbiosis and Inspiration* (Edinburgh, 2000)

Harbison, Peter, *Guide to National Monuments in Ireland* (Dublin, 1979)

Harbison, Peter, *Pilgrimage in Ireland: The Monuments and the People* (London, 1991)

Hardy, Dixon Philip, *The Holy Wells of Ireland* (Dublin, 1836)

Hartland, Sidney, 'Pin Wells and Rag Bushes', *Folklore* 4, 451–470 (London, 1893)

Hartnett, P. J., 'The Holy Wells of East Muskerry', *Béaloideas* 10, 101–113 (Dublin, 1940)

Hayes, Samuel, *A Practical Treatise on Planting and the Management of Woods and Coppices* (Dublin, 1794)

Healy, John, *Maynooth College: Its Centenary History 1795–1895* (Dublin, 1895)

Heany, Paddy, *At the Foot of Slieve Bloom: History and Folklore of Cadamstown* (n.p., n.y.)

Henderson, George, *Survivals in Belief among the Celts* (Glasgow, 1911)

Hennessy, William M., ed., *Annals of Ulster* (Dublin, 1887)

Hickie, David and O'Toole, Mike, *Native Trees and Forests of Ireland* (Dublin, 2002)

Hull, Eleanor, *Folklore of the British Isles* (London, 1928)

Hull, Vernam, ed., *Longes mac n-Uislenn* (New York, 1949)

Hutton, Arthur W., ed., *A Tour in Ireland 1776–1779* by Arthur Young (London, 1780/Shannon, 1970)

Hutton, Ronald, *The Pagan Religions of the Ancient British Isles: Their Nature and Legacy* (Oxford/Cambridge (Mass.), 1991/1997)

Hutton, Ronald, *The Triumph of the Moon: A History of Modern Pagan Witchcraft* (Oxford, 1999)

Jones, Horace Leonard, ed., *The Geography of Strabo*, vol. 5 (London/Cambridge (Mass.), 1954)

Joyce, P. W., *Origin and History of Irish Names of Places* (Dublin, 1871)

Joyce, P. W., *Irish Place Names Explained* (Dublin/London, 1923)

Joyce, P. W., *Old Celtic Romances, translated from the Gaelic* (Dublin, 1978)

Keating, Geoffrey, *The General History of Ireland*, ed. O'Connor, Dermod (Dublin, 1809)

Kelly, Fergus, 'The Old Irish Tree-List', *Celtica* 11, 107–124 (Dublin, 1976)

Kelly, Fergus, *A Guide to Early Irish Law* (Dublin, 1988/1998)

Kennedy, Joseph, *The Monastic Heritage and Folklore of County Laois* (Roscrea, 2003)

Knox, H. T., 'Miscellanea', *JRSAI* 21, 188–190 (Dublin, 1902)

Kohl, Johann G., *Ireland, Scotland and England* (London, 1844)

Lankford, Éamon, *Naomh Ciará: Pilgrim Islander* (Cork, 2000)

Lee, Joseph, *The Modernisation of Irish Society 1848–1918* (Dublin, 1973)

Logan, Patrick, *The Holy Wells of Ireland* (London, 1980)

Logan, Patrick, *The Old Gods: The Facts about Irish Fairies* (Belfast, 1981)

Lucan, *Civil War (Pharsalia)*, ed. Brand, Susan H. (Oxford, 1992)

Lucas, A. T., 'The Sacred Trees of Ireland', *JCHAS* 68, 16–54 (Cork, 1963)

Lydon, James, *The Making of Ireland from Ancient Times to the Present* (London/New York, 1998)

Macalister, R. A. Stewart, ed., *Lebor Gabála Érenn* 1–5 (London, 1938, 1939, 1940, 1941, 1956)

Mac Coitir, Niall, *Irish Trees: Myths, Legends & Folklore* (Cork, 2003)

Mac Manus, Dermot A., *The Middle Kingdom: The Faerie World of Ireland* (Gerrards Cross, 1973)

MacNeill, Máire, *The Festival of Lughnasa* (Dublin, 1962/1982)

McVeagh, John, *Richard Pococke's Irish Tours* (Dublin, 1995)

Madden, Gerard, *Holy Island: Jewel of the Lough* (n.p., n.y.)

M. E. M., 'Thorns and Thistles and their Comrades', *Dublin University Magazine* 43, 442–456 (Dublin, 1864)

Mescal, Daniel, *The Story of Inis Cathaigh* (Dublin, 1902)

Meyer, Kuno, ed., 'Mitteilungen aus Irischen Handschriften', *ZCP* 5, 21–25 (Halle, 1905)

Meyer, Kuno, ed., 'Scél Baili Binnbérlaig', *RC* 13, 220–225 (Paris, 1982)

Meehan, Cary, *The Traveller's Guide to Sacred Ireland* (Glastonbury, 2002)

MacNamara, Fr Thomas V., *Guide to Holy Island* (n.p., n.y.)

Morton, Andrew, *Tree Heritage of Britain and Ireland: A Guide to the Famous Trees of Britain and Ireland* (Ramsbury, Wiltshire, 1998/2004)

Mulchrone, Kathleen, ed., *Bethu Phátraic – The Tripartite Life of Patrick* (Dublin/London, 1939)

Murphy, Gerard, *Early Irish Lyrics* (Dublin, 1998)

Murphy, Canon William, 'The Pattern of Mullinakill', *Old Kilkenny Review* 22, 42–44 (Kilkenny, 1970)

Nelson, Charles E. and Walsh, Wendy F., *Trees of Ireland: Native and Naturalized* (Dublin, 1992)

Nuttall Smith, G., 'Holy Well and Antiquities near Cahir, Co. Tipperary', *JRSAI* 29, 258–259 (Dublin, 1899)

Ó Brien, Deirdre, *Children's Burial Grounds in East Clare: A Neglected Heritage. A Study of the Awareness and Curation of Cillíns in East County Clare* (unpubl. thesis, Mayo Institute of Technology, Galway, 2003)

O'Callaghan, Liam and Rackard, Anna, *Fishstonewater: Holy Wells of Ireland* (Cork, 2001)

Ó Comáin, Micheál, *The Poolbeg Book of Irish Heraldry* (Swords, 1991)

O'Connor, Dermod, ed., *The General History of Ireland* by Geoffrey Keating (Dublin, 1809)

O'Curry, Eugene, *Lectures on the Manuscript Materials of Ancient Irish History* (Dublin, 1873)

Ó Danachair, Caoimhín, 'The Holy Wells of North County Kerry', *JRSAI* 88, 153–163 (Dublin, 1958)

O'Donnell, Manus, *Betha Colaim Chille. Life of Columcille (1532)*, ed. O'Kelleher, Andrew and Schoepperle, Gertrude (Illinois, 1918)

O'Donnell, Ruán, *1798 Diary* (Dublin, 1998)

O'Donovan, John, et al., *Ordnance Survey Letters* relating to the antiquities of County Carlow (1839), Cavan/Leitrim (1836), Clare (1839), Donegal (1835), Fermanagh (1834), Galway (1838), Kerry (1841), Londonderry (1837), Longford (1838), Louth (1835–6), Meath (1836), Mayo (1838), Roscommon (1837), Sligo (1836), Tipperary III (1840), Waterford (1841), Westmeath (1837)

O'Donovan, John, *Ordnance Survey Field Name Book of the County of Carlow* (Dublin, 1839)

O'Donovan, John, ed., *Annála Ríoghachta Éireann, Annals of the Kingdom of Ireland by the Four Masters from the Earliest Period to the Year 1616*, vols. 1–7 (Dublin, 1848–1851)

Ó Duilearga, Séamus, *Leabhar Sheáin Uí Chonaill. Seán Ó Conaill's Book* (Dublin, 1948/1981)

O'Flynn, Críostóir, 'Blind Raftery and the Thorn Tree', *Irish Comic Poems*, 155–165 (Indreabhán, 1995)

O'Grady, Standish Hayes, *Silva Gadelica I* (London, 1892)

O'Hanlon, John, *Lives of the Irish Saints*, vols. 1–11 (Dublin, 1875)

Ó hAodha, Donncha, *Bethu Brigte* (Dublin, 1978)

Ó hÓgáin, Dáithí, *Myth, Legend and Romance: An Encyclopaedia of the Irish Folk Tradition* (London, 1990)

Ó hÓgáin, Dáithí, *The Sacred Isle: Belief and Religion in Pre-Christian Ireland* (Cork, 1999)

Ó hÓgáin, Dáithí, 'Trees in Irish Lore', *Journal of the Society of Irish Foresters*, vol. 60, 46–60 (Dublin, 2003)

O'Kelleher, Andrew and Schoepperle, Gertrude, eds., *Betha Colaim Chille. Life of Columcille* by Manus O'Donnell (1532) (Illinois, 1918)

O'Kelly, Eugene, *A Natural History Guide to the Loop Head Peninsula* (Kilkee, 2001)

O'Laverty, James, *A Historical Account of the Diocese of Down and Connor* (Dublin, 1884)

O'Meara, John J., ed., *The History and Topography of Ireland* by Gerald of Wales (Giraldus Cambrensis) (London, 1951/1982)

O'Meara, John J., ed., *Topography of Ireland: Giraldus Cambrensis. Newly translated from the earliest Manuscript* (Dundalk, 1951)

Ó Núanáin, P. J., *Glendalough or the Seven Churches of St Kevin* (Wicklow, 1984)

O'Rahilly, Thomas F., *Early Irish History and Mythology* (Dublin, 1946)

O'Sullivan, Sean, *The Folklore of Ireland* (London, 1974)

O'Sullivan, Sean, *Legends from Ireland* (London, 1977)

O'Toole, Edward, 'The Holy Wells of Co. Carlow', *Béaloideas* 4/1, 3–23; 107–130 (Dublin, 1933)

Otway, Caesar, *A Tour in Connaught* (Dublin, 1839)

Otway, Caesar, *Sketches in Erris and Tyrawly* (Dublin, 1841)

Pakenham, Thomas, *Meetings with Remarkable Trees* (London, 1996/2003)

Pakenham, Thomas (abridged by Toby Buchan), *The Year of Liberty: The Great Irish Rebellion of 1798* (New York, 1997)

Paterson, T. G. F., *Country Cracks: Old Tales from the County of Armagh* (Dundalk, 1939)

Paterson, T. G. F., 'The Cult of the Holy Well in County Armagh', *UJA* 11, 127–130 (Belfast, 1948)

Pennick, Nigel, *Celtic Sacred Landscapes* (London, 1996)

Plummer, Charles, ed., *Vitae Sanctorum Hiberniae* (Oxford, 1910)

Plummer, Charles, ed., *Bethada Náem nÉrenn. Lives of Irish Saints* (Oxford, 1968)

Pococke's Tour in Ireland in 1752, ed. Stokes, G.T. (Dublin/London, 1891)

Ranke-Graves, Robert, *Die Weisse Göttin: Sprache des Mythos* (Hamburg, 1985)

Rees, Alwyn and Brinley, *Celtic Heritage: Ancient Tradition in Ireland and Wales* (London, 1961)

Renwick, W. L., ed., *A View of the Present State of Ireland* by Edmund Spenser (Oxford, 1970)

Richter, Michael, *Irland im Mittelalter: Kultur und Geschichte* (Stuttgart, 1983)

Rodger, Donald and Stokes, Jon, *The Heritage Trees of Britain and Northern Ireland* (London, 2004)

Shaw-Mason, William, *Parochial Survey of Ireland*, vols. 1–3 (Dublin, 1814–1819)

Simon, Ben, 'Tree Traditions and Folklore from Northeast Ireland', *Arboricultural Journal*, vol. 24/1, 15–40 (Bicester, 2000)

Simon, Ben, 'A Review of Notable Yew Trees in Ireland', *Arboricultural Journal*, vol. 24/2, 97–137 (Bicester, 2000)

Smyth, Daragh, *A Guide to Irish Mythology* (Dublin, 1988/1996)

Spenser, Edmund, *A View of the Present State of Ireland*, ed. Renwick, W. L. (Oxford, 1970)

St Clair, Sheila, *Folklore of the Ulster People* (Cork, 1971)

Stokes, G. T., ed., *Pococke's Tour in Ireland in 1752* (Dublin/London, 1891)

Stokes, Margaret, 'Funeral Customs in the Baronies of Bargy and Forth, County Wexford', *JRSAI* 24, 380–385 (Dublin, 1894)

Stokes, Whitley, ed., 'The Voyage of Snedgus and Mac Riagla', *RC* 9, 14–25 (Paris, 1888)

Stokes, Whitley, ed., 'The Voyage of Mael Duín', *RC* 10, 50–95 (Paris, 1889)

Stokes, Whitley, ed., *Lives of the Saints from the Book of Lismore* (Oxford, 1890)

Stokes, Whitley, ed., 'The Prose Tales of the Rennes Dindshenchas', *RC* 15, 272–336; 418–484 (Paris, 1894)

Stokes, Whitley, ed., 'The Prose Tales of the Rennes Dindshenchas II. Extracts from the Book of Leinster', *RC* 16, 269–310 (Paris, 1895)

Stokes, Whitley, ed., 'O'Mulconry's Glossary', *Archiv für Celtische Lexikographie* 1, 232–324 (Halle, 1900)

Stokes, Whitley and Strachan, John, eds., *Thesaurus Paleohibernicus: A Collection of Old–Irish Glosses, Scholia, Prose and Verse*, vol. 2 (Cambridge, 1903)

Stokes, Whitley, ed., 'The Adventure of St Columba's Clerics', *RC* 26, 130–170 (Paris, 1905)

Stokes, Whitley, ed., 'The Birth and Life of St Moling', *RC* 27, 257–312 (Paris, 1906)

Stout, Matthew, *The Irish Ringfort* (Dublin 1997/2000)

Tacitus, *The Annals of Imperial Rome*, ed. Grant, Michael (London, 1996)

Thurneysen, Rudolf, ed.,'Der Mystische Baum', *ZCP* 14, 16–17 (Halle, 1923)

Toland, John, *A History of the Celtic Religion and Learning Containing an Account of the Druids or the Priests and Judges* (Edinburgh, 1815)

Thomas, Charles, *Britain and Ireland in Early Christian Times, AD 400–800* (London, 1971)

Wakeman, W. F., 'Ante-Norman Churches in the County of Dublin', *JRSAI* 22, 101–106 (Dublin, 1892)

Weisweiler, J., 'Vorindogermanische Schichten der Irischen Heldensage', *ZCP* 24, 165–197 (Tübingen, 1954)

Westropp, Thomas Johnson, *A Folklore Survey of County Clare and County Clare Folk-Tales and Myths* (Dublin, 1910–1913), ed. Comber, Maureen, CLASP (Ennis, 2000)

Whelan, Kevin, *The Tree of Liberty: Radicalism, Catholicism and the Construction of Irish Identity 1760–1830* (Cork, 1996)

Wilks, J. H., *Trees of the British Isles in History and Legend* (London, 1972)

Wood-Martin, William Gregory, *Traces of the Elder Faiths in Ireland: A Folklore Sketch. A Handbook of Irish Pre-Christian Traditions*, vols. 1–2 (London/New York/Bombay, 1902)

Yeats, William Butler, *Fairy and Folk Tales of Ireland* (Gerrards Cross, 1973)

Young, Arthur, *A Tour in Ireland 1776–1779*, ed. Hutton, Arthur W., (London, 1780/Shannon, 1970)

Zucchelli, Christine, *Stones of Adoration: Sacred Stones and Mystic Megaliths of Ireland* (Cork, 2007)

Index